The Life and Deaths of an Undertaker

by Tom Eldwin

In memory of my parents, Roger and Pam.

1

As I sauntered through the double doorway into the cavernous garage I immediately became aware of a major commotion. Three men in dark suits were scurrying between a vast array of black hearses and limousines and there was the distinct atmosphere of panic in the air. A young man about my age noticed my arrival and approached me animatedly, clutching a piece of paper.

'Are you t'new driver?' he demanded gruffly in an unexpected Yorkshire accent.

'Er…yes.' I held out my hand in greeting but he thrust the piece of paper into it instead.

'You're late!' he growled. 'Those are your orders. Take this hearse here, pick up Stewart from t'Dean Street office and get a move on. The funeral was due to start five minutes ago!'

I was about to crumble into one of those 'first day on the job' heaps when a screech of tyres distracted me. A dark blue estate car pulled up violently and out leapt a small, white haired man of about fifty-five. He ran towards us looking quite ill.

'Mark, which is the hearse going to the Bevan funeral?' he panted in a soft Welsh lilt.

Mark pointed to the hearse I was about to drive. 'This one here.'

'Quick Mark, we have to get to the house straight away. The funeral was supposed to start five minutes ago!'

Mark – who was now looking almost as dazed as me – grimaced. 'Well actually Gareth, I'm due out on a different funeral in ten minutes. Tom here is your driver.'

Gareth's mouth gaped open. He looked at Mark, then he looked at me, and then he looked like he was about to faint. 'Oh gee!' he exclaimed breathlessly. 'Oh gee!' He was turning paler by the second.

'Hang on a minute,' frowned Mark. 'Stewart's the funeral director on t'Bevan funeral. How come you're here?'

1

Gareth held up a hand and shook his head wearily. 'He's gone missing.'

'What d'you mean, he's gone missing?'

'He was in the office first thing this morning but he's just disappeared. No one knows where he is.'

Now everyone stood open mouthed staring helplessly at each other. Mark recovered first.

'Right, okay. Tom, you jump in t'passenger seat. Gareth you drive because you know t'way. I'll ring t'office and get someone to phone t'family and tell them you've had a puncture.'

A smidgeon of colour returned to Gareth's face. 'Oh thank you, Mark, thank you. Would you do that? Oh thank you, Mark.' Despite the need for urgent action I'm sure Gareth would have stayed thanking Mark for several minutes more had not his saviour ushered him round to the driver's door and pushed him in.

I never knew that hearses could move so fast, especially from a standing start. I had always been under the impression they were a rather sedate mode of transport. I learned a lot more about hearses too in the ten minutes that followed. Like how well they held the road when cornering at speed. Like how effectively they braked when the vehicle in front suddenly paused to turn right. And like how they possessed the amazing ability to jump red traffic lights and emerge unscathed.

We finally reached the house where the funeral service was taking place. A huge crowd had gathered and all eyes were upon us as Gareth skilfully parked the hearse in the glaringly vacant space in front of the two limousines. He had leapt out almost before coming to a halt and as I too got out I could already hear him offering explanations to the nearby mourners of flat tyres and how damned awkward a procedure it was to change a wheel on a hearse. It was therefore easy to understand his horror when a few seconds later one of the limousine drivers came forward and explained he had made an announcement to the family ten minutes earlier that the hearse would be slightly late as it was stuck in heavy traffic. I learned very early in my undertaking career that everyone needed to have the same story if ever excuses were required.

By the time we arrived at the house we were almost twenty minutes late. Thankfully, the vicar had decided to carry on and start the service. But this didn't leave us a great deal of time in which to put all the floral tributes lying outside the front of the house onto the hearse. I had never seen so many flowers in my life. There must have been between fifty and sixty tributes strewn across the small front garden. It was while we were piling all these flowers into, and on top of the hearse that I noticed there was no coffin. The realisation struck me motionless for several seconds. In the panic to get to the funeral we had forgotten the coffin!

I glanced at the faces of my two fellow drivers as they carried more flowers from the garden to the hearse. There was no apparent hint of alarm between them but maybe they hadn't noticed. I couldn't see Gareth. He had gone into the house for the service. I envisaged all sorts of headlines in tomorrow's newspapers followed by the repercussions – angry, hysterical mourners; an angry, hysterical boss… I leaned gently against the hearse for support and closed my eyes as I contemplated life back at the Job Centre.

There was movement inside the house. The vicar emerged followed by Gareth, who seemed intent on acknowledging everyone in attendance. It would have been easy to forget this was not one of his funerals and that he was merely standing in at short notice. As he reached the front gate he motioned me and the other two drivers forward. He obviously hadn't noticed the fact we didn't have a coffin. He now seemed quite relaxed and probably thought the crisis was over. But a far worse one was about to manifest itself.

'Right gentlemen,' he began quietly but regimentally. 'The coffin is just inside the front room, so if you, Nigel, and you, Griff, could bring it out. Tom, you wait by the door by yer, and then help to carry it to the hearse. Okay?'

I let out an enormous sigh of relief. My new career in undertaking was safe after all. But a coffin in the house? It sounded extremely bizarre to me. At that particular moment though it could have been perched high up on the chimney top for all I cared, as long as it was within sight.

On the way to the crematorium Gareth explained that in Wales, a service in the house was considered quite normal, as was the coffin staying at home until the day of the funeral. The latter seemed quite morbid to me, especially when I later

3

discovered that the coffin usually stayed open so that all and sundry could come and view the deceased like they would look at TV's in a shop window. All this was certainly a culture shock to a naïve young man with an English accent, beginning a new job in a new town, in an apparently foreign country.

Already I realised I had much to learn.

I drove on another, far more serene funeral that day before returning to the garage late in the afternoon. I was greeted once again by Mark, who was far more congenial this time around. He sported a knowing grin as to the events of the morning.

'Sorry I had a go at you earlier,' he said. 'I didn't realise you hadn't been told you were driving on a funeral straight away.'

'That's okay,' I shrugged. 'I reported to the office in Dean Street first thing this morning and they just told me to go down and wash a few cars.'

'Oh aye, that's typical,' he muttered, shaking his head. 'Anyway, we'll wash a few now if you like – show you how it's done properly. We're very particular about how we wash vehicles here. They're our shop window – what t'public always sees.'

'Are things always as crazy as they were this morning?' I asked as we changed into overalls and Wellington boots.

'We have our moments,' he smiled. Then his expression changed. 'I've never known t'funeral director to forget t'funeral before though.'

2

A bewildering mixture of emotions swam relentlessly around my mind on that drab December day in 1985 as I set off for South Wales. Sadness, apprehension, excitement, fear – they were all there and many more, jostling for supremacy and control. I tried not to dwell on any one of them for too long.

Each mile I drove towards my new destination also took me a mile away from the only life I'd ever really known. The county of Devon had been my home for more than sixteen years: almost anything and everything of importance in my life had happened there. But now it was time to move on. At the age of almost twenty-three I needed to take the opportunity that had recently presented itself.

Over the years the question I have been asked the most is 'How did you get involved in the funeral business?' To this day I have never been able to offer a complete answer. To say that I just drifted into this most unusual of careers does little to satisfy public curiosity, yet it is probably the closest I can get to anything that resembles the truth.

Events in life often dictate the choice of road we take and there is little doubt that had circumstances not conspired the way they did, I would probably still be a postman in the South Devon town of Paignton. For almost three years I sorted and delivered mail there and it was a job I very much enjoyed too, mundane and lacking in ambition though it could often be. Being out in the fresh air, the feeling of satisfaction as I headed home each early afternoon having delivered another couple of huge mail bags to the houses on my round, and the camaraderie of my fellow postmen and woman all helped introduce me to the world of employment with a relevant amount of cheerfulness.

I loved Torbay too. Known as 'The English Riviera', Torquay, Paignton, and Brixham – the three towns that make up this much-favoured holiday resort – was almost the perfect place in which to

'You should have seen his face when they gave him the camcorder, Tom,' said Mrs Morgan right on cue. 'He was almost speechless.'

'Yes, I can see from the photo,' I smiled. 'Was he able to use it himself?'

His father's chest swelled up with pride. 'Oh yes. He was amazing. Far quicker at working it out than me, see!'

'When we knew he only had a short time left we took him to lots of different places. He made films for us to watch when we got home.' Mrs Morgan looked at me with eyebrows slightly raised. 'Would you...like to see one quickly? Only if you've time, of course...'

I didn't hesitate. 'I'd love to see one.' I wasn't just being polite.

She took a videocassette from the shelf above the television and inserted it carefully into the video player. Within seconds we were in a Welsh seaside town and a little voice in an accent the exact replica of his parents proceeded to present a commentary on the whereabouts of each location filmed. I glanced across at Mr and Mrs Morgan. They had probably watched these videos many times and each time, as they did now, they probably shed a few tears. So too did I.

When Christopher's voice bade a cheery goodbye and the picture of a seaside pier faded out to a black screen, Mrs Morgan stopped the video and once again removed the cassette with great care. Returning it to the shelf she looked over to me, her eyes moist. 'You see, Tom, we miss Christopher terribly,' she said. 'But we were so blessed to have him for eight years. And we have these precious memories of him here. We are so grateful for that.'

An hour earlier I had envisaged leaving the Morgan home low in spirit, troubled by the overwhelming grief that would surely confront me. But as I drove back to the office that late afternoon I felt strangely invigorated and uplifted. The character and sheer mental strength that Mr and Mrs Morgan were displaying at the loss of their dear young son was amazing. Yes, they were devastated. Yes, they were hurting. But together they were handling the whole tragedy with a courage that would remain an inspiration to me for many years to come.

My heartening meeting with Mr and Mrs Morgan remained prominent in my mind over the days that followed and this was still the case when Paul called me into the office about a week later.

'Can you go and pick up Islwyn in Abertrefil this afternoon? He needs a lift to Sandacre Hospital for an appointment with his specialist.'

'Sure. No problem.'

I was pleased to have been asked and as I drove the short distance to the small town that had played such an important role in my early days of living in South Wales, I knew I should not have left it so long to return.

It was with great sadness that I had only recently discovered my dear friend, Islwyn Thomas, had been diagnosed with cancer some nine months earlier. I had been intending to call and visit him ever since, but, alas, I'd just never got round to it. My duties as a funeral director were now extensive and had long prevented me from going to Abertrefil to help out as a driver. But this was no excuse. I'd felt increasingly guilty about not popping over to visit a man who had shown me nothing but kindness and consideration in those difficult early months and beyond. At least now I had been afforded the opportunity.

When I knocked on the front door of Islwyn's grey bricked house and he stood greeting me in the doorway a few seconds later, I almost reeled with shock. He was barely recognisable as the robust and active man I had driven on so many funerals. His face was pale and drawn and he had lost an incredible amount of weight. He stood before me now looking alarmingly thin and fragile. I swear that had I passed him on the street I would not have recognised him. But nothing about his manner had changed.

'Good heavens! Tom! Where the devil have you been, my friend?' That familiar, bellowing voice was like music to my ears.

'I'm sorry, Islwyn. I've been meaning to come and see you for a while. How are you?'

'Oh can't complain, bach, can't complain. And don't worry yourself about not coming. You've been a busy lad since becoming a funeral director. I have heard some excellent reports about your progress, yes indeed I have.'

'Thanks, Islwyn,' I smiled. 'It's no excuse though.'

He waved a bony hand in that theatrical way of his. 'I don't want to hear another word. Now then, it is time to go.' He turned his head back inside the house and hollered loudly. 'Maureen! Are you ready, bach?'

Mrs Thomas emerged almost immediately, a tiny woman with short grey hair and big glasses. She greeted me like a son who had returned home after many years away. 'Hello, bach! How lovely to see you again! You haven't been by yer for ages. How are you, my love?'

'I'm fine, Maureen.' I replied, giving her a hug. 'It's great to see you again too.'

I had missed all this. The memories of those fun-filled days spent driving on the unique funerals of Abertrefil came flooding back. It had been about three years since I was last here, but in view of my advancement to the position of funeral director and the time and effort this had required as I attempted to establish myself in my new career, it now seemed a lifetime away. On the occasions when I felt my additional responsibilities were getting on top of me, I yearned for those simple, carefree days as a driver – days when my regular visits to Abertrefil were like going away to a favourite holiday resort.

Islwyn spoke very little about his illness as we drove to Sandacre Hospital. All he really told me was that the doctors were pleased with his progress and that he himself was determined to beat this 'damned cancer' and get on with his life. And that was it. He was more interested in talking about other matters, especially – and typically for him – my progress as a funeral director.

As we returned to Abertrefil following his appointment, Islwyn was in high spirits. Frankly, I'd never seen him anything less in all the years I'd known him. 'Thank you, Tom bach,' he said, as he eased himself out of the car outside his house. It has been a real pleasure to see you again, my friend.'

I shook his hand. 'You take care of yourself, Islwyn. I'll come up and see you soon, I promise.'

'Please do, please do.'

Maureen came round from the passenger side and squeezed my hand. Then together she and her husband entered through the front door and as Islwyn held onto his wife's arm, he suddenly looked very old.

That was the last time I saw Islwyn Thomas alive. Maybe I should have realised as I pulled away from his house that day and saw his tired arm raised in farewell through the front window. Looking back, it seems almost inevitable that he had very little time left. Less than six weeks later, Islwyn passed quietly away. The cancer he was so determined to conquer had claimed yet another victory and it didn't occur to me until much later that he had probably known all along he was losing the battle. But Islwyn would never have admitted defeat, perhaps not even to himself. It simply wasn't in his character to be despondent or loaded with self-pity.

I thought of all the people Islwyn must have helped throughout his life and career as a funeral director. Hundreds. Thousands. I had only snatched the briefest of glimpses during the short time I worked with him. But even then I could see the wonderful effect his personality and sense of humour had on those with whom he came into contact.

That word humour again.

There were many lessons that could be learned from the likes of Islwyn Thomas in the art of undertaking. How to arrange and conduct a funeral with confidence and his knack of being able to bridge the gap between the young and the old, the rich and the poor. Then there were his organisational skills, which, at first glance appeared carefree, but were in fact well-drilled and meticulous. However, it was his shrewd use of humour in a world where one might be forgiven for believing it could not exist that inspired me the most as I forged my own career as a funeral director. And looking back at my years working with Islwyn on so many funerals, the memories of laughter far outweigh the memories of grief and despair.

Two deaths. One illness.

I learned a great deal about many things during those few weeks when both Islwyn Thomas and Christopher Morgan passed away. They stood at distant ends of the age spectrum, but both were victims of a disease that respects no man, woman, or child – a disease we still cannot understand or combat, despite recent medical progress on hitherto unknown scales. But both Islwyn and Christopher had inspired the lives of others and touched hearts and souls in entirely different ways. They had made the most of their given opportunities.

Life truly is a precious commodity, no matter how long it lasts.

39

My biggest regret over the death of Islwyn Thomas was the fact I never did get around to visiting him again as I'd long intended. It certainly provided me with a stark lesson on the consequences of procrastination. But the truth is, at that particular time I had begun stumbling towards a major crisis of my own.

I had been working very hard. Funeral directing is a mentally draining profession under the best of circumstances. When other factors are added in the stress levels can rise and to those who don't enjoy the strain of working under such extreme pressure, it can make for a very difficult time. Unfortunately I am one such person. Right from the very beginning I had doubted my ability to cope with being a funeral director, an assumption based on the working conditions I'd witnessed up until then. Our company, like probably many others I suppose, seemed hell bent on running the operation with the fewest staff possible. In such an unpredictable business as far as the volume of work is concerned – involving a heavy on call schedule in addition to the normal working hours of the day – this places a huge amount of strain on its employees.

Although I felt I was doing well, the job as a whole was starting to get on top of me. It steadily grew worse as my workload began reaching levels that could only be considered perilous for my type of personality. I was continually rushing between two or three offices; I was involved in additional responsibilities that my fellow funeral directors didn't have, including the daily headache of working out the driver's orders; proper lunch breaks were about as frequent as a rural bus service; and I was working late with increasing regularity. This was probably already enough to set the warning lights flashing. But the killer blow was the amount of on call I was being told to do as well. My partner on the rota was forever taking time off when his weekend on duty was due and I had to cover these in addition to my own weekends. But when he went on long-term sick leave and I was left to cover fifty per cent of the on call alone for the foreseeable future, the writing was on the wall. I asked for help but my pleas fell on deaf, uninterested ears. With hindsight I should have shouted louder and longer. Instead, I just tried to struggle on.

Every night I spent on call seemed to be busy – every day I was in work was hectic...rushing here, rushing there...no lunch... Phone calls...so many phone calls all the time...another funeral to arrange...and another... Not much sleep...can't switch off...my mind is sinking. Another weekend on call...the phone is ringing already...more funerals to arrange...it's ten to five. I'm going to be working late. Again.

Something snapped inside my head.

Late one Friday afternoon I finally cracked. I was alone in the office in Penderi Village with a mountain of work in front of me. I was mentally and physically exhausted. All I could muster the energy to do was phone my father. He came and picked me up and drove me back into Westport while a blizzard raged inside my brain. Dad took me straight to my doctor: thankfully he was still in his surgery. He took one look at me and signed me off work indefinitely with stress-related depression.

I vaguely recall picking up a few belongings from my flat and going to Mum and Dad's. Here I stayed for several days, away from everything that had made me so ill. That first night I drifted into almost unconscious sleep, virtually oblivious to all that was going on around me. My mind, which had been approaching overload for weeks, had decided enough was enough. Thankfully, mercifully, nature stepped in and shut down the machinery to allow me the chance to recover.

The following day dawned and everything seemed so quiet, so still. I remember going for a walk and feeling completely outside of everything around me. I felt like I'd been involved in a serious car crash after travelling at high speed. Now, in the cold light of a hazy summer's morning, it was as though I'd been pulled unconscious from the wreckage. And the underlying thought coming from somewhere deep inside told me that crashing was the only way I could've stopped.

It is hard knowing where to begin to describe how I was feeling during those first few days. But it didn't take me long to realise that my mind, my nerves, and my confidence were completely shot to pieces. For a while I just didn't have the mental energy to worry about the consequences of what had happened, or the future it affected. My initial concern was just to survive a day at a time and come to terms with the fact that I was very ill. But in amongst the internal confusion I felt an overwhelming sense of relief. For the time being at least I was free from the pressures that had sent me spiralling downwards. I knew this wasn't a long-term solution but at that stage, being as far away from the job as possible was all I cared about. In fact, it would be almost four months before I was well enough to return.

The thought of giving up funeral directing and going back to the less frenetic position of driver crossed my mind several times throughout my enforced hiatus. But even in my frayed state of mind I remained stubborn. Awful circumstances aside I enjoyed being a funeral director. For someone who has always lacked confidence in life situations I figured I'd discovered my place in the working world – a job I was hopefully proficient at and a career that made me feel I was doing something worthwhile with my life. I was therefore reluctant to just give up on what I had achieved so far.

Tentatively, nervously, I finally returned to work, deeply concerned by my ability to resume normal service. It was a worrying time. Gradually the days turned to weeks and the weeks to months and aided by the love and support of family, I was able to slowly pick up some of the pieces. But ultimately it was the wrong decision. My comeback lasted barely eighteen months.

When I suffered my second breakdown in as many years I knew deep down that the end was in sight. I was walking on glass. I was living on the edge of a precipice. I couldn't carry on like this: something had to give. And so I swallowed what little pride I had left and requested a permanent return to driving duties. Privately I was devastated at having to give up funeral directing. What made it even worse was the fact I had only just completed my BTEC Certificate in Funeral Directing, a long and demanding assessment-based course which was being pioneered in place of the older, increasingly outdated diploma qualification. I had worked extremely hard to achieve my recognition but now I couldn't help feeling it was all in vain. After believing I was really accomplishing something worthwhile, I now felt like everything was being ripped away from me. It took a long time to overcome the humiliation of what I considered to be a complete failure on my part. But mine wasn't the only stigma that needed surmounting.

One of the biggest eye-openers for me during this time was the general attitude of certain people towards depression, especially my employer. As a whole, depression is unfairly bracketed under the same banner as other, more serious mental illnesses with scant regard for the vastly differing levels that exist. It is like trying to file all music into one category when there are so many variations – pop, jazz, reggae, classical, etc. Thankfully, and not before time, this unmerited perception is now being broken down and society is a little more accepting and considerate of depression and stress-related illness, although there still remains a long way to go. But back in the nineties I was toxic as far as the company I worked for was concerned – the journey towards awareness and understanding of mental illness hadn't even begun.

Not surprisingly, stress and depression have replaced back problems as the biggest reason for absence at work in the UK. But although, as I say, industry has now started to recognise this as fact, many companies are still doing too little to alleviate the situations that cause stress and depression in the first place. Introducing helplines and offering counselling are very commendable concepts. But these don't kick into action until there is a reason to do so, by which time it can be too late. Parking the ambulance at the top of the cliff instead of the bottom is far more effective and the sooner employers appreciate this, the better.

When I suffered my two breakdowns I was horrified by the lack of support and understanding from the company's personnel department in particular. Even now, when they claim to have learned from cases like mine, it is quite clear they are paying mere lip service to the problem of stress in the workplace. They talk a good game but they rarely turn up to actually play. As far as I was concerned I felt that I should have walked around with a huge bandage on my head. Only then do I believe that reactions may have been a little more sympathetic. Unfortunately, mental illness is hidden away inside the body. It requires no bandages or plaster casts; it is not eased by crutches or wheelchairs. It is invisible and the attitude that what cannot be seen surely does not exist prevails in the sceptical eyes of the casual observer.

It was left to family to help pull me through the tunnel of despair in which I laboured. I could not have wished for greater support from each and every one of them. Dad in particular was amazing. Having suffered similarly throughout his life, his knowledge and advice were invaluable to me. I was fortunate Dad was able to help at all. A short time afterwards he began to sink into a shrouded nightmare of his own – that cruel, debilitating illness known as Alzheimer's disease. He suffered for more than four years before finally passing away, his mind and body ravaged beyond recognition. I miss him now he is gone. I missed him when he was still alive – when we as a family became strangers to him in his world of confusion.

Physical illnesses are an awful affliction. They can be restricting, degrading, and frustrating. But at least their visibility generates an attitude of charity and concern. Mental illness cannot compete on the same level. It is a hidden world where its victims suffer in the awful privacy of their own troubled minds. In a society that subconsciously judges everyone on appearance and discernible ability, it can be one of the hardest pains of all to bear.

I still suffer from depression today. It is a burden that can be unbearably hard to endure and I could probably write a separate book on the way this undermining illness has affected me for so long. Maybe one day I will. It has been an inseparable part of my existence for most of my life: looking back now, I am convinced the signs and the potential were noticeable as far back as my early teens.

There are days when I hate the impact depression has made on my life. There are also days when I just close my eyes and accept its existence. There is little doubt in my mind that I would not be the person I am without its constant presence. It has brought me many weaknesses but it has also given me countless strengths. To remove it now would strip away an integral part of my character and soul. To lose my demons I would have to lose some of my angels too.

I continually learn how to live with this illness. Half the battle of coping with depression is accepting that you suffer from it and then having the strength to ride the waves when they come crashing at the door. Each day presents new challenges and demanding situations. Sometimes I learn from past mistakes; occasionally I fall into old traps. It is a roller-coaster of fear and emotion that no theme park can compete with.

Everyone experiences difficulties and stressful situations throughout their lives. It is just that some of us don't have the ability to deal with them as well as others. That is the curse of depression.

live, especially the picture postcard fishing port of Brixham. It was here that I grew up throughout the seventies, discovering life and the abundant joys of being a child. The complications of adulthood still lay blissfully in the far distant future.

It is Brixham that conjures up some of my most treasured memories – long hot summers listening to test match cricket on the radio with my father while helping him during the school holidays; building all manner of things out of Lego and making up Airfix kits; sneaking into the huge Pontins Holiday Camp just up the road with my best mate, James; and buying Bazooka bubble gum for the little comics inside. These are all memories of Brixham that have remained with me down the years like old and trusted friends.

Then as the seventies drew to a close we moved a few miles along the coast to nearby Paignton. The turn of the decade also heralded a huge change in my life, the change that everyone must pass through at some stage during their teenage years. Nervously I swapped the classrooms and timetables of my school in Torquay for the big, uncompromising world of responsibility. Reluctantly I had to leave behind the innocence and shelter of youth and get serious about life.

A summer job working in a busy café alongside the picturesque harbour of Torquay kept me going until my pestering of the Royal Mail finally reaped its reward and I was offered a position at the sorting office in Paignton. Now working full-time I could pay my own way at home and indulge more easily in the passions I had started to develop – buying records, going to concerts, my Blue Morris Minor bought from Mum and Dad, and best of all, hanging out and having a laugh with James.

But then it all started to go wrong. Events combined to send me in directions I neither understood nor wanted to go. A doomed relationship developed into a foolish and ill-judged marriage and halfway through my twentieth year I was separated and seeking a divorce. My inexperience in such matters and the stable, uncomplicated upbringing I had enjoyed did not prepare me for such high drama. I was shattered and the only option that appeared open to me at the time was to move away. Torbay, the place I knew and loved had turned sour on me and so reluctantly I moved further up the coast again to where my parents now lived in East Devon.

I was unable to obtain a transfer with Royal Mail and so maybe unwisely, I resigned. Signing on the dole again after having secured a job I enjoyed was very difficult to do and looking back I still wonder about the merits of the decision I made. But then I remember how I'd felt at the time and how much of a mess I had made of my life. I needed to get away and make a new start. But it also meant completely revising my career options, and that was not going to be easy. While I bluffed and edged my way through school, I'd never had even the least inkling about the sort of career I wanted to pursue. Probably it was my limited ambitions at this particular time that caused me to start thinking along alternative lines.

Ever since I passed my driving test at the age of eighteen I had enjoyed being behind the wheel of a car. I therefore reasoned that a driving job would be a logical step forward. Initially I thought along the lines of delivery or courier work, but before I knew it I had upgraded my ambitions. I figured there were sure to be jobs around that would provide the opportunity of driving something a little more upmarket than a transit van. At this stage I had to temper my enthusiasm. I didn't want to get above myself and turn into a transport snob. Then an unusual idea entered my head.

Funerals.

Strange thoughts do indeed flicker through the minds of the unemployed. But this one would take some beating. For a start, I had no knowledge of anything to do with funerals. Secondly, I knew of no one in the funeral business (who does in their early twenties?) from whom I could seek advice. And thirdly, no one ever talks about the profession. It doesn't exactly feature prominently in your average schoolboy list of potential occupations, nor does it provoke fanatical excitement amongst the career advisors of the world. However, despite the obvious drawbacks, I knew that funeral vehicles were some of the plushest and most expensive cars on the road and having never been one to shy away from anything out of the ordinary, I decided to run with my somewhat eccentric idea.

I wrote letters to all the funeral directors in the area and before I knew it, one of them actually took the trouble to reply and inform me of a casual vacancy as a driver/bearer. I was subsequently interviewed and hired, although my sense of achievement was dented slightly by the later revelation that I had in fact been the only candidate. But in the grand scheme of things it mattered not. I was in. Technically I wasn't off the dole completely – the job was only casual after all – but my new employers were confident a full-time position would soon arise and if I proved to be capable and reliable I was sure to be in the running. It never happened of course. My journey to a full-blown career in the funeral profession took a far more diverse and complicated route than that.

I worked on a casual basis at this funeral home for over twelve months, but as far as being taken on full-time was concerned little changed during that year. More significantly the situation appeared likely to remain the same for the foreseeable future. Something needed to happen. Fate somehow needed to intervene. And when it did, it emerged from an unlikely source.

My mate, James had met a woman. A Welsh woman to be precise. Before I had time to say 'are you sure you know what you're doing because I recently messed up in a situation like this', I found myself donning a posh suit and standing next to him as his best man in a church in Westport, South Wales in the autumn of 1985.

When I got back to Devon, I spent the following week searching out funeral homes in the Westport area and then writing to them to ask if they had any vacancies. I had rather enjoyed my brief sojourn to South Wales, not least because I fancied the younger sister of James's new wife. But love optimism aside I had nothing to lose and so I seized the moment. What I didn't expect was such a quick response.

Within weeks I was back in Wales having an interview with the manager of a Westport funeral home for the vacant position of Funeral Driver. My initial feeling was that the interview hadn't gone my way, but when I received a phone call later that day telling me I had been successful and asking could I start Monday week, I was ecstatic. At last I would have a proper job again with decent money. No more scraping to make ends meet and going without. No more despondency because my life had appeared to grind to a stuttering halt. I was back in the world of taxation and complicated wage slips and I could finally put the despair of the previous two years behind me. And I don't think I even stopped for one minute to think about the unusual profession I had just entered full on.

It was very difficult saying goodbye to my family and friends, Mum and Dad especially. They had been my life support, not just in recent times but throughout my entire life. Yet hard though it was I knew this opportunity was the right move at the right time. It was a new chapter in my life and a fresh and much-needed start. And as my car crossed the Severn Bridge and entered Wales on that otherwise insignificant winter's day, I was determined to make a success of the chance I had been given.

3

I knew I shouldn't have asked.

'You want Gilwern Road is it?' The stocky, oily-skinned man scratched thoughtfully at his balding pate. 'Well your best bet is to take your next left into Clos Crwys, carry on down the hill till you pass the shops, then take the second left into Cwmrhydyceirw Gardens, first right into Heol Gwyrddgoed and Gilwern Road is the last turning left at the bottom.'

'I beg your pardon?'

With a slight air of impatience he repeated the same, meaningless gaggle of words. It was no use. I didn't have a clue what he was saying. Even if he'd stood there trying to explain how to get to Gilwern Road until nightfall I would have been none the wiser.

Apologetically, and tinged with a certain amount of embarrassment, I smiled and pulled away again. I was picking up a family to take to a funeral in ten minutes time and, quite frankly, I had no idea where I was. The housing estate I was driving around resembled a maze and most of the streets looked exactly the same – rows upon rows of cream and grey houses with limited character and no distinguishing features. I duly found the address with seconds to spare but it owed more to luck than anything else.

During my first few days in Westport I had been horrified by some of the names I'd seen on signposts. They didn't make sense. There were letters where letters shouldn't be and no vowels where there should be vowels. They looked for all the world as though a young child had been given a typewriter and had then proceeded to hit the keys at random. I'd learned French at school and there was always a sense of rationality about it. But Welsh? It seemed a demented jumble and I seriously questioned my sanity at moving to a land whose native language made Japanese look easy.

If trying to read the names was a challenge then pronunciation was a whole new ball game. It was all right for the Welsh. They were used to it. They had learned to speak their jaw crunching words without sending sprays of saliva in all directions. For months I remained convinced that my best hope of pronunciation was to be afflicted with permanent bronchitis. And as I had just experienced, the worst part of all was trying to understand what the locals were saying when they spoke. I might just as well have been asking for directions in the Bolivian mountains as opposed to a corner of the British Isles. I barely understood a word.

Another quirk of the Welsh way of speaking which puzzled me was the use of the phrase *is it?* It was used in a logic-defying manner, as recently demonstrated: *You want Gilwern Road is it?* I don't want to sound pedantic here but I'm pretty confident in my opinion that on this occasion the question would sound much better as: *You want Gilwern Road, do you?* In all my years of living in Wales I could never come to terms with the absurdity of the use of the phrase *is it?*

What I did eventually learn to cope with however were those unreadable, unpronounceable Welsh names. In fact, as time went by, I actually became more proficient at spelling Welsh place names than many of my Welsh-born colleagues. The articulation of the true-blooded Welshman still isn't quite there, but considering I'm an Englishman, I haven't done too badly, is it?

The whole language experience naturally added to the pressure of settling into my new life in Westport. I had been hoping for a quiet start to the job but the chaos of the first day continued and we remained incredibly busy. Thirty-one funerals took place during that week – the most I'd ever encountered back at my old company in five days was nine – and the fact that Christmas was just around the corner only made matters worse. The traffic congestion in and around the town was horrendous and the 'genuine' reason why some funerals did in fact run a little late.

On one occasion during my second week I was stuck in traffic for over half an hour on my way to a funeral outside the town. This may not seem a long time in the grand scheme of things, but when you are late for a funeral every minute feels like an eternity – especially when seated next to you is a sweating, cursing funeral director on the verge of heart failure. Bill Travers, a short, grumpy man eagerly approaching retirement, swore at everything that morning; from the poor old gent driving a purple Austin Allegro in front of us to the squeaking brakes on the hearse that I was applying with irritating regularity. Even the festive season itself was at the mercy of his frustration.

'Stupid time of the cowin' year to have Christmas, when all the shops are busy.'

I glanced sideways with my eyes, waiting for him to laugh or even grin at what he had just said. But he maintained his pained expression and to this day I'm convinced Bill was serious.

Traffic jams and funerals can be a potentially explosive combination for all concerned. Those in the funeral industry have often discussed possible solutions to the problem. One of the most popular ideas involved being able to slap a magnetic flashing purple light, American-style on top of the hearse when circumstances necessitated it. Understandably no one ever felt confident enough to put the idea forward to anyone who mattered. It therefore remained a fantasy in the hearts of many in the profession.

Sadly, the days when other drivers will readily give way to a funeral cortege appear increasingly numbered. I have witnessed many occasions when cars have cut in on, or even overtaken, a cortege and it can certainly take a great deal of restraint on the part of the driver not to retaliate in such circumstances. The only time I did succumb to a minor bout of funeral rage years later – when a red Ford Sierra (could it have been anything else?) cut dangerously in between the hearse and the limousine I was driving on the way to the crematorium – the mourners in the back actually chorused their approval as I flashed my lights and raised my hands in irritated disbelief. But during those first few weeks I was on my best possible behaviour as I tried to create a good impression with my new employer. Acceptance from my colleagues, however, came far sooner than I expected and it was not the result of any supposed prowess behind the wheel of a hearse.

As a driver I reported for work to the company's large garage in Tessum Street each morning, where the fleet of hearses and limousines were kept. There were three other drivers based at the garage – a garage foreman by the name of Paul Williams, my friend from Yorkshire, Mark Grainger, and a young man called Nigel Prosser, who in addition to being a driver was also the company mechanic. All four of us were more or less the same age, give or take a couple of years.

Paul was a confident, friendly bloke with short, blonde hair, an equally short and wiry moustache, and a habit of raising his eyebrows in expectation of a response whenever he uttered a cheeky or amusing remark. As Paul was, in effect, my 'line manager', I expected all sorts of questions about my past when we first met – where I had moved from and my experience with funerals for example. But I was in for a surprise.

'My name is Paul. Do you play football?' he asked after I had returned from the 'forgotten funeral' on my first morning.

'Yeah, I do as a matter of fact,' I said curiously.

'Great! What are you doing tomorrow night?'

Considering I had only moved to the area the previous day, my social diary was looking a little blank. 'I don't think I'm doing anything,' I replied optimistically.

'Excellent!' he grinned rubbing his hands together. 'We've got football training. Fancy coming along?'

'Yeah, okay…'

'We've got a big game next week,' interrupted Mark. 'We could do wi' someone who can actually kick a ball. Are you any good?'

'Well I can kick a ball alright.' I was being slightly economical with the truth but they both seemed happy with my answer. I held back from telling them I had represented my school at football for seven years running and scored on a fairly regular basis. I didn't want to put any pressure on myself.

'Right, that's settled then,' said Paul briskly. You're on the team.' And with that he disappeared into one of the hearses. Not a word about work or funerals. I liked him.

While Mark and I were washing vehicles that first afternoon I asked him about the 'big match' he had referred to earlier.

'We're playing t'Dean Street Traders,' he explained. 'Bit of a grudge match actually. There were a lot o' trouble last time we played.'

13

'Right. So what's our team called then?'

'The Undertaker's All Stars.'

I suppressed a laugh. 'Are you serious?'

'Oh aye, deadly,' said Mark with a frown.

A thought occurred to me. Most of the male staff I had met up to that point were clearly the wrong side of fifty. I enquired as to how eleven fit and able men were rounded up from the company for such a physical pursuit.

'Paul and I are t'only ones who play that actually work here,' he admitted. 'You'll be t'third – if you're any good. T'others are made up of gravediggers, Paul's friends, and a couple of kids that live in t'street here.'

I felt a touch disappointed. 'So…it's not strictly an Undertakers All Stars selection then.'

There was indignation in Mark's reply. 'Of course it is. Anyone who plays for us has to have washed at least two funeral vehicles before they're eligible.'

I dipped the sponge in the soapy water and grinned. Coming to Westport, I thought to myself, was sounding like a mighty fine decision already.

4

I will never forget the first time I met Father O'Connor. It was the day we were taking a coffin into St. Augustine's Roman Catholic Church one evening in preparation for the funeral Mass the following day. We stood waiting in the doorway in complete silence, the coffin on a trolley between me and three of my colleagues. The mourners were standing meekly behind, the widow sobbing quietly into a small, white handkerchief as her family comforted her. All was quiet except for the gentle, drifting notes of a traditional funeral melody being played on the church organ. The darkness of an early winter's evening seemed to add to the reflective, melancholic atmosphere of the occasion. Until the arrival of Father Fergus O'Connor.

A commotion at the top of the church caused me to look up and I watched in amazement as a rotund figure with closely cropped hair came hurtling down the aisle towards us, adjusting his robes as he went. He was a couple of minutes late but certainly not enough to warrant the conspicuous haste with which he now approached. His round, middle-aged face was bright red – with embarrassment I thought, but I later discovered that this was his natural hue – and everything about him suggested panic and disarray. As he reached us he plucked a prayer book from somewhere deep inside his cassock and nodded a flustered acknowledgement to the family. He then glanced at us with the awkward grin of a cheeky schoolboy late for school.

If I thought that was the end of the drama I was very much mistaken. Standing alongside Father O'Connor was a self-conscious, bespectacled youth of about fourteen, wearing a robe that covered everything save for a scruffy looking pair of once white trainers. He held out a silver vase by its bucket-like handle, from which Father O'Connor took what looked like a pastry brush. He then began flicking holy water onto the coffin with the violent, jerking movements of a madman. At least that's what he intended to do. But he managed to miss the coffin completely, sending most of the water flying into the screwed up face of the youth.

He then launched into the spoken part of the service in a mumbling, breathy Irish tone. Very few, if any, of the words were understandable: it was merely a vocal drone at top speed and I began to switch off – until he reached the bit where he referred to the deceased by name. '...*Drone, drone, drone*...our dearly beloved brother...I mean sister...no, brother......Francis... Frank.....oh b'Jaysus, now who on earth are we remembering today...?' I looked up in disbelief as he stepped forward, lifted the floral tribute from off the coffin, and read the nameplate underneath. A smile broke out over his face. 'Ah yes, Patrick Toomey. I tort it was!' He grinned, giggled, returned to his place in front of the coffin and simply carried on with the service as though nothing had happened.

I was almost desperate to turn around and see what the family were making of all this. But my newly learned professionalism kept me motionless, eyes to the front and apparently oblivious to the mayhem I had just witnessed. Such dogged determination was about to be severely tested though as Father O'Connor turned to lead the procession down the aisle. Even my more seasoned colleagues exchanged glances at the sight of his cassock suspended at half-mast, revealing two extremely ample, hairy legs.

The next couple of occasions I happened to be driving on a funeral at St. Augustine's remained relatively incident-free, although no funeral involving Father Fergus O'Connor was completely straightforward. He had a wonderful gift for turning the most serene moments into sheer bedlam. As a driver I was in the enjoyable situation of being able to observe such events without having to worry too much about the consequences, unlike the poor funeral director who, depending on their strength of character, could often be reduced to quivering wrecks by the Father's accident-prone prowess. Yet never in all the years of my acquaintance with Father O'Connor did I see anyone take offence. He was such a kind, well-meaning, loveable soul that his clumsiness actually endeared him to people rather than irritated them. In the four years he spent at St. Augustine's he built up a loyal following amongst his parishioners and he certainly developed a cult following throughout the funeral homes of Westport. Both Paul Williams and I in particular talked about his exploits in glowing terms. There was one occasion, however, when even Paul's devotion was tested to the limit.

We had just finished a funeral Mass at St. Augustine's and were ready to leave for the cemetery where the burial was taking place. The family had spoken to a few people outside the church before getting into the limousine and we, the drivers, stood quietly beside the vehicles waiting for Father O'Connor to make his way from the church house to the limousine in order for us to leave. In Westport, ministers usually always travelled in the front of the first limousine rather than take their own cars. Most of the mourners were seated in their vehicles awaiting the departure of the cortege. Only a handful of people not travelling to the cemetery still milled around by the church gate, including Paul, the funeral director on this occasion.

Five minutes passed and I could see Paul beginning to glance restlessly at his watch. After ten minutes he looked distinctly uneasy and he edged towards me. 'I'm going to go and find him,' he whispered. 'I don't know where the heck he's got to. Come and get me if he turns up.'

He disappeared into the church at precisely the same moment Father O'Connor came forth from around the side of the church, pedalling furiously on a bright blue fold-up bicycle. As he sailed past the hearse he rang the bell and then shot precariously down the hill at a ridiculous speed, disappearing rapidly from view. It all happened so fast but I still managed to glimpse a handful of classic 'O'Connorisms' – the big red face with the hint of a grin, the apparent scientific impossibility of a man his size on a machine so small, and a garish-looking shopping bag dangling perilously from the handlebars.

I walked as discreetly as I could back into the empty church – which wasn't easy considering the family were now unavoidably aware that something was wrong – only to be met by a completely indiscreet Paul running out, followed by an equally panic-stricken nun.

'The idiot's gone shopping!' he breathed helplessly.

'What?'

17

'He's gone into town on his bike. He's completely forgotten about doing the burial!'

'I just saw him go past,' I blurted out. 'He even rang his bell at us as he went.'

Paul threw up his arms in despair. 'Why didn't you stop him?

It was actually a very good question and one for which I had no answer. To be perfectly honest the cycling priest had taken me completely by surprise, but that didn't seem much of an excuse. 'He was peddling quite fast,' I offered lamely.

The nun – a small, elderly lady with a slight stoop – interrupted. 'Father Bernard is in the office. Perhaps he could step in and help us?'

I saw the relief flood through Paul's face. He was never very good in a crisis. I once stood and watched him completely trash the inside of a hearse as he desperately searched for a non-existent screwdriver with which to close down a coffin. We were parked outside a house ready to leave for the funeral and I copped it that day as well. All hearses were supposed to carry certain items at all times – including screwdrivers – but on this particular day I had forgotten to check. We ended up using pennies to turn the big screws and we all sported the blisters to prove it afterwards.

'Yes, yes, could you go and ask him if he would be kind enough to do that?' he pleaded. The nun scuttled away and Paul went over to the family, still sitting patiently in the limousine. I waited for their reaction as he launched into the explanation. Every single member of the family in that car broke into a unanimous smile and I figured they would be telling the story of how the priest went shopping on his blue, fold-up bicycle in the middle of their funeral for generations to come.

Wrong names, forgotten burials, late appearances – all these and more were regular features of the funerals officiated at by Father Fergus O'Connor. But for me, his *pièce de resistance* took place just a few weeks after a brand new PA system had been installed in St. Augustine's. It certainly brought the large old church into the twentieth century because instead of fixed microphones at the pulpit, the officiating priests wore clip-on ones so their words could be picked up wherever they moved during the service. This was an excellent innovation but it created

18

unforeseen problems to forgetful, calamity-prone priests like dear old Father O'Connor.

The mourners were gathering at St. Augustine's for a particularly large and prestigious funeral one day and a respectful silence was noticeable as everyone took their seats. The prelude music playing gently in the background was disturbed only by an occasional, faint clicking sound coming from the speakers dotted impressively around the church.

We took the coffin just inside the door and Gareth, the funeral director, gathered the family behind him as we awaited the appearance of Father O'Connor. Then from the hushed reverence came the sound, clearly audible through the sophisticated PA system, of a door closing. Glances were exchanged among those seated as the sound of water on water echoed around the church.

The whistling started soon after – a cheerful, jolly rendition of 'How Great Thou Art' that was sadly and painfully out of tune. By the time the unmistakeable noise of a lavatory flushing met our ears, a low hum of muttered whispering had broken out amongst the congregation. Seconds later Father O'Connor emerged from the top of the church, his ruddy face beaming, blissfully unaware as he shuffled rapidly towards us.

The whole incident had been a virtuoso performance of epic proportions. Not even the BBC's vast and impressive effects department could have done a better job. My visible professionalism was still intact – just – but no one up to that point had ever instructed me how I should attempt to stop my shoulders from shaking in such situations. Under the circumstances I dared not look to see if his cassock was where it should be…

When Father O'Connor eventually moved to a new church outside of our catchment area I felt like I had lost an old friend. Funerals at St. Augustine's were never the same, although admittedly, they were a little more dignified. Somehow, in a slightly rebellious way, this was disappointing. But I felt privileged and contented that I had been a party to the unintentional antics of this kind and likeable man for just a handful of years. I sincerely hope that wherever he went his unique style was equally appreciated and suffered by Catholics and funeral directors alike.

5

The garage in Tessum Street was a strange building, not least because it sat awkwardly in the middle of a residential street looking totally out of place. It was large enough to accommodate the three hearses and six limousines that made up the company's funeral fleet, but it was an ugly building and certainly not the most inviting location to work. From the outside it looked run down and neglected and was, in my opinion, no advert for the funeral profession. It was constantly in need of refurbishment although it was questionable as to whether even this would have improved the overall feel of the place. The finance required to make this eyesore even half more presentable was the sort of money that large companies never quite seem able to lay their hands on.

The realisation that this was now my place of work for the foreseeable future did not initially fill me with a whole lot of enthusiasm. The brickwork was tired and uneven and the roof leaked when it rained – something that occurs with depressing regularity in South Wales. It was particularly frustrating to arrive at work in the morning to find the vehicles we had cleaned the previous afternoon streaked with dirty water. We possessed large, material covers to put over the cars once they were dry in order to shield them from the unpredictable nature of the garage's defects. But we only had three of these and so it became a lottery in itself, choosing which three vehicles to cover and which six to leave unprotected. The simple solution would have been to purchase a further half dozen covers, but our company was one of the many in the world who mysteriously shy away from simple solutions.

The small office situated in the left hand corner as one entered was certainly no oasis in the desert and offered little respite. At times it was preferable to carry on working rather than take a break and sit within its cramped, damp-smelling walls. In winter it was freezing, partly due to a lack of sufficient heating, but also because the door wouldn't shut properly. The frame had apparently been damaged a few months before I started, the result of an incident involving Nigel Prosser and a mallet.

Of my three new colleagues at the Tessum Street garage it was probably Nigel Prosser who interested me the most. He was all arms, legs and spectacles, topped off by a shock of wiry, receding hair with matching moustache, the latter of which always appeared to be in the early stages of growth.

Nigel was one of those types who was into everything. Outside of work – and sometimes in – he was always trying to make an extra few quid. He was a mechanic, a DJ, a quizmaster at the local pub, and a wheeler-dealer in all manner of things. It would not be far from the truth to say he was no expert at any of the above and this often resulted in him being a figure of fun to most of his colleagues. But he always seemed to have more money than the rest of us so who, actually, were the bigger fools? His financial affluence probably accounted for the regular grin that would often light up his face – a grin so wide it threatened to consume his entire head.

Many thought Nigel a tad immature. Although they had a point I actually liked him. I have to confess that this was initially down to the fact that he serviced my car cheaply. Having been the recipient of many a rogue mechanic's handiwork over the years, I considered my acquaintance with Nigel quite a coup. I could therefore tolerate any supposed irritations for that reason alone. The only thing that went against Nigel for me was the fact he got on really well with Stewart Lewis.

Stewart Lewis was one of the funeral directors based in Dean Street and I had not taken to him at all. It didn't take long for me to work out he felt the same way about me. Forgetting a funeral on my first day probably hadn't endeared me to him, although it would be unfair to say I judged him on this event alone. Why he chose to dislike me I'll never know but it certainly wasn't paranoia on my part – many of my new colleagues noticed a distinctly negative attitude towards me too. On the surface Stewart was an amiable person, but underneath there existed something I wasn't quite sure about. This feeling rarely disappeared during the years that followed. There always seemed to be more lurking behind those jet black eyes – thoughts and agendas that were carefully disguised. Like the way he always seemed to agree with whoever was in his company at the time, only to go against them in ensuing conversations with others.

Back down at Tessum Street, Mark Grainger's character was almost the complete opposite to Stewart's. A gruff but friendly Yorkshireman, I always knew where I stood with Mark. He was as straight as a Roman road. Although his occasional grumbling would get on everyone's nerves from time to time, I was actually grateful initially for the immediate presence of someone else from England. I was learning very quickly – and not without some genuine surprise – that the differences between the cultures of Wales and England were not confined to funerals. Maybe I was naïve but I certainly wasn't prepared for the disdain and, on occasion, downright hostility shown towards anyone with an English accent. Mark was a brother-in-arms of sorts, although he remained totally unfazed by any of the above and, knowing Mark, had probably never been affected from the word go.

Mark was of a slim build with hair that continually threatened to drop below collar length. Any longer and someone, somewhere within the company would have had a quiet word. But Mark told me his current style was about the shortest it had ever been. He later proved it with some photos from his pre-funeral days in the seventies, where he looked just like a member of the band Supertramp. He also sported a moustache and I was beginning to wonder whether this was a requirement of the job. I was assured it wasn't and having never been a fan of moustaches, I happily maintained my clean-shaven appearance beneath the nose.

Tessum Street garage itself was banked on either side by narrow, terraced houses, which stretched along both sides of the street in neat, undemonstrative lines. They were so typical of the area and could be found in virtually every district of the town. Their appearance was unspectacular from the front, but once inside they seemed to stretch back endlessly like a railway carriage

With the closeness of the houses to our working environment it didn't take me long to become familiar with our immediate neighbours. On one side lived the Morgan family, whose son Gavin played with us in the Undertakers All Stars; as did his friend, Jim from further down the street. Then on the other side there lived a retired couple, Frank and Rhoda Hammond. I always smiled at the sight of Frank emerging from his red front door each morning. It was as though he went out of his way to look scruffy and unkempt – old pullovers with a decoration of various sized holes, trousers that clearly hadn't seen a washing machine in months, and slippers that had seemingly been chewed into submission by a boisterous dog – except the Hammonds didn't own a dog. Yet for all his scruffiness Frank was an intelligent and talkative man who loved to call in for a chat, usually when we were rushed off our feet. But we made time to talk with him, and all our other neighbours too, especially Arthur and his wife, Ann from number twenty-three across the road.

I enjoyed my conversations with Arthur Morley, a cockney war veteran who was just as jovial and sprightly as I imagined he'd always been, despite his age and his aches and pains. It was after one such chat with Arthur that I finally persuaded my father to send for his unclaimed war medal. Dad had been invalided out of the army with rheumatic fever during World War 2 after barely twelve months. Because of this he never really felt he deserved to claim his service medal. But Arthur was insistent.

'He did his bit. He deserves it as much as the rest of us,' he told me firmly. 'You send for it yourself if he won't.'

Not long after this Dad did indeed send for his medal and duly received a small, brown box in the post a few weeks later, impressively stamped 'O.H.M.S.' – forty-five years after the war had ended. Now that my father has passed away I often look at his medal and think that without the gentle persuasion of Arthur Morley, I may never have had the opportunity to hold such a treasured keepsake in my hand.

There were others in Tessum Street, including the tall, rather fearsome looking bearded man just down from Arthur. He walked with a stick – I later found out he had a false leg – and would always say good morning but very little else. Then there was the dapper gent a couple of doors down from the Hammonds. Very friendly and always ready for a chat, he was a much-travelled man, especially throughout Europe. He had obviously never allowed a severely withered right arm to prevent him from enjoying life.

And so these were my neighbours and these were my colleagues; the people who now made up my new working environment. They lent character and reality to my world and they became as much a part of my daily routine as breathing and growing tired.

Along with driving funeral vehicles of course.

6

I awoke with a start and immediately became aware of a throbbing sensation all over my body. I tried to turn over but this caused even greater discomfort and I ended up remaining in an awkward position somewhere in between. I ached horribly from head to foot. In the stupor of my first few seconds of consciousness I wondered if I had somehow been enticed into a sumo wrestling ring the night before. Then I remembered. Football. I had been playing football. I looked at the clock beside the bed and groaned. I had to be in work in less than an hour and I could hardly move.

It was my fault. I had once been superbly fit; firstly at school when football was a way of life, and secondly when I was a postman negotiating the hills and steps of middle Torbay. But since then it would be fair to say I wasn't quite as fit as I used to be and exercise was low down on my list of priorities. Now, as I closed in on the grand old age of twenty-three, I was suffering for my laziness.

In agony I dragged myself out of bed. As I hobbled to the bathroom the memories of my debut for the Undertakers All Stars the evening before came flooding back. Unfortunately not even the result could provide a crumb of comfort. The heartless Traders had thrashed us 5-0 and it probably could, and should, have been more had it not been for Hughie 'The Cat' in goal. To be perfectly frank I was a little bit miffed with Paul. Despite having educated him as to my adeptness as a striker, he had selected me at left back, a position I was none too familiar with. Although I felt I had done reasonably well, the fact I had been part of a defence that leaked five goals clearly said otherwise.

Now in the kitchen I momentarily forgot my physical limitations and reached up into the cupboard for the cereal packet. I let forth a mild expletive as a pain seared up my entire right hand side. Gingerly I put the packet down wondering how on earth I could be aching there at all. It would seem I had rediscovered muscles that had long been neglected.

Out on the pitch itself I hadn't felt too bad at first. Then after half an hour it was as though an entire coffin delivery was lying on my chest. I was quite alarmed by the amount of wheezing and coughing I had done throughout the match too. The fact I am a passionate non-smoker seemed to give me no advantage at all, which upon reflection was actually quite irritating. There was only one thing for it. As I drove into work I decided there and then to retire gracefully from the world of football.

I came out of retirement just four weeks later for a rematch against the Traders. Paul, having admitted his tactical *faux pas*, talked me round quite easily with the lure of a position leading the attack. By then, of course, my body and soul had recovered to the point where I felt it surely hadn't been as bad as I had made out. It was, and I suffered equally as much following match number two. But this time I had the exhilaration of a win and a rather craftily taken goal to cushion the agony. All the aches and pains were suddenly bearable. It's amazing what a bit of sporting success can do for the male psyche.

Having turned things around in the second game in which I played, the Undertakers All Stars then went on what has since become a much-celebrated unbeaten run of ten games. We even beat a couple of local league teams on the way. But best of all was that initial sweet revenge gained over our fiercest rivals, a 4-1 win against the low-down ne'er-do-well traders from Dean Street. I scored goals on a regular basis throughout the run, which, as I say, did wonders for the sporting ego, not to say the stiff muscles that followed. We even achieved one of the transfer coups of the decade when Rottweiler Rob, one of the Dean Street Traders' midfield stalwarts, swapped allegiances to play for us. I was a little dubious at first, especially as the eligibility clause of washing funeral vehicles was mysteriously dispensed with. This was mainly down to the fact that Rob was dating Paul's cousin, a quality that apparently qualified him automatically to play for the Undertakers All Stars. It troubled me for a while but worries about nepotism and correct procedures soon paled into insignificance as the unbeaten run grew and we conquered everything and everyone in our path.

One thing I noticed with depressing regularity during my undertaking football career was the fact that the day following a game was always a strenuous one in work. It was as uncanny as it was infuriating. The funeral profession is a very physically demanding job at times but the coffins were always heavier, the house removals guaranteed to be more awkward, and the hours before one could return home to rest aching limbs seemed longer. How much of this existed in the mind is debatable, but I remember being convinced on one occasion that a conspiracy against my weary body was afoot.

I had only just crawled into work on the morning in question when I received a message via the receptionist to say there was a house removal awaiting our attendance. No one else was available to go other than Dai Proctor – one of my non-football playing colleagues – and myself. The conspiracy theory kicked into action at hearing the words 'no one else available.' Out of a staff of approximately twenty I found it highly suspicious that only two of us were free right at that moment. That's the way it goes from time to time but it doesn't stop the mind from putting two and two together in a self-persecuting attempt to make five. However, I shrugged my shoulders, which after a hard match the night before was an extremely painful thing to do, and went in search of Dai.

I must have looked a sorry sight upon arriving at the house that morning. When every possible muscle in existence is aching, extricating one's body from a car with dignity becomes a major issue, especially when there is an audience. Two members of the bereaved family were awaiting us outside the front door of the small cottage. The first, bearing a slightly puzzled expression at seeing my laboured movements, introduced himself as the son of the deceased.

'Mam's upstairs, second room on the right.'

Upstairs. The word was like breaking glass on a wooden floor. I offered my condolences through clenched teeth and asked them to wait in the front room until we had attended to the removal. The funeral director had spoken to the family on the phone earlier so our presence there was merely to convey the deceased back to the chapel of rest. Dai fetched the stretcher from the back of the estate car and we began to climb the narrow stairs, which wound alarmingly to the left halfway up. Such picturesque staircases probably mean little to the majority of people other than their attractiveness as a design feature. But to undertakers they were designed by the devil and one of the banes of the profession. Architects and builders must have very red ears because there is always a panting, struggling undertaker somewhere, cursing the ridiculously small and cramped house designs in so many British homes.

We stepped respectfully into the tiny, dimly lit bedroom and I breathed a sigh of relief when I looked down at the bed. A small head with eyes closed rested peacefully on the pillow, the rest of her body covered by a pale green quilt. She had slipped away quietly in her sleep – surely the most comforting way to go – and Dai and I exchanged knowing smiles. It was still going to be awkward, especially on the staircase, but at least the lady was of a small build and would not place too much excess strain on my partly functioning body.

Dai opened the stretcher and placed it in the narrow strip of space between the bed and the wardrobe and I gently pulled back the quilt to check the lady for any jewellery she may be wearing. As I did so I gave a cartoon-style double take.

'What the....!'

Dai was absorbed in placing a piece of protective plastic sheeting on the stretcher, but he looked up at my exclamation and reacted in almost identical fashion. There, lying in front of us was a woman approximately twenty stone in weight. Her huge torso, legs, and arms filled the bed and that small, delicate head suddenly seemed totally out of place. In fact, at that moment, I was convinced it was the wrong head for the body. It didn't match. It was abnormal, surreal. Such situations cannot be staged of course but I had the distinct impression someone, somewhere was having a laugh. I had to call on sheer will power, guts, and something from the unknown to move that lady down the absurd staircase and out of the front door with Dai. If muscles could talk then mine would have been screaming in protest throughout the entire operation.

Over the years people have often smiled when I use the term 'dead weight.' But anyone who has ever lifted a dead or unconscious person will know exactly what I mean when I say the weight does literally increase. A live or responsive person will almost unintentionally assist when they are being lifted, even if it is only to shift their weight a little or move into a slightly more helpful position. But the dead cannot do this and moving them in a dignified manner, especially in tight spaces, often proved extremely difficult.

Dai drove the estate back to our premises: I had neither the strength nor the will power to even contemplate it. When we lifted the stretcher off at the chapel of rest I wondered, as I often did at that stage, how on earth we'd ever moved the body in the first place. Somehow we always managed.

As we put the body away in the cold room it came as no surprise to see vast numbers of my colleagues milling around in the background looking for something to do. Conspiracy? You bet.

7

Within six months of taking up my new post in Westport, fate delivered three setbacks, all of which created a profound and lasting effect on my morale. The first of these disappointments came literally after just a few weeks.

Rhys Parry was one of the craziest people I've ever known, not just in the funeral profession but throughout my entire life. This was the first of two major reasons why I took to him from the moment we first met. The second became more apparent as each day passed.

As far as my new colleagues were concerned – the funeral directors in particular – Rhys was by far the most light-hearted and relaxed of them all. This characteristic appealed greatly to me. I always felt far more comfortable in his company as opposed to many of the other often intense and humourless individuals I found myself working with. I have always identified far more easily with the Rhys Parry's of this world. He never shied away from the chance to have a good laugh, he was uncomplicated and trustworthy, there were no hidden agendas in his personality, and he possessed a heart of gold – a willingness to help anyone who was in genuine need. This included green, wet-behind-the-ears funeral novices such as me. More than anyone else, Rhys took me under his wing from day one and helped me settle into my strange new surroundings.

Rhys was middle-aged, sturdily built but not overweight, with twinkling eyes that always seemed ready to break into a smile. His hair, thick and black with tinges of grey, was usually covered during funerals by a stylish top hat. Rhys was one of a handful of funeral directors I've known down the years who could wear a top hat without looking like a misplaced circus ringmaster.

Because he was a practising Roman Catholic he conducted a fair amount of the town's Catholic funerals and these were always an experience to drive on. It quickly became obvious that

Rhys was an immensely popular figure, not least with the nuns who literally adored him. Most were at least twice his age, yet they giggled like schoolgirls when in his presence. He was a born entertainer – confident but not arrogant, cheeky but never offensive – and it was a pleasure to work with him. But not everyone felt the same.

Many of Rhys Parry's peers thought him too brash and irreverent for the funeral profession. Rumours were rife of his apparent outrageous behaviour. He was once supposed to have been driven down one of Westport's busiest streets with his legs dangling merrily out of the hearse window. Many were also convinced he had sneaked into the premises late one night to embalm his children's recently deceased pet hamster. These, and other such tales, may or may not have happened, but for me Rhys had the perfect temperament for such a potentially consuming profession. He was without doubt one of the most successful funeral directors I ever worked with and this clearly sat uneasily with the so-called traditionalists. In the years that followed I grew to realise that Rhys was also one of the few funeral directors I worked with who didn't possess an ego the size of a train station.

As each working day came to an end, the driver's orders for the following day would be delivered to the garage and I would eagerly skim through them to see if I was driving Rhys. Invariably I was (I later found out he always asked for me) and I would go to work the following morning completely motivated and enthused by the prospect of another day of guaranteed enjoyment. Then suddenly, out of the blue, Rhys handed in his notice. I walked into the garage one morning and heard the other boys discussing the matter.

'He's been on about leaving for a while,' Paul was saying. 'He's not been happy since the takeover.'

Mark nodded his head in agreement. 'Pretty bold move if you ask me though. T'Middle East can be a volatile place to go and work.'

'Yeah, but if anyone can do it, he can.'

'Aye, you're right there.'

'Who's this?' I asked casually, having approached the conversation with only mild interest.

'Rhys has resigned,' answered Paul. 'He's taken up an engineering contract out in Saudi Arabia.'

I rocked on my heels, stunned into devastated silence. This couldn't be right. Not Rhys. Surely he would have said something to me. But it was true. On a funeral with him that afternoon he told me the full story. Disillusioned with working for a large funeral company, it was a move he had been planning for some time. He was an engineer by trade and the opportunity to work in Saudi Arabia was too lucrative to pass up. By the time the ten-year contract was finished, he and his family would be financially secure for life.

Back at my lodgings that night I felt as though the bottom had fallen out of my new world. I had been in Westport barely a couple of months, during which time I had made only one really true friend. Now he was deserting me to make his fortune. I couldn't blame him of course, but in an evening of self-pity I found it hard to envisage life at work without him. Although I was getting on fine with most of the others, Rhys, for me, was that rare breed in the workplace – a genuine friend who could be completely trusted, rather than just another colleague.

I kept in touch with Rhys long after he left for his new life abroad. His contract allowed him home for a fortnight every five weeks and I made a point of calling in to see him on these occasions. His wife, Michelle, was like a second mother to me during those early days. She also told me something during Rhys's first few weeks away that almost compensated for his absence. She said she had noticed him suddenly coming home from work a lot more cheerful than usual. When she asked him why he told her it was because a new chap had started who enjoyed a laugh as much as he did. Although at that stage his decision to leave was already made, she told me he was genuinely sorry to be leaving me behind.

Rhys Parry's last few days in work were unbelievable. I was his hearse driver for every funeral he conducted in his final week and we took endless detours on the way back to base after each one so he could say farewell to somebody. The nuns were heartbroken to see him leave and many tears were shed as he kissed each one of them goodbye with the charm and the panache of a film star. As we left a melancholic convent on that final Friday afternoon, I remember smiling and thinking to myself that it was the Middle East that needed to be worried about the arrival of Mr Rhys Parry, not the other way around.

Although the resignation of Arnold James was less painful to me personally, the impact, ultimately, held probably greater significance than Rhys Parry's departure three months earlier.

Arnold was the manager of the funeral operation in Westport – a tall, imposing man in his early fifties. He was a strict boss and I often found him a little intimidating. His gold-rimmed spectacles and assertive presence enhanced his stature and he certainly commanded respect from all those around him. This, as I would later learn, is a vital ingredient for anyone in a position of management.

My dealings with Arnold were probably less than those I experienced with everyone else. A good boss keeps a slight distance and Arnold had this trait down to a fine art. Always friendly yet somehow watchful and observant, I certainly felt obliged to be at my best whenever he was around. This was no great effort on my part – I was grateful to him and did not want to let him down. He had, after all, interviewed me for the position I now held and had subsequently taken a chance on an unknown quantity from across the border. I don't think expectations were any higher but he could easily have passed me over for a local, more politically-correct choice.

When the news reached me that Arnold James too had resigned I was still unaware of the politics bubbling beneath the surface of my new surroundings: neither did I fully understand the reasons or motivations behind them. In time, all would become clearer, but for now I was just sorry to be losing a good boss and, like Rhys before him, someone I trusted.

Looking back, I don't think I ever really recovered from Rhys Parry's departure, nor, for completely different reasons, that of Arnold James either. The effect of both was quite unsettling, not least for Arnold's quiet but worrying parting words to me.

'Tom,' he said, placing a hand on my shoulder, 'I wish you all the best. But look out for Stewart Lewis. For some reason – and I've no idea why – he's taken a disliking to you. Watch your back.'

And with those words of warning ringing in my ears, I listened grimly to the announcement a few weeks later of setback number three. Stewart Lewis had been installed as the new manager of the Westport branch. I closed my eyes and let out a heavy, nervous sigh.

8

The Reverend Norman Jones had the perfect face for a funeral: sad, drooping eyes embedded in a long face from which leathery jowls hung loosely like the curtains in our chapel of rest. To undertakers he was affectionately known as 'The Voice', for he had also been blessed with the beautifully rich tones of a Shakespearean actor. At funerals his velvet timbre made even the mundane parts of the service sound like a recital.

We never knew exactly how old Reverend Jones was, only that he was long retired and probably somewhere in his eighties. His age was never a handicap though and he always made himself available for funerals, especially on occasions when local parish priests in the town were away or otherwise engaged. He was, if you'll excuse the pun, a godsend to funeral directors. One of the most difficult tasks when arranging a funeral is trying to tie in the minister with whatever times may be available at the crematorium or the cemetery, particularly the former. Ministers can be incredibly busy people so the back up of someone so readily available was a welcome reassurance.

As long as we didn't interfere with his daily ritual of lunch at the local pub, the Reverend Jones was more than happy to help us out. If ever we required him for an afternoon funeral we always asked him what he'd had to eat that day. He would reply with a sumptuous description of every morsel that had graced his plate, making even the humblest of meals sound like a feast fit for a king, or indeed, a faithful servant of the good Lord Himself.

He was also the bearer of many a nostalgia-tinged quote. Gems such as: *It seems strange to see a bus driving down Hanbury Avenue*, and: *I remember the day they planted those trees*, would roll effortlessly from his cultured tongue. He never expanded upon them. They remained one-line random observations hanging teasingly in the air: snapshots of an era we youngsters knew nothing of. Yet the vocal dexterity of the

Reverend Jones made us feel like we had indeed once been a part of his world.

It was from such an era that my favourite story about this local legend came – an era when funerals and funeral parlours were seen but never discussed; when hearses were vehicles of dark, foreboding mystery. Those days are now thankfully disappearing and some, though not all, of the barriers from one of the world's greatest remaining taboos have tumbled gently down. The hearses of these days were huge and intimidating, usually with a thick, dark purple curtain running around the inside of the rear windows, as though hiding some awful secret inside. One such hearse once roved the streets of Westport bringing silent unease and cold shivers to its inhabitants.

Another funeral over and it was time to leave the cemetery, but the Reverend Norman Jones needed an urgent lift home. There were no seats available in the hearse and the funeral director suggested the only solution was for him to lie down in the back with the curtain drawn. Reverend Jones was desperate – he had an appointment somewhere: maybe it was his lunch at The Kings Arms – and so he readily agreed.

The hearse rattled and rolled its way back towards the town centre and it wasn't long before Norman felt the bruises starting to form. It seemed an uncomfortably long journey. Then finally they stopped and the Reverend parted the curtains in relieved anticipation of the front door of the vicarage. Instead, he stared straight into the horrified faces of two old ladies standing at the Barn View junction. One screamed; the other turned pale.

Eventually the hearse continued on its way. No one ever knew who those ladies were, nor if they fully recovered. But it appeared that even in his younger years the Reverend Norman Jones possessed the perfect funeral face.

Hearses are something of a strange commodity. They are built for one reason and one reason only – the conveyance of the deceased. Cars and vans have a multitude of uses but the hearse has no purpose in life other than death.

This probably explains why many undertakers, especially the smaller, private concerns, hang onto them for as long as possible. They need to get every inch of service out of these preciously expensive vehicles. A good hearse can provide several decades of use if maintained properly. They do not date like ordinary cars – the older models still look the part. Indeed many people actually prefer the traditional classic hearses made by the likes of Daimler and Rolls Royce.

However, not all funeral vehicles are looked after quite as well as they should be. In fact, I often wondered when I saw one particular hearse driving around Westport how its owner had the cheek to actually use it on funerals. This undertaker was what we generally referred to as a 'one man band.' He had a hearse, his name, and little else. He would rely on other, bigger undertaking companies to do the bulk of his legwork. We accommodated many such independents, supplying them with coffins, chapel of rest facilities, limousines, and drivers on the day of the funeral itself. The reasoning was that if we hadn't been approached by the family to do the funeral ourselves, we might as well make some money out of the undertaker who had.

One day I was standing outside the garage with Griffith Evans, one of our part-time drivers, when the hearse in question rattled its way past, ejecting a continuous cloud of thick, grey smoke from a rusting exhaust pipe. Griff, a crusty old Welshman in his seventies who suffered no fool easily, tutted as the bone-shaking heap of black metal lurched around the corner and disappeared from view.

'Shed of a vehicle,' he growled distastefully. "I wouldn't be seen dead in that thing.'

It goes without saying that the likes of Griff are an integral cog in the British undertaking machine. Without them, funeral directors the length and breadth of the nation would grind to a shuddering halt.

The amount of staff our company employed rarely equated to the number of drivers needed for funerals. Rare were the days when the 'casual drivers,' as we referred to them, were not required and everything could be covered by full-timers. Because the casuals seldom became involved in removals, taking care of the deceased, fitting coffins, or making funeral arrangements, they invariably only drove on funerals while many of the full-time staff stayed behind to carry out the behind-the-scenes work.

This was okay in theory, but the fact that as part-timers they did not qualify for a clothing issue caused no end of problems. Funerals are a very public event and people attending them notice the funeral director, the coffin, the vehicles, and the drivers. They notice the drivers even more when, as was the case on numerous occasions, they were dressed in a variety of mismatched clothing. I never understood management's half-hearted attitude to this area of the business. It made clear sense to me to ensure that all staff in the regular public eye were dressed consistently and appropriately. Things have improved in recent years but in Westport in the eighties and nineties, it was low on my particular company's list of priorities.

Casual drivers were generally either retired men bored with sitting around the house, night shift workers who didn't mind depriving themselves further of sleep during the day, and the unemployed – the route by which I myself had entered the profession. It was hardest for the unemployed. The money was poor and the hours never guaranteed so it was impossible to make a living from such endeavour, as I knew only too well. Financially I found that particular period in my life difficult to endure and it was only the sheer determination and hope that my efforts would one day secure a full-time position, coupled with the support of my family, that kept me going.

With these factors in mind it is no surprise to learn that a colourful variety of candidates applied for this most unusual of part-time occupations. They came with a whole host of skills, young and old, and in all shapes and sizes. The latter was particularly important. It must be one of the few jobs where height is crucial, yet no one interviewing these prospective drivers seemed to think of this until it was too late. I have seen many a coffin being shouldered down the aisles of crematoriums and churches looking like a ship in a storm because of an alarming discrepancy in shoulder height.

In my time I worked with literally dozens of casual drivers. Some stayed with us for years; others lasted only a few weeks, days even. But one I will always remember is a young man in his late twenties by the name of Alan Hodder. Of slim build with gingery-blonde hair and piercing blue eyes, Alan suffered the awful indignity of a stutter like a machine gun. But he rarely allowed it to interfere with his ambition of pursuing a career with us and for that I admired him greatly. His lofty aspirations did not get off to the greatest of starts however.

The lack of instruction given to casual drivers was almost laughable. The training usually consisted of a two-minute drive around the block before being sent out alone into the big, wide funeral world, driving vehicles twice the size of anything they had ever negotiated before. Alan was subjected to this highly sophisticated procedure and, having then prepared his limousine to perfection, set off for his very first funeral.

He arrived at one of our satellite branches in Penderi Village just outside the town and began to reverse into a space in front of the office. At that precise moment the resident funeral director happened to be looking out of the window and saw Alan inching perilously close to his own car. He seemed to be coping well but then with a sudden, inexplicable surge he crashed into the rear of the Renault Clio with clinical ease.

The sound of car against car always brings out the inquisitive. By the time I arrived in the hearse a nice little crowd had gathered to witness the crisis brewing outside the funeral home. I tried to console a distraught Alan – whose stutter had now reached Morse code proportions – and the funeral director who was examining the damage to his precious car with flailing arms of disbelief.

I eventually managed to restore a little calm and civility to the situation – although I stopped short of organising a bonding group hug – and by the time we went out on the funeral, complete professionalism had returned.

A couple of days later when I was in Penderi Village again for another funeral, I happened to notice Alan's completed Accident Report Form lying on the desk. I casually picked it up and glanced over the front page:

NAME – *Alan Royston Hodder.* ADDRESS – *blah, blah, blah.* AGE – *27.* TYPE OF DRIVING LICENCE HELD – *Full.* Time of accident – *10.37.*

I was about to put the form down again when my eyes caught sight of question six:

HOW LONG HAVE YOU BEEN EMPLOYED WITH THE COMPANY?

I giggled helplessly as I read Alan's scribbled reply.
2 hours and 7 minutes.

9

'So which undertaker do you work for then?

'I…. er…. well…. quite a few actually.'

'Right. So where are they based?'

'Well, they're all over the place. We have branches right across the town.'

'So what's the company's actual name then?'

I had this kind of conversation regularly. Around about halfway through I would reel off a long list of small undertaking firms in the area, all of whom I actually represented when at work. At this point the person would usually depart the scene with a scratch of the head wishing they'd never asked. I sympathised greatly with them all.

When I first moved to Westport I never envisaged for one minute the complicated web of intrigue that encompassed the funeral profession there. I had come from one branch, proudly displaying its name above the premises with one location and one building. In Westport there were branches, buildings, and locations galore, each bearing a different name. It was ridiculously confusing.

Slowly I began to learn the local history. Westport is very tribal in its layout, with distinct boundaries between districts and areas. It was almost as though some town planner from the distant past had sat down in front of a map of the area, drawn a rough circle around a collection of villages and hamlets and decided to collectively call them a town.

Most of these areas had their own undertaker, who was entrusted with the final journeys of those members of the community who had passed on. Then one day in the late sixties, a group of these small concerns decided to amalgamate in order to share costs and vehicles etc. The result was a funeral company that soon became unofficially known as the Westport posse. I never discovered the reason for such an interesting moniker but it had more to do with a tongue-in-cheek nickname thought up by a rival than gun-toting, cowboy hat-wearing guardians of the deceased.

A short time before I moved to Westport this small conglomerate was then itself the victim of a somewhat more ominous player entering the equation. Eventually the owner succumbed and a takeover bid submitted by a large funeral company was successful: they took control just six months before I started. In fact, I was the first to be employed full-time under this new regime.

It didn't take me long to realise there was a great deal of resentment from my new colleagues towards the takeover. They figured things had been fine as they were and needed no intervention from the big boys, especially as they had been told never to use the company's real name in public for fear of a backlash. The company were well known throughout South Wales but certainly not well liked. We were under strict instructions, therefore, to use only the original company names, pretending they were still private concerns. This never sat comfortably with any of us, especially those who had lived through the transition.

At first I thought the attitude of my colleagues was a little negative and narrow-minded. Surely a larger company would have far bigger resources to pump into the business, not to mention better conditions for the staff and, ultimately, a better service for the clients. The first seeds of doubt were sown in my mind when Rhys Parry departed: his disdain for the takeover was well known. The seeds then grew even bigger at the controversial departure of Arnold James. Suddenly I realised all was not well in my new world. The politics of business were very much on my doorstep and they would affect me no matter how much I tried to ignore them.

As the years passed, my innocence was replaced by an underlying cynicism as I, together with my disillusioned colleagues, watched things slowly and painfully deteriorate. Yet despite the difficulties, we never compromised on our service to the people who mattered most – the bereaved and their loved ones who had passed away. It was their welfare that always took priority, borne out of a compassion that brings so many to this strange but rewarding profession.

If only those who took over the decision-making could have understood this vital concept a little better.

One local funeral director whom I very much doubt was in line for a takeover bid from anyone was Cyril Norman, painter and decorator.

I was eighteen months into the job before I first met Cyril. Up until then I had never even heard his name mentioned. Then on my driver's orders one morning I read the instructions to pick up a Mr Cyril Norman at his home, 1 Ormsby Place, Millfield, at 10.15am. I looked up at Paul who was busy polishing his shoes.

'Who's Cyril Norman?'

A knowing grin broke out across Paul's face. He's an independent funeral director. Sort of.'

'What do you mean, 'sort of'?

'Well, he's actually a painter and decorator. He does funerals as a side line.' Paul didn't offer any further information so I didn't ask and an hour later I was on my way to Millfield to pick him up in a spotless, shining hearse.

1 Ormsby Place was a ramshackle of a house. In estate agent-speak it would loosely be termed as 'having potential.' It was certainly a large property with ample grounds but I was surprised to see the home of a painter and decorator looking so shabby. It was hardly an advert for the man's talents.

I walked along an untidy, overgrown pathway leading to the front door and rang the bell. It didn't work. At least I couldn't hear it working so I knocked loudly on the flaking wooden door. Eventually I heard footsteps approaching and there then followed several seconds of grunting and pulling as someone tried desperately to open the door. It appeared to be sticking somewhere, possibly in more places than one. Then suddenly, the thing flew backwards and a figure stood imposingly in the now vacant gap.

'Good morning,' he said in a cultured tone that did not match his appearance. He wore a very old, brown gabardine coat that barely concealed a protruding stomach, a dirty pair of grey trousers, and a well-worn pair of black brogue shoes. All three items were generously splattered with specks of cream-coloured paint. With tufts of white hair protruding alarmingly from the sides of his head he looked to be well into his sixties and not too enthusiastic about his appearance.

I looked beyond him into the grubby passageway. 'Er... good morning. I'm here to pick up Mr Cyril Norman for the funeral. Is he ready yet?'

'I am he. And yes, I am ready. Shall we go?'

I made the snap decision not to reply verbally for fear of spluttering incomprehensibly. Mr Norman reached behind the door and placed a light brown trilby on his head. I was glad he did that: it added a touch of much-needed decorum. He grunted his way awkwardly down the steps to the passenger side of the hearse and as I saw him in profile, it looked for all the world as though someone had shoved a very large balloon up the front of his coat.

Throughout the whole of that funeral my demeanour was a combination of cringing horror and sheer disbelief. Yet no one in attendance seemed to notice his unique sense of dress for an occasion so sombre. In fact, everyone treated him with great affection and respect and standing by my gleaming hearse in my charcoal grey suit, I couldn't help but feel I was the one who was out of place, not him.

When I arrived back at the garage there were a few smiles on the faces of my colleagues.

'So you've met Cyril at last' grinned Mark. 'How did it go?'

'It was...interesting.'

Paul began chuckling. 'So tell us, what colour was the paint today?'

'Cream.'

'Oh, that's not too bad. Last time I drove him it was fire engine red!'

'How on earth can he go out on a funeral looking like that?' I said.

'I've no idea,' replied Paul. 'But he only does one, maybe two funerals a year.'

'Really?' I replied with eyebrows raised. 'As many as that.'

10

'So there we were, wandering around this enormous nursing home in the middle of the night. Did not have a clue where we were. Then finally I sees a nurse. "Scuse me, bach?" I said. "We've come to pick up Mr Pardue. Could you tell us which room he's in, please?" Well, she was a miserable piece, this nurse. Had a face like a bulldog chewing a wasp, she did.'

I chuckled as my new friend paused briefly to take a gulp from his cup of tea.

'She just pointed down the corridor, growled "Room eleven," and disappeared like. Well I says to Walter, "it looks like we're on our own by yer, boy.' Anyway, we steps quietly into room eleven and walks over to the bed. I'm opening up the stretcher when Walter hisses at me. "What's up now?" I said. "There's another body over by yer," he said. Well he was right. There were two people in the room, and to be perfectly honest, Tom bach, either one of them could have been dead. So Walter says to me: "This must be the one, Dyfrig. He looks cowin' awful".'

Dyfrig paused once again from his entertaining tale as he took out a battered, black leather tobacco pouch and began to roll a cigarette with bony, nicotine-stained fingers. He finally put the finished article in his mouth and lit it with a tarnished silver lighter. After drawing blissfully for a few seconds, he continued.

'Well I put the stretcher by the bed and we lifted the old boy down carefully. "Tidy," I said. "He's quite light, Walter. Shouldn't have too many problems by yer." Well I spoke too soon didn't I? As we were walking out of the door, Walter trips over the doorstop and goes down like a sack of potatoes. "Walter!" I says, "Stop messing about and open your eyes, man!" But, Tom bach, as true as I'm sitting by yer now, someone did open their eyes – but it wasn't Walter. The corpse had come back to life. We'd picked up the wrong body!'

I burst out laughing. 'What did he do?'

45

'Nothing,' said Dyfrig. 'We undid the straps and got the poor bugger back into bed before he fully came round. I've never seen Walter move so fast in all my life.'

At that moment, Islwyn Thomas bustled into the small rest room. 'Dyfrig, are you telling that story again?' he groaned.

'Aye boss. It is still as good now as it was at the time.'

'Oh, Dyfrig, Dyfrig!' cried Islwyn with mock dismay. 'Tom bach, don't you listen to a word this old fool says!' He paused and winked. 'It is a good story though, is it not?'

I laughed and finished my glass of milk. Not being a drinker of tea or coffee it was my only option, but I didn't mind. In fact, I was having the time of my life. I had been sent to drive on funerals at our branch in Abertrefil for the day, a small, parochial town about eight miles east of Westport. I felt like I'd walked in on a variety show. Never in my entire existence had I met characters like the staff at this crazy, busy office.

Islwyn Thomas was the manager, a chunky man in his early sixties with a square face and a mouth that rose slightly to the right. I doubt I've ever met a louder person: in fact, he probably bordered on over-exuberance. But it was rarely irritating because he was so entertaining in the process.

Dyfrig Griffiths was almost the opposite, laid back to the point of falling over – which would have been a long way for he was a very tall, lean man who looked as though even the smallest-sized clothes would hang loosely on him. His thin, weather-beaten face was barely visible behind dark-rimmed spectacles and he wheezed frequently, hardly surprising considering the amount of cigarettes he smoked.

Funerals in Abertrefil were completely different again to what I had now become accustomed to in Westport, despite the short distance between the two places. Here they seemed more down to earth and slightly less formal, as though maybe the people of Abertrefil were more accepting of the fact that death is very much a part of life. A lot of this was due to the way Islwyn handled his funerals. His larger than life personality didn't make for a continually melancholic atmosphere and it did seem to have a positive effect on all those in attendance.

Today, my first ever funeral in Abertrefil was taking place at the large church in the town centre. There seemed little privacy there for an occasion so personal. A supermarket on one side and the bus station on the other flanked the tall grey church that was St. John's: opposite was the edge of the main shopping area. Many central churches in towns and cities all over the country now find themselves suffocated by the surrounding modern architecture. Where they once stood like majestic beacons – focal points of the areas they served – they now cower awkwardly amongst urban gardens of concrete, glass, and oblivious consumerism.

After we had taken the coffin down the aisle of St John's to reside in front of the alter, we returned to the rear of the church where most undertakers will wait while the service is in progress. Against the back wall that day was a mountain of tinned food and a notice just above proclaiming a collection for the needy in Africa. It appeared the people of Abertrefil had been very generous, as the colourful pile of tins was extremely impressive.

Back outside in the shy spring sun, I saw the family safely into the limousine and then stood patiently beside the driver's door awaiting Islwyn's nod. When it came, I opened the door and got in. As I sat down I noted a distinct inability to get myself comfortable. I put my hand into the right hand pocket of my raincoat and removed two tins of sardines. With a giggle beginning to rumble ominously from inside I then removed a tin of pineapple chunks from the left pocket, just at the moment Islwyn opened the passenger door for the vicar.

Horrified, I flicked the tins underneath my backside and smiled awkwardly at the beaming priest getting in beside me. As he pulled the seatbelt across his chest, Islwyn leaned in with a ridiculously inane grin on his cube-like face.

'Everything okay, Tom bach?'

'Er...yes thank you,' I lied, already beginning to feel uncomfortable sitting on the tins.

'Splendid, splendid! You are in good hands, vicar. Young Tom here trains with a Formula One racing team you know.'

'Oh very impressive!' smiled the still beaming vicar as Islwyn closed the door. 'That must be very exciting, very exciting indeed. Do you want to be a racing driver, Tom?'

I spent the next couple of minutes trying to explain that Islwyn had in fact been jesting, but the damage was done. First impressions in life are always crucial and so to the vicar of Abertrefil I would never be anything less than a future Formula One racing driver. I'm sorry to say I gave up on my protestations and decided to run with the story, unashamedly boasting of various exploits and daring deeds on the racetrack.

At least it took my mind off the food mountain I was perched upon, an affliction that was becoming more uncomfortable by the second. I hadn't yet worked out how I was going to hide the tins when we reached our destination either. The moment I got out of the car, there they would be in all their glory, fresh from the vicar's proud collection of tins for Africa's poor and hungry. I still couldn't believe how Islwyn had managed to slip them in my pockets during the service without me noticing.

I was greatly relieved when we finally reached the crematorium, even more so when the vicar alighted as soon as we stopped and disappeared into the small vestry to prepare for the committal service. This gave me the opportunity to quickly hide the now much-travelled sardines and pineapple chunks under the seat. It was touch and go but I managed it unnoticed.

After the service I returned the family home and then dropped the vicar off at the church. As he made to get out, he placed his hand on my arm.

'And jolly good luck with the racing,' he beamed excitedly. 'You never know, I might be watching you on the television one day!'

There was much merriment back at the office when I returned. Even the usually unflappable Dyfrig was enjoying the moment. 'Haw haw! We've all had it done to us at one time or another, bach,' he chortled. 'My lot was spaghetti hoops and a steamed pudding!'

'Tom bach, I must apologise for our juvenile behaviour!' interrupted Islwyn noisily. 'What must you think of us, boy? Terrible state of affairs. Now then, who fancies sardines on toast?'

From that day on I loved being sent over to Abertrefil to drive on funerals. It was almost like going away on holiday and visiting old friends: I was greeted as such on each occasion. I finally got to meet the legendary Walter too. I was shocked to discover he was eighty-six years old. He worked on a part-time basis, mainly fitting coffins but quite how he managed this was amazing because the poor man appeared to be quite riddled with arthritis.

Walter Murdoch was a small fellow with jagged features and white, wispy hair. He also had hands like a pair of coal shovels that just didn't match the rest of his body. But despite being a man of few words, Walter had an amazing tale to tell. He could neither read nor write (*never saw the point, bach*) and in his younger days during the 1920's, he made his money through organised but unofficial boxing matches. He told me how he would spend a whole week walking to the west coast ports of Wales, sleeping under hedgerows and in ditches, and then fighting some unknown in a makeshift boxing ring before hiking all the way back to Abertrefil. At first I wasn't sure whether to believe such stories, but in a rare moment of seriousness both Islwyn and Dyfrig assured me they were very definitely true. They also told me what Walter himself seemed reluctant to add – that he won most of these fights and was something of a local hero in his day.

When Walter Murdoch died a couple of years later I found myself thinking about his early years and how starkly they contrasted with modern life. As people like Walter pass away a part of history goes with them. It is up to us to ensure that the stories and tales they tell are never lost or forgotten. Without them there is no history for us to look back upon.

Especially in wonderfully character-rich towns like Abertrefil.

11

I glanced anxiously up at the sky. It was heavy and grey, laden with an ocean of rain. This was my first summer in Wales but it certainly didn't feel like summer today. The sun was nowhere to be seen, barred from the planet by the oppressive blanket above.

A few large drops of rain splattered across the windscreen before suddenly turning into another blindingly heavy downpour. I groaned and flicked on the windscreen wipers, but the rain was so heavy they made little impression. Instead they whined and mysteriously slowed down, as though in protest at having been asked to perform the impossible. I was on my way to carry out a removal at a small convalescent hospital north of the town and as I approached St. Aspen's Church on the left, I decided to pull over into the church grounds for a few minutes until the rain eased. I cursed myself for having taken the Granada estate. The heating system was shot to pieces and the windows were beginning to steam up already.

I listened gloomily to the cacophony of the rain as it hammered down onto the estate car. I had planned to go out for a walk tonight with some friends but if this carried on it would almost certainly be a night in watching a video instead. Since moving to South Wales I had come to the conclusion that it was nigh on impossible to plan any outdoor activity, so frequent was the gathering of rain clouds overhead. In fact, Griff had once told me that it only rained twice a year in Westport – it was just that on each occasion it lasted five months at a time.

I found myself staring at the gravestones in the churchyard and it suddenly hit me that this was now my life. I had worked my way into a profession that was unusual in the extreme – a career move I had neither anticipated nor planned; a career move that had raised several eyebrows amongst friends and associates. Even people I had never met before would tell me in conversation that there was no way in the world they could do my job.

Death is still one of the great unmentionables of our society. We fear it. We shun it. We try not to talk about it. Yet it will affect each one of us during our lives until we too fall victim to its inevitability. We should discuss it more. It is far healthier to be honest and open with death, but the fear and uncertainty of the unknown can close mouths and minds like no other emotion we experience.

I have never really been afraid of death myself. A religious upbringing – the cornerstone of which is a firm belief in life beyond the grave – has helped ease that fear. Yet the difficulty many perceive about working in professions dealing with death is as much about the physical handling of dead bodies as it is about where we may, or may not, be going when we die. One group of people who continually told me they would hate to do my job were nurses. I always responded by saying I could never do theirs and I genuinely meant it.

I was fortunate that dealing with the deceased also never bothered me. In fact, even before I'd ever seen a dead body I knew I'd be okay. And sure enough, on my first day on the job back in Devon, I never batted an eyelid when I was taken into the chapel of rest and shown my first body. I soon realised, however, that not everyone was as calm and collected as me. Over the years I witnessed many new employees start work with us, only to leave a few weeks – in some cases days – later because they felt unable to handle the whole death situation.

When I told people I enjoyed my job they often looked at me with disdain. 'How can you enjoy working with dead bodies?' was an unspoken question etched into their expressions of disbelief. But they had missed the point. To be perfectly honest I hated working with dead bodies. Anyone who claims to enjoy it has some serious issues hidden away somewhere. No, what I enjoyed was helping people at a time when they possibly needed help like never before. For the bereaved, the role the undertaker takes in assisting them is very much a part of the grieving process. This was the source, purely and simply, of my job satisfaction. It always amazed me that so many casual observers, usually with a joke or two I'd probably heard a hundred times before, seemed completely oblivious to the fact that our role was very much to care for the living too. Until, of course, they suffered a bereavement themselves. Then they understood a little more about the work that undertakers actually do.

A tap on the window interrupted my thoughts and I peered through the misty glass into the hooded face of the Reverend Brynmor Davis. I wound down my window and he grinned through the teeming rain.

'Good job I haven't got a wedding today!'

I laughed, immediately remembering my experience with Reverend Davis a couple of weeks previously. 'Come and have a seat, vicar,' I said, motioning him around to the passenger side.

He tiptoed through the puddles round the front of the car, his black cape billowing in the strong wind. With the hood covering his head he actually looked quite sinister and for a few seconds one of those absurd images entered my head – the kind that often drift in and out of minds like mine – of him leaping around the gravestones at night in his menacing black cape, scaring the living daylights out of anyone who happened to be passing by.

He got in beside me and the scene melted away as he removed his soaking hood to reveal the kindly, understanding face I had come to know and like in recent months.

'Boys bach, it is an awful day,' he said in his breathy Welsh tone.

'I know. It's gone beyond a joke now hasn't it?'

'It has, yes indeed. And what brings you here today, Tom?'

'Oh just taking time out from the weather,' I smiled. 'The demister's on the blink so I thought I'd better pull over.'

'Oh dear. And now me sitting in here will make it worse.'

'No it's okay, don't worry. As long as you didn't think I was sitting here waiting for a wedding!'

A pained expression exacerbated the creases on the vicar's face. 'Oh dear, oh dear,' he groaned. 'You know, I still can't believe I did that.'

I chuckled again. A fortnight ago we had been on a funeral with Reverend Davis not far from his church. The service had been at the house and we were driving back past St. Aspen's on our way to the crematorium when the vicar suddenly exclaimed.

'What are all those people doing outside my church?'

To be totally honest, the group of six men dressed in grey morning suits with huge white carnations perched discernibly on their lapels gave it away somewhat, but I said it anyway. 'Looks like a wedding to me.'

'A wedding? Well who is having a wedding...' He broke off as a horrified look swept across his face and the colour drained from him like someone, somewhere had turned on a facial colour-draining tap. 'Oh no! I completely forgot! I've got a wedding at eleven!' For a few tense seconds I honestly thought he was going to leap from the moving car. But instead, he just put his hand to his mouth and began muttering insanely to himself.

'Do you still have a curate in this parish?' I asked.

He shook his head, staring numbly at the road in front of us. His church was now out of sight and we were approaching the roundabout that led to the crematorium. I needed to console him and be positive in the process, no easy task in the circumstances. The committal service at the crematorium was also at eleven o'clock.

'Look, the bride obviously hasn't arrived yet so she probably intends on sticking with tradition and turning up late,' I reasoned. 'A quick committal service here and we'll be leaving in no time. Don't forget you're only five minutes from the crematorium.'

He nodded slowly. 'Yes, you are right,' he said. 'I'll probably get away with that side of things. It's just that I don't remember assigning anyone to prepare the church or play the organ...'

As we sat in the car now two weeks later, watching the rain bounce off the gravestones, the Reverend Brynmor Davis was all smiles again.

'So it all worked out in the end,' I laughed.

'Oh yes indeed, indeed it did. But only just, mark you,' he added, raising his eyes. 'One of the parishioners attending the wedding stepped in to play the organ and the verger had seen the booking in the diary the night before and came in early to get everything ready. The bride arrived about two minutes after you dropped me off, but nobody seemed to notice I was late. They were all too consumed with chatting to each other.'

'Weddings and funerals, vicar. It's the only time families do talk isn't it?'

'Yes, you are right there, Tom. Sadly you are very right. Oh well, I'd best be off now. Thank you for the shelter.'

'You're welcome. I'll see you soon, I'm sure.'

He eased himself out of the car, his advancing years making it just a touch more of an effort than it once might have been. Then with a wave he replaced his hood and braced himself against the rain.

I smiled and watched him athletically avoid the puddle-strewn path until he reached the church doorway and was gone. I wiped the windscreen with my hand and started the engine, glancing at those silent, motionless gravestones once more. Yes, it was a strange old job I'd chosen – difficult, challenging, respectable, unusual.

I'd really love to borrow the Reverend Brynmor Davis's cape for an evening though…

12

I've always been a huge fan of Sergeant Bilko and his sidekick, Doberman from the wonderful 'Phil Silvers Show' on TV. But I never expected to be working with them in the funeral profession.

Bryan Stockton was appointed operations manager not long after I started. His remit covered the South Wales area and he came to us with considerable experience. The problem was it hadn't been gained in the funeral industry. Mr Stockton was the first in a long line of non-funeral managers. The feeling within the company at the time was that a more business-like approach was needed at managerial level. It mattered not from where the experience came, as long as the figure at the bottom of the annual balance sheet was a big, fat juicy one.

While many industries and corporations now adopt this approach, I have always believed that the funeral profession in particular cannot be treated just like any other business. The requirements are unique, as are the needs of the clientele. The customer service offered, such a key area these days, has to be way above that of most other industries. There needs to be a balance between shrewdness and compassion; between profits and sensitivity. On the other hand the running costs need to be viable to provide a professional service at all. There is an enormous difference, however, between realism and pricing yourself out of the market. The so called financial wizards were installed to reverse some of the lax practices of the past, but in the process the pendulum began swinging too far the other way and our company, in time, became just another profit-hungry organisation.

In Westport – and throughout the whole of our region – it could be said that Bryan Stockton drilled the hole in the dam wall as far as we were concerned. The leak became a steady flow over the years as our whole operation deteriorated. From product and price to attitude and staff conditions, the downward spiral was breathtakingly fast. Poverty was pleaded at every turn, yet money always seemed to be found in vast quantities when opportunities to buy up yet more private undertaking businesses became available. None of this did staff morale any good because we were constantly in the public firing line trying to defend such intimidating action.

Where Bryan Stockton failed with us as employees was his inability to gain respect. It was hardly surprising. When we learned he had come to the funeral industry from a career selling mobile homes, the hoots of derision could be heard from across the Bristol Channel and beyond. His image was tarnished even further when one of my colleagues happened to casually mention his uncanny resemblance to Sergeant Ernie Bilko. The likeness was actually little more than a similar 'egg in a nest' hairstyle and dark-rimmed spectacles. But the nickname stuck and he was forever known as Bilko from that moment on.

I had the dubious honour of labelling Bilko's cohort – area manager Peter Raymond. Short, squat, and chubby faced, Peter was a dead ringer for Private Doberman, the long-suffering subject of many of Sergeant Bilko's shady schemes. Whereas us mere mortals at the bottom of the company's employment ladder had little to do with the mighty Bilko, we were often subjected to frequent visits by Mr Raymond and I don't think I ever saw the man smile in the process. In fact, my suggestion of his likeness to Private Doberman was a visual one only: personality wise he was about as far as one could get from the loveable simpleton from Fort Baxter. More accurate was a similarity with the fierce, uncompromising Doberman dog. The breed has been known to possess an attitude problem and Peter Raymond was certainly blessed with this characteristic in great abundance. On his first couple of visits to Westport, Doberman completely ignored me. During the third I managed to provoke a whole sentence from him.

In sharp contrast to the rain of a few weeks earlier it had been a sizzling hot day. We were, in fact, in the middle of a rare occurrence in Welsh weather terms, a phenomenon more commonly known in warmer climes as a heat wave. We had been washing cars down at the garage when a call came through from the office asking for one of us to pick up some forms and take them to the cemeteries office. I volunteered and jumped in the nearest limousine in my shirtsleeves but still with my black tie on. I arrived at the office, picked up the forms, and was on my way out of the office when in walked Doberman, accompanied by Stewart Lewis.

'Get your jacket on!' he barked and pushed straight past me. I caught Stewart's eye and he just shrugged.

I shook my head in disbelief and stormed through the door. I was tired, fed up, extremely hot, and not particularly in the mood for pig ignorance, especially at the sight of Doberman and Stewart swanning around in *their* shirtsleeves. I drove down to the cemeteries office, possibly with smoke steaming visibly from my ears, delivered the forms and collected the receipt to take back to the office. Heat can do strange things to the brain and, at this point, I was vulnerable. I called back at the garage and put on my jacket...then a scarf...then someone's nice big warm overcoat...a pair of gloves...and finally topped it all off with a peaked cap. I vaguely heard Mark mutter, "What the 'ell..." as I strode purposely past him and back out into the blazing sunshine. I arrived back at the office, marched down the corridor into the back room, and ceremoniously slapped the receipt on the desk.

Jill, the receptionist, and Gareth, who had obviously heard Doberman's earlier admonishment, burst out laughing at the ridiculous sight of me standing there bedecked from head to foot in winter clothing on probably the hottest day of the year so far.

'Wonderful, wonderful!' clapped Gareth, who was by no means a fan of Doberman himself. 'It's a pity Mr Raymond has left!'

With hindsight it was probably a very good thing that Doberman had left. But at that moment Stewart came through from the workshop out the back. He stopped suddenly, stared at me blankly for a couple of seconds, and then continued along the passageway and outside as though nothing had happened. From that moment on he was clearly aware he had a rebellious mutineer on board.

Although my reaction to this was grossly absurd, my point was actually a valid one. It was almost unbearable having to drive black vehicles in black suits in hot summer temperatures. Apart from the health and safety issues this raised, surely common sense could prevail in such extremes? Do the general public actually think more of undertakers because they sit in their cars perspiring to the point of collapse? In my experience many clients told us to remove our jackets while driving because they felt uncomfortable watching us suffering. Company policy instructed us to politely decline such requests, as it would apparently lower our standards.

In other countries where the upper lip isn't quite so stiff, there is a far more sane approach to working in the heat, even in the funeral trade. I'm not saying undertakers should be walking around in shorts and t-shirts (apart from anything else, most undertakers I know just don't have the figures for such attire anyway) but there are uniform-style shirts available which would suit the funeral profession. Paramedics and the police force, who, as many will have noticed regularly remove their jackets in very warm weather when on duty, use such shirts.

At one stage during this period, Bilko even issued a memo to say that all hearse and limousine drivers must keep their windows closed at all times. He failed to issue the same instruction to grieving families sitting in the back of the same limousines, obviously believing they were somehow less susceptible to heat exhaustion than us.

This particular problem – and it was a problem – has been alleviated in recent years by the purchasing of funeral vehicles fitted with air conditioning. But the attitude at the time was typical of the new aggressive and inflexible style of management that had assumed control of our company.

The next time I saw Doberman was a couple of months later down at Tessum Street garage: ironically it involved clothing once more. I was washing vehicles on my own when he pulled up in his dark grey, executive monster of a car and marched in carrying a dark suit, an overcoat, a raincoat, and two brown boxes. He took them all into the small office and emerged a few seconds later looking in my direction.

'Clothing issue,' he announced dispassionately. 'Hope it all fits.'

I assumed it was for me but I barely had time to say thank you before he was back in his car and pulling away. I felt a little deflated. Maybe I was expecting too much but it would have been an ideal opportunity for him to ask me how I was getting on.

I put down my sponge and made for the office. This was an exciting moment for me. I'd been waiting seven months now for my clothing issue to arrive. Until then I had been relying on 'hand-me-downs' from colleagues. Although this had provided me with most of the items I'd needed, the arrival of my very own issue – with my name written boldly on the labels and on the two brown boxes – was a momentous occasion indeed.

It wasn't until later that I realised Doberman had, in his own way, made a genuine attempt at humour. When he had said 'hope it all fits', I had wondered how it could possibly not. Some five months earlier Arnold James had presented me with a 'clothing form' and I spent a good half hour filling in every single measurement that had been requested. I'd even talked Jill into equipping herself with a tape measure and going boldly where no other receptionist had gone before in a quest for accuracy. One can imagine my surprise, therefore, when I tried on the items at home that evening.

I am convinced that somewhere on this planet there exists a group of apes that have taken up undertaking. If this is the case I was certainly sent one of their jackets by mistake. The fit itself actually wasn't too bad. It was just the arms. I defy anyone in the tailoring industry to prove to me that there is a human being on this earth with a 40" chest and arms the length of rugby posts. If nothing else it was a complete waste of material. I fared little better with the trousers. I had ordered a 32" waist. What I received would have castrated me in seconds had I possessed the courage to fully button them up.

The shoes and the shirts were perfect, likewise the socks, which gave me a semblance of hope. Until, that is, I tried on the overcoat and the raincoat. Both were generous enough to accommodate both myself and selected members of my family. And as a final slap in the face, two buttons were dangling precariously from the raincoat, as if unsure whether to stay or jump for freedom. I went to bed that night both disappointed and disillusioned.

It took another six weeks for me to get the right-sized clothing. This time I took Mark's advice.

'Don't bother wi't form. They don't take a blind bit o' notice. All they understand is small, medium, or large. Ask for medium and you'll be okay.'

He was right. The replacements that duly arrived fitted me as though they had been made to measure. There's a moral in this story somewhere but I've yet to work out just exactly what it is.

13

The shrill ringing of the telephone barged rudely into my dream and wrenched me from my slumber. Cursing, I stumbled out of bed and lurched into the living room, picking up the receiver with the usual dread.

'Hello?' I mumbled, looking up at the clock on my wall.

'You've got a call out!' came the cheery reply.

'Oh good.' I tried to keep the sarcasm out of my voice but at ten to three in the morning it was a struggle.

'Paul's on his way to pick you up now. He'll tell you all the details. You took long enough to answer the phone.'

I had long refrained from saying the reason for this probably had something to do with the fact I was fast asleep in another room. It wasn't worth it. I would only be asked exactly the same question next time so I no longer rose to the bait. For months I had craved to pick up the phone on such occasions within a couple of rings just to see what reaction I would receive then. Unfortunately it never happened and so I just pretended I hadn't heard. This morning was no exception. "Okay Connie. Bye.'

I replaced the receiver and padded miserably back to my bedroom. Connie Rees was the old lady who lived above the Dean Street office. Now in her seventies, she had been a part of the original company for years and was still employed to answer the telephones out of hours. She did this all the year round, except for a fortnight in the summer and a couple of single weeks here and there when she went to stay with her sister. Connie was a friendly old soul but I wished she didn't derive so much pleasure from calling us out in the middle of the night.

The 'on call' duty was always the aspect of undertaking I disliked the most and as I sat on my bed now, desperately trying to fight the urge to lie down and go back to sleep, I cursed the day I had entered the funeral profession. It was strange how unappealing the job was in the small hours of the morning.

I summoned the energy to pull on my suit and hoped that the call out would be a quick one. I always figured that the shorter the call out, the quicker I could get home and back to bed before fully waking up. This was complete nonsense of course because within ten minutes of leaving the house I was usually wide-awake. It was just a comforting thought to get me out of the house in the first place. I grabbed a couple of biscuits – for some reason I was always hungry if I got called out in the night – and walked downstairs where I could watch for Paul's estate out of the front window. He duly arrived a few minutes later, possibly looking worse than I did.

'Good morning, Tom,' he greeted, pretending to sound alert and cheerful. He had recently been promoted to the position of funeral director and was sadly no longer based down at the Tessum Street garage.

'I can't see anything good about it right now,' I mumbled, getting into the car.

'Now don't be like that. We've got a nice coroner's removal to go to.'

My head sank to my chest. So much for my quick call out. 'Where is it?'

'Mid Wales.'

'What?'

'Only joking! No, it's just up to Maesgwyn. We might be lucky actually – CID are there and the girl on the switchboard said they'll be finished by the time we arrive.'

Ever since Paul and I had been called out on a seventy mile round trip one night a few months earlier, he always tried to mess with my tired head on subsequent occasions. Sadly, I usually always fell for it. 'So what's the story tonight?' I asked as we sped away.

'A hanging.'

'Oh, lovely.'

A hanging. The mere mention of the word conjures up all sorts of images for undertakers. How the person had carried it out and where; the state the body was in; whether the police had cut the body down or wanted us to do it. They were always unpleasant deaths to attend and in the dark of night they took on a more sombre, eerie atmosphere.

We reached the house, a small, terraced cottage in a row of typically monotonous small, terraced cottages. All were in darkness except this one. Outside was parked a police car and the familiar white CID van with its blue police crest on the side. As we pulled up alongside the front door a woman constable stepped out to greet us. We recognised her from previous removals we had recently carried out.

'Not you again!' she grinned.

'It is getting a bit predictable isn't it?' said Paul. 'What have you got for us this time?'

'Male, late thirties. Lives alone. We're in the process of contacting the family. He has an estranged wife and a daughter of nine. According to the note he left, it appears he was being denied access to her.'

'Are they the only relatives?'

'No, his mother's still alive. To be honest, I think it might be better for you to contact her initially rather than the wife. As you can appreciate, the situation is a little awkward. Anyway, CID are just wrapping up here so he's all yours.'

We moved straight into action. Even in my relatively short time in the job I had already attended four or five similar scenes. It was also not unusual to be given so much information about the deceased and their situation. It was essential for the funeral director – in this case Paul – to have as much background information as possible in order to know how to approach the funeral arrangements when the time came.

The body was in the small bedroom upstairs and we climbed the creaking staircase, carrying the equipment we needed. Two detectives met us at the top and they were zipping up the body bag in the dim light.

'Good timing, boys,' said one of them. 'He's all ready. Thought we'd save you a job. We'll need to check him properly for personal belongings down at the mortuary though. Do you need a hand?'

Paul shook his head. 'No, we should manage okay. Thanks for your help.'

'There we are. We'll see you downstairs. Sorry about the lack of light. As you can see, he didn't seem too keen on buying light bulbs.'

I looked up at the bedroom light and then the hallway. The cables hung limply from the ceiling, vacant and useless. The main source of light came from downstairs and apart from the soft glow of a street light outside, we would be working in very murky light. From the small glimpse I'd had of this silent, soulless house, it must have been some time since the occupant had taken any interest in its maintenance.

The two detectives left us alone and I began to open up the stretcher on the small landing. There wasn't a great deal of room but the fact the body had already been placed into a body bag would make the lift a whole lot easier. There was no sound except for our movements as we manoeuvred the stretcher and ourselves into the best possible position. I could always feel an air of desperate gloom at scenes of suicide and here was no different. The whole atmosphere was heavy with a sense of hopelessness that I would experience on countless similar occasions over the years.

With everything ready Paul stepped into the tiny room carrying one end of the stretcher and we placed it alongside the body as best we could. Then just as we were positioning ourselves ready to lift the body onto the stretcher, something suddenly leapt from off the top of the wardrobe. It skimmed across Paul's head before landing on the floor and scuttling out of the room.

'Bloody hell!'

I had caught a glimpse of whatever it was right at the last minute, but Paul had had no warning whatsoever. As I looked at him in the dingy light I could clearly see his face was as white as his shirt.

'What the devil was that?' he panted.

Not entirely free from the shock myself I looked out into the hallway. A bright pair of oval eyes stared nervously back at me from inside the bathroom. 'A cat!' I breathed with relief. 'A flaming cat!'

Paul shook his head. 'Well that's done me. I'm shaking like a leaf.'

It took us a couple of minutes to compose ourselves before we were able to pick up the stretcher and descend down the narrow staircase to our estate car outside. The weight of the body almost paled into insignificance, so distracted were we by the sudden appearance of our feline friend upstairs. I closed the back of the estate and the detective came across from his van.

'We'll follow you down to Sandacre Hospital. See you when we get there.'

'Okay,' said Paul. 'You could have told us that cat was in the room though.'

The detective frowned. 'Cat? What cat?'

I crawled back into bed at twenty-past five. I knew it was pointless but I did it anyway. I could rarely go straight back to sleep following a call out, especially at that time of night. The darkness was already beginning to make way for the early morning light of a new day. I had to be up again and back to work in just over three hours. I sighed and tried to relax, but my brain was now wide-awake with the events of the past hour – being woken from my sleep, the removal itself, and that blasted cat.

But the thoughts that came from behind to overtake and dominate my mind concerned the situation that had disrupted my sleep. What had driven that man to take his own life? The state of his house told me he had given up long before tonight. But something had finally snapped. Something had tipped him over the edge that most of us are able to steer well clear of.

The repercussions of his actions would, for a variety of reasons, turn the lives of his family upside down forever. His nine-year-old daughter would now spend the rest of her life in the knowledge of an awful truth. His mother would know the anguish of losing a son. There would be feelings of guilt and dismay and of questions unanswered. Time may eventually heal but what had happened tonight would probably never go away in the minds of many, especially that little girl. In a couple of hours time as I went to work, tired and bleary eyed, social workers, doctors, and councillors would begin planning the strategy to pick up the pieces of her young life. As undertakers, all we had to do, unpleasant though it could often be, was pick up the remains of a life at an unsociable hour.

The comparison was worlds apart.

14

Standing in the middle of a main road is not the most sensible of activities to pursue. But this is exactly what Glen Edwards was doing right now. He was risking life and limb as he stopped traffic on a busy road in the centre of Westport to allow the cortege tlme to pull away as one from the church.

It is an understated work of art to keep a funeral cortege together, especially when setting off after a large church service. The volume of traffic on our town and city roads means it is hard enough to find a gap that will allow one car out, let alone a procession. This, coupled with the sad fact that very few drivers seem willing these days to give way to a funeral for fear of their precious journey taking a couple of minutes longer, means that funeral directors often take their lives into their own hands.

Glen Edwards was probably the one colleague who had finally gone some way to replacing Rhys Parry as my chief ally in work. Glen was a young funeral director who had transferred down to Westport from the Valleys and we hit it off together almost immediately. This was mostly because we both possessed an almost identical sense of humour. But he also happened to know a group of friends of mine who lived in the valley town of Tremorlais and this was the mutual ground from which our friendship grew. The fact we lived next door to each other also contributed.

During my first summer in South Wales the company had offered me a rent-free flat above their Stapleton Road office in the centre of Westport. I gratefully accepted, as it meant I would save a good deal of money on rent or a mortgage, the latter of which I had been considering at the time. I later found out that the offer hadn't solely been for my benefit – company policy dictated that where possible all available accommodation on company premises should be offered to employees. This not only provided security for the premises, it also meant someone was available to deal with the public outside of normal office hours should the occasion arise.

The Stapleton Road building was an ugly one – square and bland with no character in its regulation 1960's brickwork. But this didn't really bother a young man in his early twenties. The flat itself was perfectly adequate and it was right bang in the centre of town with the nearest supermarket a mere three minute walk away. I was more than happy with the arrangement and I actually remained in company accommodation throughout my entire time in the funeral profession.

Part of the package offered to Glen when he relocated was the availability of the empty flat next door to me. He duly accepted and was moving in within a few days of being approached. We soon discovered, however, that Glen came with a reputation and it appeared he had actually been 'moved on' to become someone else's problem. Unfortunately, Glen was branded from the moment the rumours escaped and I feel he was treated unfairly as a result. Molehills regularly became mountains and probably because of the unmerited pressure he felt he was under, he became quite unpopular with a number of his colleagues, especially Stewart Lewis. I even had a couple of minor disagreements with him myself, but they never affected our friendship as a whole.

Lean, and of average height, Glen had a small round face with dark eyes that always bore a slightly suspicious expression. He was an intelligent, brooding man and I often felt he was a victim of his own deep and complex personality. This was no wild guess on my part: his demons were occasionally uncomfortably similar to some of my own. But despite whatever flaws others chose to see in Glen, we had some good times together both in and out of work. We made each other laugh continually, especially with the occasional expression or delivery of a satirical one-liner, and on the day in question, as he stood defiantly in the centre of the road, he was about to give me one of my biggest laughs of all time.

I inched slowly forward in the hearse as I waited for Glen to give me the all clear. Finally, almost in desperation, he held up his hand to stop the continuous stream of vehicles approaching from my right and then waved me across the road, while raising his other hand to slow down the bus now coming from the left. At last we were on our way. I checked my mirrors and the limousine was right behind me, as was the first of the following private cars. With the coast clear Glen began to walk the cortege up the road and I followed slowly behind him. A little further on he turned to make sure the remainder of the cortege was still being allowed to leave the church. He then began to walk backwards whilst continuing to observe the situation.

I should have seen what was coming and made an attempt to warn him, but I had also glanced behind me to see that everything was okay. I turned back just in time to see Glen stumble backwards into the first of a row of parked cars. For a split second he was flat on his back across the bonnet with his legs in the air, not unlike a glamour model draped over a sports car at a motor show. Except that this was a chocolate brown Ford Montego, which, with all the best intentions in the world, could hardly be considered a sporting classic. And nor, come to think of it, could anyone in their right mind think of Glen as a glamour model.

By the time Glen had slid back down the bonnet and hit the tarmac I had stopped the hearse, fervently hoping everyone behind had been able to do the same. I was about to jump out and run to the assistance of my beleaguered friend and colleague, but I realised this would draw too much attention to him. I needn't have worried. As Glen slowly rose to his feet I became aware just how much of a spectacle this had become. Everyone seemed to have stopped in their tracks and there was a distinct hush in the air. People were staring from their cars, from the pavement, and in particular from the bus.

Not surprisingly, Glen had decided to abandon any further walking but it seemed an age before he reached the passenger door of the hearse. His face was as red as the roses which lay on the coffin behind me. As he opened the door and got in, I kept my gaze facing forward. He sat down, also staring rigidly ahead. There was silence for a few seconds before he finally spoke with slow, deliberate words.

'Get Me Out Of Here Now.' Another pause. 'And don't even think about laughing...'

To walk or not to walk. That was certainly one of the questions I asked myself when I eventually became a funeral director a few years later. Many think it an essential part of the funeral while others see it less so. As I observed and learnt from the styles and preferences of different funeral directors, I soon began to lean towards the latter school of thought. Now don't misunderstand me. It's not that I disagree with walking in front of the hearse because nothing could be further from the truth. Paging (to give it the correct term) a funeral away from the home or a church or to the crematorium or graveside is both dignified and appropriate. It was the vanity that turned me off. It soon became obvious to me that for many funeral directors, walking in front of the cortege had far more to do with their own self-importance than any respect for the deceased. I thus formulated a theory based on the length a funeral director would walk – the longer the walk, the bigger the ego. I believe it was an astute and accurate observation, especially in view of some of the funeral directors I worked with over the years.

Of course, the other major reason for my growing concern over the funeral walk were the many mishaps I was witnessing along the way. Although Glen's was probably the most spectacular and humiliating, there were several other incidents that warned me of the potential pitfalls in the pursuit of dignity or vanity. One such occasion was when Paul decided to page a funeral into Saron Chapel Cemetery one day. In his defence we were a little early and his actions were motivated by the fact we needed to lose a few minutes. However, unbeknown to us, being early also meant that the verger had not yet tethered Bartholomew, the resident goat. Quite frankly Paul was walking into a situation not too dissimilar to the plight of the Christians in a Roman coliseum.

The goat charged. Paul ran. Both disappeared round the side of the chapel for several seconds before Paul finally emerged tentatively through the front door of the old building. He jumped back in the hearse breathlessly until the goat was captured by the verger a few minutes later and led unceremoniously away. During this time Paul explained in animated detail how he had skilfully escaped by darting through an open side door and shutting it quickly before the goat realised what was happening. The open-mouthed mourners in the limousine behind had observed the whole spectacle of course. To this day I am convinced they thought that Paul had performed some kind of ancient, Celtic pre-burial ritual.

And then there was Gilbert Rees, doyen of the extended funeral walk. Gilbert hadn't been with us long but he took to the supposed eminent status of funeral directorship with conceited ease. He was a stout man of fifty with a curtain fringe, a beard perpetually in the early stages of growth, and a stiff walking style that earned him the nickname of 'Robbie the Robot.' The drivers soon learned that any funeral with Robbie would also mean long periods of painfully slow driving. Whether it was leaving the funeral home, the residence of the deceased, or the church, Robbie would inflict his walk of death upon us without fail, come rain or shine. In his opinion the family were paying a lot of money for the professional service we provided and we needed to put on a show worthy of such expenditure. He nearly came a cropper one day though and was extremely lucky to get away with it.

We were carrying out a funeral in the small town of Llandulais – about seven miles west of Westport – and we were ready to leave following the completion of the service in the deceased's small cottage close to the Llandulais estuary. With everyone safely in their cars, Robbie launched into his walk and I followed slowly behind, resisting as always the urge to nudge the back of his legs with the front bumper. He turned right at the end of the road and then right again a couple of minutes later. I furrowed my brow. This didn't feel right. I was sure he should have turned left. The road began to descend gently and the houses that stood on either side stopped suddenly to be replaced by thick hedgerow. Now I was certain this wasn't the way we had driven into the estate. But Robbie continued undeterred with his robotic march and I figured he must know a different route.

When we reached the bottom of the road and there was nowhere else to go but into Llandulais estuary, I knew we were in trouble. There was a brief pause from the slightly hunched figure in front, then on he continued, leading us all in a half circle round the gravelled track, complete with random tufts of stringy grass, and back onto the tarmac of the road. As he began the walk back up the gentle slope, I caught a glimpse of the side of Robbie's face. I expected a look of desperation or maybe a touch of colour in his cheeks even. But his expression was totally impassive as he stared unblinkingly ahead. If he could retain that countenance as he now walked past several of the vehicles in the cortege still on their way down to the estuary, I would be mightily impressed. At the top of the road he finally abandoned his expedition and got into the hearse. His face immediately crumpled into reflective horror at what had happened.

'I'm for it now,' he muttered gravely. 'This is one of the fussiest families I have ever dealt with. They're going to be furious.' His fear must have been very real for I rarely recall him being as quiet as he was during that agonising journey to the crematorium. He was clearly anticipating the awful fate that awaited him when we arrived.

About forty minutes later I pulled up outside the crematorium doors and Robbie opened the hearse door. 'Here goes,' he sighed deeply. Almost before he had placed his foot on the ground, the deceased's daughter had already reached him. She was a formidable looking woman in her early fifties, dressed in an expensive looking black chiffon dress with an enormous matching hat. Everything about her suggested flamboyance and I envisaged a lively and public handbag attack to begin very soon, accompanied by a volley of well-chosen words.

'Mr Rees!'

I would have done the honourable thing and closed my eyes, but the worryingly sadistic side to my nature was quite looking forward to this.

'How did you know Mum used to walk the dog down by the estuary every morning? Oh, that was so beautiful! She would have loved what you did!'

Eh?

'And that place where you paused. That was the exact spot where Benji used to do his business every day. Thank you! Thank you so very much!'

My lasting impression of Robbie, however – and he left us soon after for varying reasons – was a far less successful episode which did untold damage to his carefully nurtured image.

Once again he was paging a cortege away from the residence and once again I was driving the hearse. All was tediously quiet and dignified until I suddenly noticed a blur come hurtling down the driveway of the house we were passing. It was small, it was hairy, and it made straight for Robbie, leaping up at him while yapping furiously.

In his commendably focussed way, Robbie swatted at the dog without breaking stride or moving his head. But the dog was having none of it. This wasn't embarrassing enough. He paused briefly from his jumping up and down and I could almost see his little dog brain working. Then suddenly he ran after Robbie again and with a bouncy leap he grabbed at the bottom of the funeral director's tailcoat with his jaws and hung there. And hung there. And hung there. Somehow, Robbie continued on his way, completely unfazed.

To one such as I, that scene of a dog dangling and swaying with the robotic jerks of Robbie's footsteps caused me immense mirth. It also killed stone dead any inkling I may have had for prolonged walking on a funeral. It all seemed far too risky to me.

15

'If that's off, I'm off!'

The telephone continued ringing as we all burst into laughter. I was the first to recover and picked up the receiver, immediately putting on my funeral voice.

'Good afternoon, funeral services. Can I help you?'

'Yes, can I speak to Denzil please?' The voice was agitated.

I suppressed a giggle and looked at Denzil who was standing panic-stricken by the door. 'Er...I'm afraid he's not available at the moment. Can I take a message?'

'Yes. It's Chloe from the burials and cremations office. Can you *please* tell him that if he doesn't get that cremation form to me within the hour, I'll have to cancel the funeral.'

'Oh hi Chloe. No problem. I'll tell him as soon as he comes in.'

I put down the receiver and Denzil wiped a trembling hand across his forehead. 'Thanks pal. Now I've got time to think up a story.'

I had only called into the office to pick up the driver's orders for the following day. Little did I know I'd walk in on a major incident. Denzil had been in the back office looking in his briefcase as I entered when he suddenly swore and held up a pale green piece of paper.

'I don't believe it! I've forgotten to hand this in again.'

Paul looked up from writing in the office diary. 'I hope that isn't the cremation form Chloe's been pestering me about all morning.'

Denzil nodded sheepishly.

'Denzil! Do you realise they can cancel a funeral if the forms aren't received by eleven o'clock the day before?'

'I know, I know,' he babbled. 'She's going to kill me!' At that precise moment the telephone rang and Denzil, in total panic, uttered his gloriously muddled response: 'If that's off, I'm off!'

73

Already in a short space of time, Denzil Jenkins had rapidly become famous for his habit of mixing up words and sentences. It usually happened when he was flustered, but he would be the first to admit that it occurred rather frequently under normal circumstances too. Every office in every town and city of the world needs a Denzil Jenkins working there. He was a constant source of entertainment. But what made him even more of a joy to work with was the fact he laughed at himself as much as we did. It was a priceless quality from a naturally funny man.

Denzil was solid in every sense of the word. He was portly around the midriff and plump in the face and the neck. The parting in his dark brown hair continually fell down across his forehead, causing him to forever push it back into place with his big, meaty hands. He bustled and huffed his way through almost everything he did and his propensity for getting into a flap caused the verbal blunders to flow. These made work a pleasure for several hours afterwards as we spread the news far and wide of the latest Denzil classic.

Like the time he was on the phone trying to explain the location of a grave to a patient gravedigger: 'It's easy to find. Once you see the big black monument on the end of the row, the grave is three doors down from there.'

Another time he was trying to tell us that a body was having a post mortem. Everyone in the funeral profession abbreviates this to a simple 'PM'. But Denzil for some reason found this too difficult: 'Mr Johnson's been taken to Sandacre Hospital for an MOT.'

Then there was the time we were trying to persuade him to take part in a friendly football match we had organised. To be brutally honest it wasn't the most realistic of enlistments, but we tried all the same. Denzil was vehemently opposed to it on health grounds: 'No, I'm not playing football. If Yohan Cruyff can have a haircut (heart attack) at 43, I'm damned if I'm going to risk it.'

One day we were rushing between funerals and after having taken a funeral from a local farm, the vehicles were filthy. We called round the back of one of our small satellite branches in the hope we could quickly hose them down before going onto the next funeral. Denzil disappeared inside for a few seconds and then emerged triumphantly. 'I've found a bucket. We can wash our vehicles in it.' Just a few minutes later as we merrily 'washed our vehicles in Denzil's bucket', the conversation got round to our own private cars. Denzil proudly announced that his Vauxhall Nova was brand new when it came out.

Denzil was certainly not at his best on the phone. When Christine from the Westport Chronicle rang to speak to me one day, he answered the call and then shouted out from the front office: 'Christine! Can you speak to Tom from the Chronicle?'

On another occasion Griff was on sick leave. Denzil, being a genuinely caring person, rang Griff's wife to see how he had got on with a doctor's appointment: 'Hello Jean. Is Griff back from the doctors yet?'

'I've no idea, Denzil,' came the reply. 'You've dialled the wrong number. This is Anne, Mark's wife.'

But my favourite Denzil-ism was uttered when he and I were returning to Tessum Street in the hearse after a funeral. He was looking out of the window when suddenly he exclaimed: 'Whahay! Look at the backside on that!'

'Denzil,' I replied with a sigh. 'That's Frank from the hairdressers.'

'Is it? Oh well, never mind. He still looks good.'

Just before the coffin is about to be taken to the graveside or placed upon the catafalque at the crematorium, many funeral directors will take a single flower from the main wreath and place it on top of the coffin. By this stage all the wreaths and floral tributes have been removed from the coffin completely. The placement of a single flower, therefore, was a simple, final act of respect that we always upheld on behalf of the family.

Normally this modest gesture drew no cause for comment or explanation. But Mr Gripton could hardly be described as normal. Denzil had arranged his wife's funeral with him and made no secret of the fact he would be mightily relieved when it was all over. 'It wasn't so much that he was difficult,' Denzil told us. 'He was just...strange.'

Mr Gripton wasn't old – probably late fifties – and with his smart, black designer suit and pale blue and white shirt, he had the air of a successful businessman about him. As the hearse driver on the funeral I was meeting him for the first time and it didn't take me long to realise that Denzil wasn't exaggerating. For starters, it seemed very odd to me that his son and daughter had been made to travel in the second limousine while Mr Gripton rode alone in the first with nobody other than one, unrelated gentleman whom he referred to as his 'funeral supporter'. During the arranging of the funeral Denzil told me there had been no shortage of unusual comments or opinions. From initially refusing to sign the council's burial form (*what have the local council got to do with my wife's death?*) to asking why we needed to know his wife's age, this hadn't been your average, everyday funeral arrangement.

It could be very interesting when clients occasionally questioned the whole etiquette of the funeral process. There are some aspects of funerals that I find hard to understand myself so it was fine by me if someone was willing to challenge what is considered the so called 'correct way' of doing things. It was usually the result of family members stopping and thinking carefully about what they, and their loved one, would really want rather than just blindly accepting everything that was presented to them. For example we often came across families who would request that no one should wear black to the funeral, claiming that Mum or Dad had always been happy and cheerful throughout life so wearing black would not reflect their characters. Such people were rational enough to realise that a funeral should be a personal affair and a celebration of life, not just a farewell.

Then there was the young woman who died of cancer in her mid-thirties, whose dear friends sat up all night painting beautiful, peaceful scenes on her coffin in the front room of her house. It looked amazing and although the people of Westport probably weren't ready for such extremism in those days, I thought this act showed far more love and warmth than spending a fortune on a solid oak coffin just to impress the traditionalists. Of course today there are all manner of coffin options available – wicker, bamboo, seagrass, wool, cardboard, and standard wooden ones with printed scenes. But this was South Wales in the eighties and nineties and anything beyond the traditional wooden coffin was virtually unheard of.

I was always open to the thoughts and ideas of families and the little requests that perhaps bucked the trend slightly and made the day more special as a result. But in the case of Mr Gripton, his rebellion against the scheme of things was just born out of sheer cussedness. He enjoyed being awkward and it quickly became tiresome, especially for poor Denzil who clearly couldn't wait to see the back of him.

With hindsight, it probably wasn't such a good idea to take a rose from Mr Gripton's wreath and place it on his wife's coffin just prior to the words of committal. When funeral directors are concentrating on looking after the family they would often ask the hearse driver to do the honours for them as far as the flower was concerned. Denzil was clearly on edge with the unpredictable Mr Gripton so I automatically assumed the responsibility for him. I bent down beside the double-ended spray of red roses and pulled out the largest, best formed rose I could see. I then placed it gently below the nameplate on the coffin before acting as a bearer in lowering the coffin into the grave.

Following the service the mourners chatted in various clusters and Denzil returned to the hearse where I was standing. We struck up our own quiet conversation while we waited for everyone to disperse. After a few minutes, Mr Gripton broke away from the couple he was talking to and, accompanied by his ever faithful 'funeral supporter,' approached us with his hands thoughtfully behind his back.

'Everything okay, Mr Gripton?' asked Denzil politely.

'Well actually, no it isn't,' he replied in an almost comically stereotypical English accent. 'I'd very much like to know why your colleague here placed a red rose on my wife's coffin?'

Denzil was a little taken aback. 'Well…it's just something we do as a final gesture of respect…'

'Really?' Mr Gripton rocked back pompously on his heels. 'So I take it you can assure me that your colleague was not in any kind of relationship with my wife?'

If this scene had been from a Tex Avery cartoon my jaw would have dropped to the floor with a loud clunk. I was stunned. I also noticed Denzil's jaws open and remain that way for several seconds before he was finally able to muster up some kind of response.

'Mr Gripton, I think you're getting things a little out of pollution here…'

77

'Well do you blame me?' he interrupted, his darkening mood rapidly chasing away any notion I had that he might have somehow been joking. 'A complete stranger steps forward and quite openly places a red rose on my wife's coffin. What do you expect me to think?'

I was now convinced I was in a weird dream. Either that or Jeremy Beadle from 'Game For A Laugh' was lurking behind a gravestone somewhere. Unfortunately Denzil had reached the pink-faced, babbling stage and was clearly incapable of defending my good character.

Mr Gupton, there is nothing untoward happening here at all. Mr Eldwin is a highly hysterical man. We simply place a coffin on the flower to show our intent.'

There was a brief pause as Mr Gripton allowed this muddled information to sink in. Thankfully, despite his faults, he was clearly an intelligent man and he had a rough idea of the sentiment Denzil had been aiming for. He scratched his nose slowly and narrowed his dark brown eyes. 'Okay Denzil,' he nodded. 'I will accept your...interesting explanation. But I assure you that if I ever find out that...'

'Come along Don,' interrupted his friend. 'Let's leave it there shall we?' The two walked away leaving Denzil and I staring at each other in disbelief.

'What a space cadet,' I declared incredulously.

Denzil, whose cheeks were beginning to assume their natural sheen, coughed a small laugh. 'It doesn't matter how long you do this job, you never stop learning', he said. He was about to walk away when he stopped and looked at me. Then he leaned forward, his beady black eyes twinkling. 'Are you sure you didn't know Mrs Gripley?'

16

With little or no management experience behind him, Stewart Lewis spent the first few weeks of his managerial reign in training. In real terms this meant we hardly saw anything of him. It pretty much suited me, as I felt uneasy whenever he was around. I also hadn't forgotten the parting words of Arnold James.

When Stewart re-surfaced following his crash course in leadership skills, we didn't really notice much difference. The older, more experienced funeral directors had been surprised by his appointment but as one of them said at the time, senior management weren't looking for a manager: they were looking for a 'yes' man. To that extent they had chosen shrewdly in Stewart Lewis. The company's new management recruitment drive certainly appeared to place man-management skills at the lower end of their requirements list.

Whenever Doberman visited – now with increasing regularity – it was rather sickening to watch Stewart follow him around like an adoring puppy. In some respects it is fair enough for someone to want to make a good impression and to be seen as keen and ambitious. But with Stewart, one always felt he would have sold his soul to Beelzebub if he thought it would earn him more gold stars with the bosses.

Although I was now small fry to Stewart in his new, slick-shirted world, he still found time to administer the occasional kick in my direction. For example, I was told in front of several colleagues one day to get my hair cut because it did not meet with company standards. This despite it being shorter than Mark's at the time. On another occasion he tried to discipline me for taking my full lunch break when there was work to be done. Maybe it would have been a fairer comment had I been informed that the work in question (taking some flowers from a funeral earlier that morning to a local nursing home) was in a branch five miles away, a task that no one else knew needed doing either. Despite settling well into my new surroundings, I still hadn't quite grasped the apparent need for telepathy. For most of the time I just kept a low profile, got on with my work, and tried to keep out of Stewart's way. I genuinely tried to respect the man and get along with him, but a series of incidents about a year into his spell as manager appalled me. From then on I found it hard to look upon him with any respect ever again.

When Arnold James finished with the company he was prevented from starting up his own funeral business for a period of four years. This clause had been written into his new contract following the takeover: the company undoubtedly had the foresight to guess he would probably stay in the industry. Their fears were not without foundation. The name Arnold James was synonymous with the funeral profession in Westport and he would certainly take a great deal of business with him should he choose to set up his own funeral home. I personally didn't have a problem with the company's stance on this matter. Any business will try to protect its own interests and I understood that, although I did think four years was rather excessive. No, what appalled me was the fact that Doberman, with Stewart hot on his heels, spent hours each day trailing Arnold's every move. They would wait outside his house and follow him when he left in case he was involved in a funeral somewhere. Armed with cameras they would hide behind bushes at cemeteries and the crematorium to see if he ever turned up conducting a funeral for a company with whom they believed he had links to. They would even sit outside his house at night, hoping to catch him on his way to a call out.

In my eyes this constituted human behaviour at its lowest. Arnold was the reason why Stewart was even in the funeral profession. He had taught him all he knew and trained him up from nothing. Now Stewart was repaying him with a treachery that was hard to comprehend. It was clear such behaviour was instigated by Doberman, but Stewart lost the respect of virtually everyone in the company over the treatment of his former boss. He had dug himself a hole far deeper than any gravedigger could and for many of us he never really managed to climb out and redeem himself. Loyalty and respect are hard earned qualities but it seemed that results were now the new god. And we were soon to discover just exactly what results were to be expected.

The word 'target' is used in most large business organisations. Hard sell techniques are rife, as are the training methods employed to implement them. When the word was bandied about in our working environment with increasing regularity it was hard not to laugh. It was even more difficult not to treat it with the contempt it deserved. Unfortunately we were obliged to, as the number crunchers at the top were very serious about it.

It does not take a scientist to realise that setting targets in the funeral business could be considered extremely insensitive, not to say unsettling. Joe Public may, quite understandably, be horrified at the thought. But it was no less disturbing to many of us within the profession. There is one glaring problem with targets in the funeral industry – what happens if the target given isn't attained? What do you do if an annual goal of nine hundred funerals is set but only eight hundred and forty reached? Do you discretely slip something into the local water supply in the hope of getting your remaining sixty funerals? At times I wondered, given the perpetual doom and gloom presented each month if we were below the precious target set, whether we might receive a memo one day to this effect.

Over the years we lost no end of funerals to rival funeral directors. There was one basic explanation as to why, obvious even to simple drivers with no business acumen like myself: cost. If a company takes over an established business and then starts raising the price of its product for no justifiable reason, is it any wonder that potential clients will start drifting towards a cheaper but no less competent option? People talk to each other about the cost of things, especially in close-knit communities such as Westport and its surrounds.

There has been an ongoing backlash in recent years at the spiralling cost of funerals. People now question these costs far more readily than they used to. Phoning and shopping around where funeral directors are concerned is becoming more common by the day. And quite rightly so. We do it for everything else we buy in life – at least the sensible among us do – so why should funerals be any different? The trouble is, the majority of us are too upset or shocked to go searching for the best deal just after a death has occurred. Money, for the first time in many people's lives, becomes secondary as emotions take centre stage. People are suddenly financially vulnerable and this is where some (but certainly not all) undertakers can take advantage.

A code of practice was introduced into the funeral industry stipulating certain standards be met, including a written estimate of the costs being presented before the funeral takes place. This is a commendable measure, but it doesn't prevent the price from being extortionate in the first place. Unless the client has asked beforehand the estimate is not given until the arrangements for the funeral have been finalised. It takes a very strong person to cancel everything at that stage In order to seek a more reasonable undertaker. Invariably this wouldn't work out any cheaper because the initial funeral director would probably issue a bill for his services up to that point anyway.

Telephone quotes became a major player during my day. Our company in particular made big moves to address the increasing number of enquiries we were receiving about the cost of a funeral. We retained very few clients who were shopping around and comparing prices. This was hardly surprising as we were a good thirty percent dearer than our rivals, most of whom could offer the same satisfactory service as ourselves. The buzzword to counter this problem was 'empowerment'. I've never been a fan of trendy, corporate words and this was no exception. Basically, the person answering the phone was empowered to 'adjust' the charges according to the way the conversation was going. For example, if a potential client rang saying they had been quoted a certain amount by another undertaker, we would immediately be allowed to match, or even better, the quote, even if it was far less than what we would normally charge. In theory it was a good, competitive move. But it begged a question in me. Why couldn't we charge this amount in the first place instead of ripping off the clients who were just too distressed to ask? Surely ten funerals carried out a little cheaper was better than four at an inflated price? It made sense to me. But then I was only a driver working on the frontline. What would I know about funerals and dealing with the bereaved?

17

If someone had told me I'd be spending the night in Connie Rees's bed, I would have turned a pale shade of panic and fled for the Valleys. But I had time for neither, as in one of those bizarre moments in life when events conspire to invoke the unexpected, this is exactly where I found myself right now.

It was ten minutes past midnight and I couldn't sleep. I lay looking up at the strange ceiling, helplessly listening to the old mantelpiece clock ticking incessantly like the wheels of a long distance train. I asked myself a hundred times why on earth Connie had such an irksome timepiece in her bedroom. I still found it hard to believe I was here at all. I had only just sat down for my evening meal at half past five when the phone rang. It was Stewart with a dilemma. Because Connie was away on holiday, the night telephones were being put through to the homes of one of the funeral directors each evening. But tonight there was a technical problem and they just wouldn't switch over. The only solution was for someone to stay in the office all night and because Glen and I lived above the other office just around the corner, Stewart had asked if we would be willing to help out.

Glen, possibly taking advantage of his senior status, agreed to cover up until eleven o'clock and suggested I cover through the night. Reluctantly I agreed but Stewart had then suggested that as Connie wasn't returning home until the following day, I could stay in her flat upstairs rather than trying to sleep on a chair in the office. The phone system was the same both downstairs and upstairs: Connie simply switched her telephone off during office hours and any personal calls she received went through via a bypass number. This was only one of numerous occasions when I realised how complicated the telephone systems of undertakers could be in the days before the advent of the mobile phone.

Contrary to what many have often believed, the twenty-four hour service that undertakers provide does not mean the office itself is covered every hour of the day and night. Outside of hours the telephones are answered at home and if a removal is required the team on standby are called out, also from their homes. I was often surprised at the amount of people who thought someone was sitting at a desk throughout the entire night.

And so there I lay, unable to sleep, in this tiny little flat above the main office. My eyes had long become accustomed to the shadowy light and I was now equally familiar with everything in the bedroom. Like the dark oak wardrobe and dressing table, the stack of old *Woman's Weekly* magazines in the corner, and the heavy, ornate picture frames on pale, tired walls.

Being in Connie's flat felt like I'd stepped back forty years in time. I doubted whether there was anything new or modern here. The shelf above the old fireplace in particular looked as though it had been lifted straight out of a well-stocked antique shop. Vying for limited space were all manner of objects, from tarnished brass candlesticks to softly painted figurines. There was also a small doll in a white lace dress now tainted a dusty ochre with age, and a gravy brown china horse almost hidden by a stack of recent mail. There was no order to the way any of this was displayed. It was just the accumulated trinkets and belongings from the life of an old lady.

I glanced upwards again at the sepia photograph hanging silently above the mantelpiece. A young woman stared down at me, her smiling face both attractive and coy. It was a pose that encapsulated the style of an era, an era vaguely remembered by those who lived through it, but one unknown to people of my age and younger. I knew the photo was of Connie. She had proudly showed it to me one day when I had taken the evening newspaper upstairs to her. I ended up staying almost an hour as I got to know her a little better for the first time since moving to Westport. As she told me about her life, her marriage to her beloved Ron and his premature death at the age of fifty-four, I could tell she was now a lonely woman. Despite the comings and goings downstairs she missed real company and having someone to talk to properly instead of just the standard small talk that is all most people have time for in these modern, self-centred days.

Connie was a large lady with grey, wispy hair and arthritic joints, which caused her to walk with the aid of a stick. Age had taken her sepia-toned figure away, the curly brown hair, and the slim, porcelain face too. But time had failed to dampen the sparkle in her hazel eyes. Even in her seventies there remained in them a hint of youthful zest. I went to see Connie regularly after that first visit. Often she would bake an apple pie or make a huge slab of bread pudding for me to take back to my flat. For a bachelor boy far from home, this was like finding gold in the street.

I heard a bump at the bedroom door and I quickly covered myself with the blankets, bracing myself for another attack. Connie's cat was on the prowl again. I had tried to shut the bedroom door but the catch was broken and nothing I could find to block it with seemed strong enough to keep the infernal thing at bay. Fred had taken an intense disliking to me. I assure you the feeling was mutual. He was an ugly, flat-faced thing with mangy grey fur and the temperament of Attila the Hun. He had already attacked me three times by slinking in unnoticed. He would climb up onto the wardrobe and launch himself fearlessly like a heat-seeking missile, landing on my midriff each time with such pinpoint accuracy the Royal Air Force would have been proud.

In my desperation for sleep I began making excessive plans for Fred's demise. The ideas and inspirations flowed. I would set a trap for him by removing myself quietly from the bed and emptying a box of drawing pins from downstairs onto the sheets. No, he wasn't stupid – he'd know I wasn't really there. I know: I'll lie silently on the bed holding a couple of forks upright in my hands. No, too messy. What about catching him and throwing him outside? Or better still, putting him in a coffin in the workshop? Too risky. I was quite partial to my scar-free hands.

I puffed out my cheeks and blew a stream of disheartened breath into the air. It was going to be a long night. Despite my relatively short time in the profession I was beginning to think that animals were a regular hindrance to undertakers. Cats, dogs, goats – they all seemed preordained to interfere with the dignity of a funeral and its protagonists. Only last week Nigel had returned to the garage at quarter to five with blood oozing from a leg wound. He had been helping to take a coffin home when the resident Yorkshire terrier had taken exception to the intrusion, even though it was his former master who was in the coffin. Talk about ungrateful. Much discussion had taken place thereafter as to why Nigel had been singled out for such a harsh reception – there were, after all, three of his colleagues also in attendance to whom the dog had paid little attention. The conclusion drawn, with great hilarity I might add, was that Nigel just had one of those faces a dog hates.

Then about a month ago I'd had my own run in with a feisty canine. Having spent three years working as a postman I was something of an expert when it came to dogs, or at least how best to avoid them. I was quite proud of my adeptness in remaining bite-free throughout. But I never dreamed my record would be put on the line in my new profession.

We had just taken a funeral into the crematorium and with the service having started, we returned to our vehicles and drove them round to the side of the building ready for when the family re-emerged. One of the mourners driving a private car had followed us to the crematorium doors because he was carrying a disabled passenger. I offered to move the car round for him while the service was on because it might be in the way of the funeral that would follow. He smiled a thank you and handed me the keys. After parking my limousine I went to the dark blue Volvo and jumped in. I was just about to put the key in the ignition when I heard a deep growl from behind. Swallowing loudly I glanced up in the mirror and saw a snarling German Shepherd baring his teeth menacingly.

It didn't take me long to assess the situation and decide on the best course of action. Keeping my eyes firmly fixed on the dog I fumbled for the door handle while keeping as still as I could. It wasn't easy. Trying to open a car door with the window handle is even harder. I cursed car manufacturers as I frantically searched the side panel. How the hell do you open the door on these things? I could sense the dog's breath on the back of my neck. I glanced quickly to my right, located the handle, and flung open the door before tumbling out of the car commando-style and slamming it shut behind me.

As I made to get up I was aware of a pair of eyes watching me distastefully. They belonged not to the beast in the Volvo, but a little old lady who had arrived early for the next funeral. She stared at me for several seconds, muttered something in Welsh, and then carried on towards the waiting room. I should have felt more embarrassed than I did, but to be honest I was just relieved to have emerged from the car in one piece.

After the funeral I returned the keys to the owner with apologies for not moving his car as promised. When I explained why he just chuckled.

'Oh you needn't have worried about Oscar! He's as daft as a brush! Wouldn't hurt a fly!

Yes, I thought to myself as I stared at Connie's clock for the umpteenth time. That's what they all say.

As sleep finally began to drift over me I suddenly noticed that Fred hadn't actually made a move for a while now. I saw him in the murky light, lying in the corner of the room by the magazines. He looked to be quite comfortable and it seemed, perhaps, he had finally accepted I was here to stay. With some relief I turned over and felt more able to relax. Now all I was concerned about was Connie coming home earlier than expected in the morning to find a strange man in her bed. I wasn't worried so much about frightening her. It was just the stories I'd been told of Connie being something of a man-eater in her younger days.

18

I first saw Angus the paperboy while working at our main chapel of rest in Brynmawr, a district just outside the town centre. I thought the name Angus was a little strange in heartland Wales, but I soon realised that anywhere on the planet would have been out of place for this lean, dark-eyed schoolboy. His belt definitely did not go through all the loops and I worried greatly for the population of Westport if he intended staying around into adulthood.

I would hear him approaching every afternoon at four-thirty, singing at the top of his voice, his bright orange newspaper bag almost touching the ground as he shuffled along. But when he reached the chapel of rest the singing would suddenly stop, as if the building acted like some sort of trigger to his unhinged mind. He would push open the letterbox and peer through for several seconds, eyeballs rolling manically in their sockets, before finally posting the evening paper with a flamboyant shove.

I could see all this from a position looking out between the vertical blinds of the window next to the front door. But Angus wouldn't leave it there. He would stay a little longer, reciting tales out loud about rotting corpses and young women being hunted down in swamps by decomposed men who had risen from their coffins, before finally moving on.

Our chapel of rest in Brynmawr was situated on the corner of two roads, a long building with a large stained-glass window looking out onto the adjacent street. Sometimes I would dash out of the office and into the service room where I could further observe Angus in open-mouthed fascination as he walked alongside the coloured window towards his next delivery. Through the distorted reds, greens, and yellows of the glass, I could see him performing extravagant impersonations of all manner of zombies, ghouls, and monsters as he meandered up the small slope, seemingly oblivious to the fact he might have an audience.

On one occasion, as I watched him pull off an extremely lifelike impersonation of Frankenstein, I remember thinking to myself that young Angus was probably going to be very famous one day.

It was for what reason that bothered me.

For those who think that working with dead bodies is a creepy occupation, they are also the ones who would probably think it the scariest job in the world come Halloween. There were even colleagues of mine who were a trifle wary of wandering around a chapel of rest on the night of October 31st. Being one of the least superstitious people in the world, such nonsense didn't bother me in the slightest. Which is why I barely gave it a thought as I walked through the funeral premises beneath my flat at half past ten one windy, Halloween evening. On returning home after visiting friends, I parked my car in the garage of the funeral home and set off, as always, through the darkened corridor. This led into the front office, which was then followed by a left turn through the interior entrance door and up the staircase to my flat.

As I passed by the front window of the office I could hear a voice outside, a vaguely familiar, rasping kind of voice. Someone was standing in the doorway of the building, which they often did at nights, particularly courting couples. Normally I took no notice but tonight the voice intrigued me. Where had I heard it before?

Just beside the front door was a small cupboard in the wall. This was the letterbox and with a touch of agility it was just possible to put one's head into the narrow space and look to the right through the horizontal slit in the stone. I did this and to my surprise, standing leaning against the big, wooden front door was Angus. He was babbling away to someone and judging by the tone of the conversation, he was quite clearly in the process of chatting up a member of the opposite sex. Angus? With a girl? I'd never have thought it possible.

I averted my gaze to the left and could just see the top of a neatly permed head of blonde hair. Poor girl, I thought. Did she know what she was letting herself in for? Angus's fascination with the macabre, especially the fact it was Halloween, was certainly evident in his choice of courting venue. I removed myself from the hidden vantage point and was about to carry on up the stairs when the spirit of Halloween swept through me. Almost uncontrollably a mischievous smirk broke out across my face as I looked back at the letterbox. The thoughts entering my head were equally wicked. No, I can't. I mustn't...

It was weird. Something unearthly seemed to propel me back down the corridor to the small staff kitchen at the rear of the building. I found myself picking up the bottle of tomato sauce that Denzil had recently bought in order to decorate his daily lunchtime pie. I was surprised to find myself pouring a generous quantity of the thick red liquid over my left hand and then drifting effortlessly back down the corridor towards the letterbox. I tried to stop myself – honest I dId – but my feeble efforts were In vaIn. An unseen force was driving me and there was nothing I could do.

Angus was still holding forth, his animated voice coming out with all the right lines. He was trying really hard. I couldn't do this to him.

Oh yes I could. I thrust my severely sauced hand through the gap and wiggled my fingers around. I couldn't quite reach Angus...

The blonde-haired girl suddenly screamed. Angus must have turned around and responded with what could only be described as a yelp. Now I went for the kill. I made grabbing motions with my hand, which were greeted by more screams and a colourful collection of words from Angus, most of which were highly controversial. The poor boy's composure had completely vanished, as had his potential girlfriend whom I could already hear running down the street. The rapid sequence of heels clicking frantically on the pavement gave me some indication as to how fast she was running. Unfortunately I couldn't be so sure where young Angus was concerned. He must have been wearing trainers or something because when I sneaked a look through the letterbox, he too had disappeared from view.

I withdrew my hand and collapsed deliciously onto the floor where I remained for several seconds. I was still chuckling as I staggered back to the kitchen to rinse the tomato sauce from my hand. Then suddenly, as I dried myself with the towel, I heard the garage door open. My eyes lit up. I was obviously still under the influence of a full moon.

A car drove into the garage and I could hear Glen, my in-house neighbour, whistling as he stepped out and locked his door. Oh boy! What a night of opportunity this was! I quickly skipped back down the passage and into the front office. Now where could I hide? Beneath the window facing inwards stood a row of four chairs. Was there enough room for me to wriggle underneath them? I lay down in front of the top end of the row and reversed myself in between the legs until I was completely hidden. I just made it in time – Glen was on his way. He entered the office...he approached the chairs...he walked alongside them...

As he reached the final chair I thrust out my hand and grabbed hold of his ankle. The silence was shattered by a loud howl of unmitigated fear. This was followed by another volley of randomly chosen expletives, uncannily similar to those used by Angus five minutes earlier, give or take the odd variation. When Glen realised what had happened he swore again before collapsing onto one of the chairs and joining me in mutual laughter.

This incident saw the beginning of a continuous campaign to scare the living daylights out of each other. It began slowly and grew in momentum until it became impossible to move at night for fear of what might be about to happen. The fact we both had quite active social lives provided endless opportunities for such tomfoolery and coming home in the dark became a nightmare of uncertainty and apprehension. The moment one of us heard the garage doors closing downstairs, the other would spring into merciless action. Upon arriving home at night it was virtually impossible to touch base unscathed. For a start the large, metal garage doors were too cumbersome to close quietly. Even attempts at then walking round the outside of the building instead of through were futile, as one still had to enter the front door to gain access to the stairs.

I lost count of the hours I would spend planning strategies and traps and then lurking in corners waiting for Glen's eventual appearance. He too did the same. We were lucky to live in a building that contained so many rooms and hiding places. It was a practical jokers paradise and anything was possible. From trip wires and glow in the dark masks to recorded tape messages and plastic cups of water balanced on top of doorframes, we tried everything we could think of to outdo each other. We were the

Clouseau and Cato of Westport and we enjoyed every minute of it, nerve-wracking though it often was.

Honours were pretty even throughout the campaign, but I modestly confess to coming up with a masterstroke plan one evening – the double bluff. Upon hearing the garage doors closing one dark night, I simply stayed in my flat. Eventually there was a knock at my door. It was a disgruntled Glen complaining he had just wasted ten minutes walking nervously through the darkened building, bracing himself for the attack that never came. To give him credit he did counter this successfully a month later with the 'going away for the weekend without telling me' ploy, while misleadingly leaving his car in the garage.

They were great days.

It was several weeks before I found myself back up at Brynmawr chapel of rest again. With little to do the day had dragged, but as four thirty approached I felt the anticipation rising from within.

At four thirty-two I could hear in the distance that familiar voice, singing yet another obscure song: the renditions never seemed to be anything I knew. Then right on cue the singing stopped and I peered out between the blinds to see Angus nearing the chapel door. But somehow he didn't seem his old self. He was strangely hesitant. He pulled a newspaper from his bag and pushed it hurriedly but gently through the letterbox and was gone. I rushed out of the office into the service room and watched him through the stained glass as he walked slowly and conventionally up the road. There had been no deranged stare through the letterbox. No rants or grisly mutterings. No disturbing impersonations.

I have to confess to a certain amount of disappointment at this. But as I returned thoughtfully to the office I experienced an overwhelming sense of heroism; a feeling that I had unwittingly performed a selfless act of public service on that dark Halloween night. It was just possible that my tomato sauce-laden hand had saved the people of Westport from a potentially dark and horrible end in the not too distant future.

19

The young man with shiny, ebony skin took out a roll of twenty-pound notes from his jacket pocket. In the dim light he peeled off four with impassive ease.

'Is that right?' he smiled, revealing two rows of beautifully white teeth.

'Yes. Thank you,' I replied. 'The car is ready when you are.'

Again the smile. 'If you'd like to go downstairs I'll be with you in about ten minutes'.

I turned to leave and he returned the bundle nonchalantly to his pocket. I had no idea how much was there. My experience with large wads of money was sadly limited.

I caught the lift down to the ground floor and stepped back out into the rapidly darkening night. The air seemed vibrant as I waited patiently beside my limousine. I had never been inside the university grounds before and I guess I'd probably never even considered the intense activity that represented student nightlife. The tall accommodation block that now towered above me was one of three on the campus and the atmosphere emanating from both was one of pulsating energy. Belting out from an open window two floors up came the disco beat of the new Pet Shop Boys album; from another window close by I could hear the sound of raucous laughter and singing. There were endless groups of students bustling around, most on their way out for the evening. Several cast a curious eye over the sleek black limousine as they walked past.

Before I became involved in the funeral profession I had no idea that the limousines were often hired out privately, but it became a regular feature of my work. Weddings were the chief reason but two or three private hire runs a month were commonplace. We even had an ongoing contract with a couple of very large international companies who had bases in the wider area.

Most of these private hires took place in the evenings and at weekends, usually to take company directors and their wives to a posh function somewhere. It was often quite pathetic to see these prominent, highflying businessmen reduced to drunken, slobbering messes by the end of the night. Any respect I might have had for them at the start quickly evaporated by the time I watched them staggering home up their long, immaculately gravelled driveways. Occasionally though, like tonight, we would receive a telephone call from a private individual who wished to hire the services of a limousine for the evening. Normal procedure would be to invoice the client a couple of days later, but because this booking had come from a university student, Stewart, with some justification, had asked me to collect the money in cash before the evening started.

There need not have been any fears about the integrity of George Mbeki however. His polite willingness to pay up front immediately caused me some embarrassment at having had to ask. His manners were impeccable and as he now emerged from the tower block dressed in a very expensive looking charcoal grey suit, I knew that Mr Mbeki was no ordinary student. My client for the night was certainly the kind of person who turned heads. He had a presence about him that highlighted further his handsome face and lean, sinewy build. Out of the corner of my eye I could see the other students stop and stare as he stepped gracefully into the back of the limousine.

As I drove George to pick up two groups of friends and then take them onto a nightclub, he was clearly the centre of attention and a very popular person. He spoke only occasionally to me and I didn't learn a great deal about him other than he was the son of a chief of a very prominent tribe in central Africa and he was studying medicine here in Great Britain with the hope of taking his skills back home to his country one day. He did not boast, he did not brag; he merely told me things as a matter of course. But one thing I will always remember this prince and future doctor for was an incident early on in the evening just after we had set off from the university.

Before picking up the two groups, George stopped at a phone box to make a couple of phone calls. A few minutes later he returned and got into the limousine looking very thoughtful. He remained this way for several minutes. Eventually, I turned and asked him if everything was okay.

'Yes. Yes, I'm fine,' he replied in his exemplary English accent. There was a pause. 'Well...as a matter of fact...no.'

'What's up?'

'I lent my sports car to a friend tonight. I've just had word that he's written it off.'

'What!'

'Yes. Driven down a ditch or something. He's okay, but he's not insured.'

'You're joking!'

'I wish I were.'

He remained pensive for a few minutes. Then suddenly he spoke up. 'Oh, well. I suppose I'll just have to buy another one.'

There wasn't the slightest hint of arrogance in his voice whatsoever.

I drove on my fair share of these private hire runs, mostly in the early years. For some reason the bookings became fewer as time went on, probably the result of their spiralling cost. Another reason may have been the fact that the fashion for big black cars had changed to less pretentious options such as white or silver, choices which we, as undertakers, could not provide.

The decreasing number of chauffeur driven bookings did not leave any gaping holes in my life. Quite frankly, I didn't enjoy them at all. One of the major problems was never actually knowing how long they would take. This was particularly the case where weddings were concerned. With a funeral there is always a structure to proceedings. But weddings usually involved a lot of hanging around and waiting, which, if nothing else, was mind-numbingly boring. But there were also unexpected good points to chauffeuring.

As a chauffeur one is often privy to information that could be considered confidential. I once spent most of the day driving a party of businessmen around Westport, during which time they visited their two factories in the area. The local area manager, Mr Jenkins, a tall, slick man in his late thirties who was clearly susceptible to status-induced mood swings, had engaged our services earlier that week. He was extremely terse and surly with me; but grovelled and nodded in all the right places with the two American owners of the international company.

With their business done for the day I dropped the bootlicking manager back at the larger of the two factories near Westport docks. He bade his two bosses a sickly farewell and then walked off without a single word of thanks to me. I got back in the limousine feeling pretty aggrieved at his attitude. Then from the back, one of the Americans spoke:

'I don't like that Jenkins guy, Dan. He's gotta go.'

I tried not to make my smirk too noticeable.

Americans seemed to play a regular part in my private hire duties. I once drove another group of American businessman all the way to London Gatwick Airport in order for them to catch a late night flight home to Arizona. Once more I was witness to some amazing conversations and comments that took place in the back of the limousine. But the client from the United States of America I will never forget is Chuck Woods.

Chuck was about my age, stocky with curly blonde hair and deep blue eyes set into a square, friendly face. He was, in fact, a very amiable guy. But by the end of the night of our only acquaintance I could quite cheerfully have inflicted severe pain upon him.

It was half past four that day and Jill was phoning me down at the garage.

'Are you interested in some overtime tonight?'

'Well, not really,' I replied hesitantly. 'What's the problem?'

'I've just had an American guy on the phone. He wants to hire a limousine for a few hours this evening.'

'What does he mean by a few hours?'

'Well he has given me the full story,' said Jill with a smile in her voice. 'There's a girl he really fancies and she's agreed to go out on a date with him tonight. Basically he just wants to impress her.'

I sighed. I was just coming off a particularly heavy night on call and I didn't really relish the thought of working again tonight, even though it was more overtime and the job in hand sounded fairly undemanding. On top of all the on call we did I often felt the private hires were a step too far. It probably annoyed the company but I did actually have a life outside of work, not to say the desire to catch up on oft-missed sleep. Tonight, however, I had simply been looking forward to a quiet evening in and an early night.

'Isn't there anyone else available?

'No, I'm afraid not. I left asking you till last because I knew you were on call last night.'

After a brief silence I reluctantly agreed. 'Okay, but it's definitely not going to be a late one is it?'

'Oh, good gracious no. I've already told him that the cut off point has to be half past eleven at the latest because it's a weeknight. I think he only wants to take her to see a film and then onto somewhere for a quiet drink.'

'Fair enough,' I said, feeling a little happier. 'It sounds straightforward. I'll come up and get the details off you now.'

While Chuck and his girlfriend were in the cinema, I managed to pop back home and put my feet up for an hour before returning to pick them up. As I stretched out in front of the television I envisaged only being out for a couple of hours again at the most. This wasn't such a bad deal – an easy job of work and a few hours overtime in the process. I set off back to the cinema at half past nine and the couple duly emerged about a quarter of an hour later, laughing and radiant. I was pleased. I had already decided that Chuck was okay. His gratitude for my availability at such short notice had been extremely sincere.

Chuck was not your typically confident American by any means. There was a quiet charm about him that appealed to me and a nervousness with which I identified only too well in situations like this. After I had picked him up from his rented cottage near the seafront in Penderi Village, he asked me three times whether he looked okay for his big night out. In a pair of cream-coloured Chinos and a casual, blue open-necked shirt I thought he looked fine. But he took some convincing and his hands twitched nervously as we drove the couple of miles inland to pick up his date.

We arrived at a pleasant looking semi-detached house with red bricks and hanging baskets soon after and taking my chauffeuring duties seriously I walked up the hedge-lined pathway to ring the doorbell while Chuck waited anxiously in the limousine. I couldn't help feeling a little amused by it all. But when the front door opened and Kirsty stood smiling in front of me I suddenly understood the reason for Chuck's apprehension, the hire of the limousine, and the determination to get everything right. Kirsty was positively stunning. A perfect face was highlighted by incredibly deep brown eyes that sparkled playfully beneath a bob of neat, auburn hair. She wasn't tall but her short black dress, black stockings, and generous heels gave the impression of long, shapely legs. I realised I was staring open-mouthed and decided I needed to act quickly before I began drooling. I smiled back and walked her to the limousine in a state of awe, while developing a sudden loathing for my American client at the same time. It wasn't fair. The girls who invariably fancied me looked nothing like this at all. They all lived on a planet called earth. Kirsty was from a higher existence I had yet to locate.

Now, as I dropped them off at a small wine bar on Penderi sea front, they looked an infuriatingly handsome couple. Being a red blooded male I had, of course, fallen head over heels in love with the gorgeous Kirsty myself. But Chuck had seen her first and was going to great lengths to win her heart. My part in all this was simply to assist the man in his quest and judging by the way she had snuggled up to him in the limousine as I drove from the cinema to the wine bar, it certainly appeared to be going extremely well.

'Could you pick us up in an hour, Tom?' asked Chuck with a huge grin on his face. I couldn't help but smile back. I looked at my watch. That would be just after eleven o'clock.

'Yes, no problem. Enjoy yourselves.' I was going to discreetly enquire as to the progress of the evening but there was really no need. The fact they held hands tightly as they walked into the little continental establishment said it all.

There was plenty to see and watch along Penderi sea front at that time of night so I parked up and went for a walk. Penderi is a small but popular tourist resort a few miles from Westport and in the height of summer, as it was now, the bustling village was a picture of activity. Couples and groups of people were quietly strolling around the narrow streets or along the promenade, soaking up the nautical atmosphere of a balmy summer night.

Rain had actually been predicted but, so far, the forecasters had thankfully got it wrong.

When I returned to the limousine I started to feel very tired. The effects of the previous night were beginning to take their toll. Yawning, I checked my watch. Ten to eleven. Within the hour I'd be tucked up in bed.

I drove back to the wine bar and waited outside. Sure enough, at two minutes past eleven, my dear friend, Chuck emerged, as promised, with the film star, Kirsty still glued tightly to his side. I was about to get out and open the door for them when Chuck raised his hand, then opened it himself. What a top bloke, I thought to myself as he seated Kirsty. But instead of getting in himself, he sidled round to the driver's window.

'Tom, I wanna ask you a big favour, buddy.'

I didn't like the sound of this.

'I know you've gotta be back by midnight but Kirsty wants to go onto a nightclub. I realise this is an imposition, my friend, but would you stay on for a couple of hours?'

A couple of hours! I looked at him with pleading, bleary eyes. They were met by the same beseeching expression, minus the bleariness.

'Well...'

'I'm really sorry, buddy. Normally I'd getta cab, but...' He leaned a little closer and lowered his voice, a creased look of minor anguish on his face. '...to tell you the truth I'm running a little short of cash here. I don't wanna have to show her I've not brought enough money by going home for more.'

I cursed myself for not having any money on me because at that moment, I would have willingly given him the money for a taxi. I blew my cheeks and looked at my watch. This would take me up to one o'clock and beyond. Then I had to drop them off, get back home...

'It's not that I don't want to, Chuck. I'm just shattered.'

'Yeah I know, buddy,' he said, his concern genuine. 'But everything's gone so well tonight, far better than I could ever've imagined. Look, if you do this for me I'll make it worth your while, I promise.'

What could I do? This was a plea from one guy to another. The love life of a fellow male was on the line. Even though I was insanely jealous of the beauty sitting in the back of my vehicle and exhaustion was tugging viciously at my weary body, I had to help him. It was a man thing.

'Okay, jump in. Where do you want to go?'

If practical matters like money and sleep weren't important, the look on Chuck's face at that moment would have been payment enough. However, my thoughts were of the mercenary type as I set off again, knowing that my bed had been cruelly pushed away into the dark depths of night.

As I dropped Chuck and Kirsty outside the Beachcomber nightclub at the top end of Penderi I was in something of a quandary. I dared not go home and wait – I'd fall asleep for sure. But I didn't relish the thought of sitting around in the car for a couple of hours either. I began cursing Chuck Woods and his blasted hormones. In the end I parked the limousine up and went for another walk along the seafront. I had to stay awake somehow and although the night was still warm, a keen breeze had started to whip in from the east, helping me keep my bleary eyes open. It didn't occur to me until much later what a sad and solitary figure I must have appeared to the hundreds of revellers I passed as I walked aimlessly up and down the esplanade.

After what felt like several weeks my watch finally crawled its way towards one o'clock and I made my way back to the Beachcomber. I began to sense blissful freedom from my night of duress at last. I parked outside the entrance but this was a mistake because I quickly became the centre of attention. Several passers-by were pausing and milling around, obviously in the belief someone famous was in the vicinity.

Ten past one... Quarter past... Twenty past...

A group of girls came walking towards me and upon noticing the limousine, began pointing and giggling. Various squawking comments were soon to be heard until one of the members of the group, a rather brash looking bleach blonde wearing next to nothing stepped forward and spoke in a gloriously melodic Welsh accent.

'Hello luv! Who are you wai-ting for?'

Even in the midst of sleep deprivation I managed to raise the energy from somewhere to have a bit of fun. 'I'm sorry. I can't divulge that kind of information.'

'Aw, go on sweetheart. You can tell me!'

I shook my head.

'Is it somebody fay-mous?'

I let slip my best teasing smile.

'Oh my goodness!' she sang, believing she was onto something massive. Her vast jewellery collection began to rattle as she wrung her hands excitedly. 'Girls! Girls! It's somebody fay-mous!'

Her friends now crowded around the car and the squealing voices began again in earnest, pleading with me to reveal the identity of my mystery client.

'Who is it?'

'Is it a man?'

'Is it a pop star?'

'What are they doing by yer in Wales?'

Each question was defended by my smiling silence, which seemed to increase the frenzy. I have to confess that my doggedness was not so much a case of playing hard to get – it was my tired mind going completely blank and not being able to think of a suitably famous name to throw at them. Blondie wasn't giving up however. She leaned further in through my open window, displaying a cleavage the size of a shopping mall.

'Come on luv, just tell me,' she pleaded. 'I won't tell the others, I pro-mise. Tell me, pleeeese! Come on, you know you wants to reelly!' I'm gorgeous I am!'

As a cocktail of beer and perfume wafted into my face, I had a brainwave. With a few measured glances of secrecy here and there, I spoke in a low voice. 'He's in 'Neighbours' on TV.'

Blondie's jaw dropped open and her green eyes, which up to now had displayed a certain amount of alcohol-induced mistiness, suddenly began to sparkle. 'Is it Jason Donovan?' she breathed huskily. 'Please tell me it's Jason. He's cowin' lush, he is!'

'No, it's not Jason Donovan…'

At that very moment Chuck suddenly appeared from the doorway of the nightclub with Kirsty and made hastily for the limousine. I leapt out, opened the door and in they stepped looking for all the world like a glamorous celebrity couple. They were watched all the way in a silence of awe by the cluster of girls. As I walked back round to the driver's door, Blondie looked at me with a puzzled expression on her heavily made-up face. 'I don't remember him in 'Neighbours.''

'Have you watched it from the very beginning?'

'Well, no... '

'Ah well, he was in the original cast you see.'

As I drove away I looked in my mirror and grinned. Surrounded by her friends, Blondie was gesticulating excitedly and pointing at the car. I congratulated myself on a jape well executed. It was...

'Tom, my friend!'

I glanced in the back to see Chuck leaning ominously forward. I pushed open the glass partition.

'We sure have had a wonnerful night thanks to you, haven't we, babe?'

The babe nodded.

'I was just wondering if you wouldn't mind driving us down to Sandy Cove so we can finish the night in style.'

The private satisfaction of my little 'Neighbours' joke suddenly felt a very long time ago as the reality of tiredness and desperation returned. This wasn't fair. 'Chuck, normally I wouldn't mind, mate. But I've got to be up for work in the morning.'

'Buddy, I promise it won't be long. Half hour tops.'

The green digital clock on the dashboard swore 1:30 at me. I wanted to cry. I was just about to put my foot down and say a definite no when I caught a glimpse of Kirsty smiling sweetly at me. Well that was it, wasn't it? Women. How can they be so damned persuasive without even saying a word?

'Okay,' I sighed with a sudden meekness that surprised me.

'Hey, thanks, buddy. I won't forget this.'

'No, nor will I,' I muttered to myself.

Sandy Bay was about ten minutes away and it was a beautiful location – sweeping ocean views and an aura of peace and wild solitude. But right now it was one of the last places I wanted to be. At almost a quarter to two I pulled up just near the edge of the steep slope that led down to Sandy Bay itself.

'We won't be long, Tom,' smiled Chuck as he got out. Somehow I didn't believe him.

'Just wake me up if I'm asleep,' I grunted. I watched them clamber down the hill between the large tufts of grass, hand in hand, until they disappeared from view. Now I really was suffering. Not even the news that Kirsty had a sister who possessed a strange aspiration to date an undertaker would have cheered me up at that point. But even though that kind of scenario was, in my world, highly unlikely, something was actually about to brighten my dark and wearisome night.

Throughout my life I have often witnessed fate take a hand in certain, seemingly insignificant matters. Usually it was to my detriment, but tonight, somebody, somewhere took pity on me. Barely three minutes after Chuck and Kirsty had left the car it began to pour with rain. This was no summer shower either. It literally bucketed down and sitting in the car, the raindrops on the roof sounded like the mass applause of an audience at a music concert. Almost instinctively my bleary, bloodshot eyes searched the darkness and right on cue, two bedraggled figures came stumbling up the slope and ran desperately for the car. They were soaked to the skin.

'I guess we'd better call it a night,' gasped Chuck as the pair of them jumped into the back of the limousine with a squelch. There was joy in my heart as I started the engine and set off in the teeming rain. The weather forecasters, for once, had been correct. The end was at last in sight.

I took Kirsty home first. Despite looking as though she had dived fully clothed into a swimming pool, she still looked ravishing. She kissed Chuck goodnight and thanked me – how I wish the combined effects of cold rain and alcohol could have confused her into getting that mixed up – and disappeared into her house with a final, glitzy wave.

When I stopped outside Chuck's cottage at half past two, he was full of open appreciation for me.

'Tom, you're a real friend. I wanna thank you for your kindness and your willingness to make tonight a special one for me and Kirsty.'

I felt like saying 'Aw shucks' or something. But with my bed less than half an hour away and the traumas of the night almost already forgotten, I managed a not entirely honest 'No problem, it's been a pleasure Chuck.'

'Now if you'd just like to wait here for a minute, Ah've got something in the house to give you for your wonnerful service tonight.' He entered the darkened cottage and as I watched various lights flicker on and off, I began to wonder what reward awaited me. A fiver? Maybe a tenner. He was American – they could often be very generous indeed. After all, I had ventured way beyond the call of duty.

Chuck finally reappeared carrying a bottle of something. 'I want you to have this, buddy. It's a bottle of extremely nice wine. I hope you enjoy it. All the best, my friend.'

I took the bottle and muttered a distraught thanks. I really didn't have the heart or the energy to tell him that I didn't drink.

The following week I called into Dean Street for something and Jill greeted me with a smile.

'I've had a friend of yours on the phone. Chuck Woods. He wants to know if you can drive him again tomorrow night. He says you're the nicest, most accommodating guy he's ever met.'

My head started spinning and I clutched the desk for support. 'Oh no! Not again!'

Jill burst out laughing. Everyone knew by now about my experience with Chuck Woods the previous week. 'Don't panic,' she said. 'I've told him you're not available. Anyway, I don't think Stewart will be wanting to do hires like that anymore. By the time we paid your overtime I don't think we actually made any money.'

I never did find out how things worked out between Chuck and Kirsty. I would like to have known because if it had all gone pear-shaped, I wouldn't have minded a crack at her myself.

I'm kidding, of course. The likes of Kirsty have always seemed way beyond my average looks and station in life. By this stage I had long accepted that I probably stood more chance with the Blondies of this world. Even though I don't look a bit like Jason Donovan.

20

I glanced in my mirror and saw that the situation had begun to overwhelm Mrs Hughes. Her sobbing was now a shade louder, just a little more uncontrolled.

Alongside her in the back of my limousine sat her husband, a stocky, dark-haired man with lightly tanned skin. With his arm coiled tightly around his wife's delicate shoulders, his expression remained grim and detached. Barely a hint of emotion was visible in the tough, brooding features so typical of the true-blooded Welshman. Yet in the depths of those coal black eyes there raged a fire of both hatred and despair.

The scenes outside were still difficult to believe. In my short experience I had never seen anything like this before. As the cortege edged its way along at walking pace, the crowds were gathered on either side of the street, four, five, sometimes even six deep. There were no gaps; there was no thinning out along the way. If anything, the multitudes increased as we turned each corner. It appeared that the whole population of Llanclwyd had turned out to pay their respects, to give their support, to display their togetherness.

It had been like this since leaving the Hughes's home some ten minutes earlier. Local television cameras had filmed our every move as we carried the coffin from the house to the hearse. Then as we pulled away, a cameraman stood in front of us to capture the oncoming cortege as we set off. It must have been an impressive sight – hearse bedecked with an ocean of flowers, followed by four gleaming limousines in perfect configuration. The sight that was now unfolding as we drove solemnly along was equally awe-inspiring to me. The opportunity to witness the collective grieving of a community is a sobering, yet somehow uplifting experience.

The death of local boy, Donny Hughes had dominated the headlines and column inches of both the local and national press for days. While on duty with the armed forces, Donny had been murdered by terrorists. He was only nineteen. Similar stories of such atrocities appear on the front pages of newspapers almost every week. But they always happen somewhere else, to unfamiliar names in far off places. Now the abominations of the twentieth century had reached tiny Llanclwyd and the effect on the community of this little town nestling quietly in a valley north-east of Westport was devastating.

We turned into the main street of Llanclwyd and inched ever closer to St. Peter's Church at the lower end of town. The sight of the gathered masses lining our route as they stood In front of the unanimously closed shops was almost overwhelming to me. I could only hazard a guess as to how Donny's parents must be feeling. They had chosen to travel alone, just the two of them together in the leading limousine, as if creating a deliberate cocoon for themselves from the world outside. Just for a while.

As we drew to a halt and I opened the door it was the eerie silence that hit me first. Like an archer drawing back his bowstring, the uneasy tranquillity conspired to heighten the already highly-charged tension. I became acutely conscious of my movements and any necessity to speak to my colleagues. It seemed as though the whole universe had stopped for a short time out of respect for a young man whose life had been cruelly cut short.

Why him? Why Donny? His parents must have been weary of asking such questions.

The wrong place. The wrong time.

Six of Donny's colleagues carried his coffin shoulder high into the church with the dignity and efficiency one would expect. There were tears in the blue eyes of the young soldier at the front. Maybe he had known Donny more than most. The silence still spoke louder than any words. Only the sergeant's voice could be heard as he barked his instructions into the still air. Even they seemed tempered, less imperious.

The service inside St. Peter's was being relayed to the many hundreds of mourners surrounding the church by a number of loudspeakers positioned above the church door and on lampposts along the street. Everyone listened with a pensive intensity I have rarely witnessed since. Still nobody moved. Still nobody spoke.

We, the drivers, felt compelled to do likewise. Normally while a funeral service is in progress the drivers congregate quietly outside the church and have a chat. There was none of that today. We remained motionless beside our vehicles as we too were caught up in the sheer emotional power of the occasion. A spine-tingling rendition of the hymn 'Abide With Me' signalled the conclusion of the service and the mourners emerged from the haven of the old, grey-stoned church and back into the cold, intrusive world outside.

I opened the door for Donny's parents and I could see his mother's desperate face wet with tears as the reality of her loss began to take its fearful grip. She was an attractive, petite woman in her early forties, but the strain of the past few days had aged her cruelly. Her neat, brown hair fell across her eyes as she stepped wearily into the car: she made no attempt to push it back into place. In the back of the limousine as we set off again through the crowds to the cemetery on the edge of town, her husband did it for her. Tenderly he wiped the tears too from her swollen cheeks with rough, awkward hands. Still he held himself together. Still he remained the silent, restrained rock.

He probably felt he had no choice. It was what the world expected from a man of his generation.

It was several years later. I was watching the news, the usual depressing, disheartening stuff – a murder here, a rape there, the continued fighting between rival forces in some African country, mass fraud and deception, an argument between two neighbours that had spiralled out of control, drugs, alcohol abuse, family violence.

Each news item I watched underlined everything that is depraved about the human race. Every story was laced with greed, hatred, disrespect, and man's dismal inability to live in harmony one with another. I was about to turn the television off and do something more constructive when the newscaster began the final item. It was about dolphins. I stopped to listen because I love dolphins. But what I heard left me open-mouthed in disbelief. Some supposedly knowledgeable scientist was out to prove that the beloved dolphin is not quite as delightful as we like to believe. Underneath the charm and the cuteness, he claimed, there is a nasty, vicious streak and he was determined that the illusions of millions had to be shattered: *the truth needed to be told.*

My disgust was not about the dolphin that had apparently deceived us all these years with a Jeckyll and Hyde character. It was the sheer cynical arrogance of the scientist himself. What right did he have to stand in judgement over the conjectured failings of a so-called lesser animal? How can we, an allegedly more intelligent species, have the hypocritical nerve to shake our heads in disapproval at the possible discovery that dolphins, or any other animal for that matter, have a dark and flawed side to their nature?

I have absolutely no idea why my thoughts returned to the funeral of Donny Hughes at this point but they did, and with some intensity. More specifically they focussed on the reason for the funeral in the first place. A young man with his whole life ahead of him had been killed in cold blood for no other reason than the selfish, bigoted, intolerance of man.

The human mind possesses complexities that animals will never have. One is the ability to know the consequences of our actions. If an animal kills, it kills for a reason – survival. It has no concept of the knock-on effect. But the killer, or killers, of Donny Hughes were aware of the terrible repercussions their actions would cause. That they chose to ignore such feelings says much about the ruthless inhumanity that man is capable of. We may watch a wildlife documentary on television with revulsion as a lion hunts down a gazelle and tears it apart. But what makes us so superior? We, because of our knowledge and understanding, have the ability to know better.

For a few minutes I was back in that limousine, driving Mr and Mrs Hughes to the cemetery so they could farewell their precious son. I could see Mrs Hughes, broken and distraught, clinging desperately to her husband in the back as we drove in through the cemetery gates. I could see the stony face of Mr Hughes finally crack as he and his wife stared down into that hollow, meaningless abyss that was Donny's grave. I could see them gripping each other tightly, as though afraid to ever let go before returning to the car. I could see the remainder of their lives polluted with bitterness and confusion, emptiness and despair. As I opened the door of the limousine back at their small, semi-detached house in Llanclwyd, they stepped out and thanked me quietly for what I had done. But I had done nothing. Nothing, that is, except my job.

Over the years, whatever the circumstances of death, I always wished there was more I could do to help those who had just lost someone dear. I learned with time that a few kind words, a gentle smile in the right place, or a willingness to listen as others rushed away back to their lives with vague apologies, was the extra that people wanted. Simple kindness gives hope. It restores confidence. It promotes feelings of trust and well-being. It costs nothing to give.

Maybe in the case of people like Donny's mother and father, it also restores just a tiny fraction of faith in mankind.

21

Chris Littlehales was an interesting character, not least because he had fought in the Falklands conflict. But there was far more to him than just the formulaic image of another ex-soldier. He came to work for us via a friend, who was a receptionist in one of our satellite branches. Having subsequently left the army at the age of twenty-seven, Chris was looking for a new, more peaceful way to make a living. A driver in the world of undertaking seemed to be the perfect career switch for him and I soon found myself showing him some of the ropes.

Chris was roughly the same height and build as me – five-foot-nine and slight. His face had a flat appearance, interrupted halfway up – or down, depending on which way you cared to look – by the seemingly mandatory moustache. His small, dark eyes virtually disappeared when he laughed and this soon became a frequent occurrence because we discovered and invented much to laugh about as we found ourselves working together with increasing regularity.

A natural comic and tremendously quick-witted, I don't believe I ever saw anyone get the better of Chris in a bantering match or a full-scale argument. Together we made a formidable team, becoming well known for lampooning and sending up our colleagues. Woe betide any poor soul who had a prominent characteristic or way of speaking because we would impersonate them mercilessly. Many were the occasions when Chris and I threatened to sit down together and write a script of some kind. Sadly, like so many ideas in life, they remained just good intentions that never materialised.

I first became aware of Chris's razor sharp wit just three days after he started. Situated opposite our Dean Street office in the town centre was a large, privately owned hardware store called Gwilym Stevens. Whether one was a professional builder or just a DIY enthusiast, Gwilym Stevens sold the lot. From timber to tools and fittings to fixings, he was a popular and often less expensive alternative to some of the more established High Street names in Westport.

The proprietor, Gwilym T Stevens himself, was very much a prominent part of the local scenery. Seeing him going in and out of his store and around the corner into the back lane to his delivery bay was a regular feature of each working day. Gwilym was in his mid-fifties, solid with a slightly stooping gait and a continual habit of pushing back his wavy grey hair with the palm of his hand. He was a friendly, amiable type, but there was just a hint of the arrogant, self-made man about him too. One always had the impression he liked to think of himself as the 'lord of the manor' of his immediate surroundings. This was borne out by the fact he continually flouted traffic laws by tearing up the one-way back lane in the wrong direction to save time. As a result he caused a handful of, thankfully, minor accidents in the process, including one involving Paul and myself in one of the estate cars. To give him credit he always cheerfully acknowledged the blame, which certainly led us to believe his business was doing very nicely in order for him to pay for all the damage he caused.

The garage at the rear of our Stapleton Road premises (where I lived) was directly opposite Gwilym's loading bay, divided by the narrow lane he thought he owned. Over time we developed a reciprocal agreement whereby he would allow us to park our funeral vehicles in his bay if we were tight for space, or for him to park his car temporarily in our garage while lorries and vans were delivering his stock.

It was on such a day that Chris and I were returning to Stapleton Road from Sandacre Hospital, where we had been carrying out removals. The back lane was in complete chaos: not for the first time there were vehicles everywhere. Gwilym Stevens's bay was full and a hearse, another estate car, and Stewart Lewis's company car were all parked in our garage. In the fourth space, squeezed tightly between the estate and the hearse, was Gwilym's white Audi. It was one of those occasions when, despite the ongoing pact between us, the inconvenience was extremely frustrating as time ticked away.

I was just debating what to do when I saw Gwilym in my rear mirror loping around the corner. He strode past and waved without looking directly at us – as was his way – and made casually for his car with the obvious intention of moving it out. It was good timing for us, but Chris wasn't at all impressed.

'Look at this joker 'ere!' he exclaimed in his cockney tone. Despite being Welsh born and bred, Chris sounded like he should be running a market stall on London's Portobello Road. Amongst other things, his time in the army had also affected his accent.

Before I could say anything he leapt out of the estate, leaving the door wide open, and began confronting a startled Gwilym Stevens.

'Oi! You've got a cheek parking in 'ere mate!'

'Pardon?'

'This is a funeral directors. Can't you read?'

'Now listen here young...'

'No, *you* listen here. Get in your car and shift it now.'

Gwilym's colour had reached the glowing red stage and he rose up like a bullfrog. 'Do you realise who I am?' he spelt out indignantly. 'I am Gwilym Stevens!'

Chris's reply was instinctive and precise. 'Listen mate, I don't care if you're Shakin' Stevens. You don't park your car in 'ere.'

Among the many victims of the humour plied by Chris and myself was a chap named Reg Bowen. Reg was employed as a full time chauffeur at one of the private undertaking concerns our company had taken over. For several years this particular business had been awarded the contract to drive the area's judges to and from Westport Crown Court, and this, in effect, was Reg's full time duty: he would only assist on funerals when the court was in recess. He also drove on a great deal of weddings too, as the Daimler used to drive the judges was very popular with brides-to-be.

The judge's contract was certainly a lucrative one income-wise, but eventually we lost it completely. The reality-challenged halfwits at the top became greedy and totally over-priced the tender when the contract came up for renewal one year. It was no surprise that a small company in the north of the town tabled a far more sensible bid and took over this prestigious operation shortly afterwards.

Technically this left Reg without a job. Thankfully, however, he was absorbed into the pool of drivers and became one of us. Obviously he was grateful for the reprieve – he only had four years left until retirement – but he didn't really enjoy the more 'hands on' role in which he was now involved. This was entirely understandable. Being chauffeur to the judges was a task he had enjoyed and no one really blamed him for resenting the change forced upon him as a result of the company's greed.

If I thought Chris with his London accent was a certainty for the capital's market scene, then Reg's looks would surely have seen him operating the stall opposite as the local 'spiv'. With his greased-back hair and pencil thin moustache it would have come as no surprise had he opened his jacket to reveal a vast array of watches, necklaces, and other dodgy looking merchandise. Because of these distinctive features, my rather spurious memory of Reg is not one of him dressed in his charcoal grey funeral suit, but rather the black, pin-stripe uniform of the classic market dealer. This was extremely odd and completely absurd of course, because I never saw him dressed like that in all my years of working with him. But it confirms the fact that the mind does indeed play very strange tricks at times.

I liked Reg Bowen but he could be a miserable bugger at times. He was king of the expletive uttered with meaning. If ever anything went wrong or someone upset him, Reg would come out with an animated curse during which every vowel, consonant, and vocal sound was expressed to its fullest potential. But it was his tutting ability that gave Chris and I most of our impersonating ammunition. Reg was without question one of the great 'tutters' of the world. Whether discussions were about the weather, certain colleagues of ours, funeral management, or the price of a bag of chips, Reg's response would be to shake his head animatedly and emit a series of gloriously disgusted tuts. It was during one particular session of Reg-tutting impressions that Chris and I probably got ourselves into a touch of strife. The problem was we were never actually able to find out.

We were both driving on a wedding one grey Saturday afternoon – Chris was driving Reg's Daimler for the bride and her father; I was driving a standard limousine for the bridesmaids. As I have already mentioned, I didn't particularly enjoy driving on weddings. They went on too long, especially if there was an over-fussy photographer in tow. There seemed to be a glut of them in Westport – bearded, flat-haired little men with baggy trousers and tweed jackets who obviously had distant connections to the Third Reich. I witnessed them ruin many a wedding with their obsessive natures and their eccentricities. The photographs may well have been worth it when they arrived a couple of months later, but they drove everybody crazy in the process, especially us drivers.

It was this kind of marathon photo shoot that Chris and I found ourselves enduring one particular day. It had been an hour since the new husband and wife emerged radiant and happy from the church, but still the photographer was holding forth with his rants and his sharply barked orders. Even some of the guests had started quietly complaining.

Chris and I had already begun to relieve the boredom by imagining the reactions of some of our colleagues in the same situation. Gareth would be hopping from foot to foot in a nervous panic. Nigel would start messing about under the bonnet of the Daimler and offering his mechanical expertise to the gathered wedding guests. Paul would be trying to chat up the bridesmaids, possibly even the bride herself. Denzil would be wandering around offering everyone a Polo mint from his seemingly endless supply. And Stewart would be on the verge of passing out at the amount of overtime we were earning.

Unusually, it took us a while to get round to Reg, but when we did, Chris went for it in a big way. He stood beside the Daimler, arms folded, bottom jaw jutting outwards. He then proceeded to moan and grumble about the bride being late, the photographer, the cold gusts of wind playing havoc with his hair, and the fact that three bags of confetti had been deposited inside the Daimler, which he would have to clean out on Monday morning. Splendidly petulant tuts and a constantly disgusted shaking of the head accompanied all of this. It was very impressive stuff.

Unfortunately for Chris, he hadn't noticed that the person hired to film the wedding had wandered off in search of more interesting material and was pointing the video camera directly at us. By the time Chris realised, it was too late. Somewhere in Westport there is a couple whose precious wedding video footage contains the apparent dark mutterings of a miserable, disgruntled limousine driver.

Chris would only occasionally refer to his days in the army: he rarely, if ever mentioned his time in the Falklands War. I had heard from someone that he had been pretty close to the action – so close that he shot and killed an Argentinean soldier near Port Stanley. Whether this was the reason for his reticence or not I don't know. I did ask him about it one day. He confirmed it was true, but his solitary comment said much to me about Chris's character.

'It was him or me, Tom. I didn't have a lot of choice.'

Chris's life and experiences in the army definitely gave him an edge as a person. There was a bluntness and a confidence that many didn't like and, once again, it was an attitude that certainly did not endear him to Stewart Lewis.

By now I was beginning to realise that our judgemental manager would deem anyone who showed an inclination to step outside the zone of submissive meekness as a troublemaker. In his eyes, Glen, Chris, and myself all fell neatly into this category and the three of us were constantly fighting a battle to gain parity with everyone else. Which is why it was particularly sweet that all three of us happened to be driving on the funeral when Stewart slipped over on the ice.

The funeral was taking place in the district of Dyffryn on the east side of town. Stewart did a good many of the funerals here because he was Dyffryn born and bred: he knew the area and its people well. It was also in Dyffryn where, just over four years earlier, he had forgotten the funeral on my first day. Today, however, was about to become memorable for an entirely different reason. Dyffryn is basically built on, and around, a large hill. Two roads run parallel through the area, one high, and one low. Several small roads, most of which contain slopes varying in gradient from gentle to quite steep, then linked both. It was on one of the more severe slopes that we now stood on a freezing cold January morning, waiting for the service in the tiny, terraced house to conclude. We'd had some difficulty in reaching the house at all. Although the major roads had been gritted, many of the smaller side roads were still covered in ice.

The vicar finally emerged from the house and the family gingerly made their way to the waiting limousines, blowing streams of cold, white air as they went. We were soon ready to leave but I was somewhat surprised to see Stewart preparing to walk in front of the hearse. With conditions the way they were I thought it was just a trifle optimistic. But Stewart was a walker, especially on home territory, and he seemed determined to see it through, come hell or frozen water.

We pulled away carefully and began to descend down the hill at crawling pace. I kept more of a distance than usual from Chris in the hearse and through my mirror I could see that Glen was doing the same thing behind me. Normally we kept a much tighter formation when travelling in a cortege but on a day like today it was far too risky.

Everything seemed to be going fine. Then just as we were rounding a curve in the road, Stewart suddenly disappeared from view. I saw Chris's brake lights go on and I immediately applied my own. The tyres growled as they tried to grip onto something firm and after a minor skid of a couple of feet I came to a safe halt. I then caught a very brief glimpse of Stewart again. I say brief because the moment his head and shoulders emerged in front of the hearse, he vanished completely out of sight again a split second later. It was just after I'd noticed Chris's shoulders gently shaking that I then saw Stewart's bowler hat rolling merrily down the hill. Now if Stewart had admitted defeat there and then and returned to the hearse, he may well have escaped with most of his dignity intact. But no. He was very fond of his black funeral bowler and bravely, foolishly, he began to give chase.

Because he had now managed to move ahead of the hearse in his doomed pursuit, I had a grandstand view of fall number three. Unfortunately, so too did the mourners in the back of my limousine. It was around about this time the comments started.

'Look, there he is.'

'Oops… there he goes again.'

'Oh dear, the back of his coat is white.'

'I think he's hurt his elbow, look.'

'Whoa, he's down again! I'll give him 7.5 for that one!'

All this from a widower and his three daughters who were about to farewell a dearly loved wife and mother.

It was at this point that I made the fatal mistake of looking in my mirror. I saw Glen's red, painfully contorted face and when I caught his eye, a helpless snorting noise escaped from my throat. It was no good. I just couldn't hold it in any longer.

After the committal service at the crematorium the family were in raptures over Stewart's ice-dance routine. They had enjoyed every minute and heartily congratulated him on his dogged determination. The four of them had laughed all the way to the crematorium and certainly weren't offended by my uncontrollable giggling.

'It would take a robot to keep a straight face during that!' chuckled one of the daughters.

To give Stewart credit he took the whole thing really well. It was certainly an embarrassing moment for him but later, when such incidents always seem a little more relaxed, he laughed with the rest of us and I admired him greatly for that.

But for Chris, Glen, and myself, an even greater camaraderie developed between us from that day forward. For the three of us it was retribution of the highest order and the image of our dear manager at odds with Mother Nature gave us great satisfaction and reminiscing material for several months to come.

22

I was back in Abertrefil.

Islwyn Thomas was describing yet another dramatic removal story with his usual histrionic enthusiasm. I was beginning to wonder whether any removal at the Abertrefil branch took place without something going wrong.

'Tom, my boy, you would not have believed it. I did not know where to look or what to say. I was speechless.'

It must have been bad.

'I left Dyfrig at the top of the stairs with the stretcher while I popped down to make sure all the doors were shut and the family out of the way. Now you know as well I do, Tom bach, that Dyfrig by yer is not the brightest star in the sky...'

Dyfrig, sitting in the corner supping a mug of tea, gave a toothy grin and nodded his head.

'...but what do you think the silly numskull was trying to do? Slide the stretcher down the stairs by himself! As I returned to the bottom of the staircase I was suddenly confronted by a ruddy surfboard descending the stairs with Dyfrig lying on top of it!'

I shook my head, open-mouthed in disbelief. But I had no time to comment because Islwyn was now in full flow.

'Dyfrig! What the blazes are you doing? I cried. Well it wasn't the best time to ask a question because the silly old fool tried to answer about halfway down. I couldn't understand a damn word he was saying. It was like listening to my grandson making machine gun noises!'

Between my helpless giggling I managed to somehow ask my burning question to Dyfrig. 'But how on earth did you end up on top of the stretcher?'

Dyfrig produced his familiar, badly worn tobacco pouch and began his half hourly ritual with the usual painstaking attention. His almost tranquil demeanour was the perfect foil for Islwyn's dynamism. He chuckled wheezily. 'I lost my balance. The old dear was a bit on the heavy side.'

'But what the devil were you thinking, trying to get her down the staircase by yourself?' cried Islwyn. I felt sure he must have asked this question many times in the past couple of days since the incident occurred. But this was a show, a performance. Whatever answer Dyfrig chose to give, the question had clearly lost none of its original sparkle.

'Well I thought if I eased her down the stairs some of the way it would save a bit of lifting.'

'Save a bit of lifting, by crikey!' You certainly did that. And you saved yourself a *walk* down the stairs in the process. And the family! Oh, the poor family!' He almost mimed the final sentence as he sank dramatically into the nearest chair, the back of his hand held delicately across his forehead. It was for this kind of sublime spectacle that I believed Islwyn Thomas might have wasted his life in the funeral profession. He had surely been born for the stage. He was a natural performer, extravagantly over the top in every glorious way.

'What did they say?' I prompted eventually.

Islwyn removed his hand from his forehead and held it aloft, groaning as if in pain. 'They were mortified. Mortified I tell you! But they ended up more worried about poor Dyfrig than their dear old mother. They even apologised for having such a steep staircase.'

As we prepared to leave on the funeral about half an hour later, Islwyn explained we would be out over lunchtime.

'I hope you've brought sandwiches with you, Tom bach. We're off on an adventure to the outer reaches of nowhere today – Newgate to be exact.' Newgate certainly wasn't quite as far away as Islwyn made out. But it was a good half an hour's drive up the motorway from Abertrefil at normal speed – fifty minutes at funeral pace. I'd not yet been to the crematorium in Newgate. It had always been either Westport or the smaller one in Murton. Murton Crematorium was actually only a few miles up the motorway from Abertrefil, but today we were travelling to Newgate because the wife of the deceased had been cremated there a few years ago.

For a change, Islwyn suggested I drive the hearse and asked Dyfrig to pick up the family in the limousine. This was mostly because they lived on a smallholding out of town. Although I was now pretty adept at finding my way around, one accidental wrong turn can prove quite embarrassing with a bereaved family sitting in the back. However, Islwyn's forward thinking on this occasion very nearly backfired.

There was a well-attended church service in town first (thankfully the resident vicar was on holiday so there was no need for me to sustain my racing car driver image) before setting off for Newgate crematorium. Islwyn was his usual entertaining self on the way. But he never dominated the conversation. He was always interested in what I had to say, especially how I was getting on in Westport. Islwyn was one of the few people genuinely concerned about my welfare and I never stopped appreciating it.

The motorway journey came quickly to an end and we had made good time. As we passed the sign signalling the Newgate exit Islwyn warned me to be careful. 'Now then, bach, nice and slow. This roundabout has apparently been altered for the better since I was last by yer. The crematorium should still be signposted though so make sure we don't miss it.'

If the roundabout had been changed for the better I was extremely relieved not to have confronted it in its former glory. The whole area was a bizarre network of junctions, sub-junctions, and interchanges, of which the roundabout itself was only a small part. Islwyn's puzzled expression at the labyrinth ahead of us didn't fill me with any confidence either, but after a couple of seconds he pointed to his left.

'Down there, Tom. I think.'

The traffic lights at the end of the slip road were green and I turned left as Islwyn had indicated. We were now on the roundabout, but for what happened next I can only offer the feeblest of explanations. To this day I have no idea what was going on inside my head. As we approached the first exit I suddenly saw a sign that said 'SERVICES'. Without warning I lurched the hearse left and followed the road around. The moment I turned I knew what I had done. I have no idea why but my funeral-conditioned mind thought the sign saying 'SERVICES' was referring to funeral services. I could have kicked myself – I most probably would have if I hadn't been driving. But the cold sweat that broke out all over my cringing body certainly made up for my temporary inability to carry out any personal chastisement.

As we approached the large sign temptingly announcing 'Two Meals For A Fiver' I knew my only option was to take the cortege around the services and out again. The damage had been done – there was no turning back. On a single, one-way piece of road this was the only escape route we had. As we passed the restaurant and veered right to go round the Travelodge, I looked back to see the long cortege snaking along behind us. I felt sick and in need of a lie down. It was then that I realised how uncharacteristically quiet Islwyn had been. I shot an anxious glance in his direction. He was sitting there impassively, his big hand pressing tightly over his mouth.

'Islwyn, I'm really sorry...' I began hesitantly. He remained motionless. Desperately I launched into a babbled explanation of what had happened. It sounded even less convincing than I thought. Then as we passed the petrol station something stirred. A strange gurgling sound began to shake the frame sitting beside me. This was soon replaced by spluttering laughter that was music to my ears. Somebody was smiling down on me. Most other funeral directors I worked with would have really gone to town.

'Tom, Tom!' he grinned, shaking his head. 'Now there's me thinking you were taking us all to the services for a cuppa and you've driven right past!'

Iswlyn had taken my *faux pas* extremely well. Nevertheless, I still fervently wished that hearses were fitted with driver ejector seats. As we all left the services in perfect unison I tried to ignore the friendly sign thanking us for calling and wishing us a safe journey. The last thing I needed at that moment was sarcasm.

When we finally pulled up outside the crematorium a few minutes later, Islwyn's explanation to the family was both simple and inspired. I doubted, however, whether there were many funeral directors around who could have actually got away with it.

'Bronwen bach, I know your Dad loved his cup of tea and as we had a little time to spare, I thought passing by such a popular place to stop for a cuppa would be the crowning acknowledgement of a grand man's passion.' It was sheer poetry and Bronwen, a delicate lady in her late forties, wiped a tear from her soft, brown eyes. 'Thank you so much for your thoughtfulness, Mr Thomas. Dad would have loved the gesture.'

After the service in the pleasant little crematorium, Islwyn was in his element. He knew most of the mourners in attendance and went out of his way to speak to them all. His talent was a joy to watch and a wonderful exercise in public relations. It was easy to see why he was such a popular figure in the close-knit town of Abertrefil. This was further borne out when he strode towards an old gentleman talking to a small group of people near where I was standing. The little man looked very frail in his loose fitting grey suit and black trilby hat: on his slightly shaking arm he carried a shabby, fawn raincoat.

'Good heavens! Ceridwen Griffiths! How the devil are you?'

Ceridwen Griffiths smiled back with watery eyes and replied in a high-pitched, throaty voice. 'Oh fair-to-middling, Mr Thomas. A little bit shaky, see.'

Islwyn shook the old man's hand vigorously. 'Well, well, my friend. It *is* good to see you. The years have rolled by now haven't they? And tell me Ceridwen, how old are you now, bach?'

'Nearly ninety-two, Mr Thomas.'

'Ninety-two!' bellowed Islwyn. 'Ceridwen bach, it's hardly worth you going home now is it!'

Everyone within earshot – which, given Islwyn's booming voice, was almost everyone attending the funeral – burst into laughter and joining them with a huge smile on his pale, life-worn face was Ceridwen Griffiths himself. It was a precious moment.

A few moments later Islwyn escorted the daughter of the deceased, Bronwen, back to the car. I stood waiting by the hearse and watched as she held his hand and kissed him affectionately on the cheek. 'Thank you, Mr Thomas,' she smiled gratefully. 'You've done us proud once again.'

Islwyn bowed very slightly. 'It has been a privilege, my dear, and an honour too. Now you take care and if there is anything at all that you need, you know where I am. Okay, bach?'

As he gently closed the limousine door it suddenly hit me that Islwyn Thomas wasn't wasted in the funeral profession at all. No vocation in the world suited him better than that of funeral director.

I arrived back in Westport just after four thirty that same day and called into the Dean Street office to pick up my wage slip. While driving back I had been thinking how there was no way our branch in Westport could compete with the madcap, entertaining bunch of characters up in Abertrefil.

Just at that moment I heard Denzil's booming voice in the front office. He had been arranging a funeral there with a family and as I'd walked along the corridor towards the back office, I overheard them saying they were undecided whether or not to view their father in his coffin. Denzil had suggested that he could close the coffin and then the family might like to go to the chapel of rest one evening and just sit quietly with the coffin instead. Sitting with the coffin was a sort of 'halfway house' option we always offered to families who were unsure, intimidated even by the thought of viewing the deceased. It was a suggestion that nearly always pacified such concerns.

Now on my way back out, I paused as Denzil was showing the family to the door. Solemnly and quietly he shook hands with each family member. Then as they stepped into the street outside he delivered his parting line: 'Now don't forget, just give me a ring if you decide you want to come and sit in the coffin.'

23

'You'd better bring your wellies too. It looks like we might need them.'

Glen's voice on the extension sounded gloomy. It didn't take long to filter through to me. I rarely enjoyed any call out at night but five minutes after getting into bed was being a touch unfair. The thought of having to dress again and venture out into the February chill didn't fill me with a great amount of enthusiasm. Especially as it appeared we had a trek through Denbigh Woods ahead of us.

Although the vast majority of coroner's removals are relatively straightforward, many involve a variety of unusual circumstances and locations. It didn't take me long to realise that in the world of undertaking, death doesn't always take place in cosy hospital or nursing home beds. Even house deaths could have their unforeseen hazards. I soon learned, therefore, to expect the unexpected. Like tramping through cold, damp woodland areas in the pitch dark of night.

I pulled on my still warm clothes and knocked on Glen's door across the landing. It was certainly convenient that the two of us were partners on call. It reduced the time spent waiting for colleagues to turn up or having to arrange to meet them somewhere *en route*. Living in the same building meant we reduced the amount of time we had to be out to the minimum and with us both being of the astute variety, this was the main reason why we had asked to go on call together in the first place.

We set off in the estate car amid a distinctly morose atmosphere. Unfortunately it had little to do with the circumstances surrounding the demise of the poor gentleman we were about to collect. Selfishly, but perhaps understandably, we were more concerned about being dragged from our cosy, comfortable beds at silly o' clock to do a spot of reluctant night rambling. Such call outs were the dreaded nightmare of every undertaker. It was bad enough being called out at all, but when an expedition such as the one we now faced was required, the job rapidly lost its appeal.

Our destination was about a half hour's drive from Stapleton Road by day. At ten to midnight it took less than half that time – a combination of traffic-free roads and Glen's driving. Denbigh Woods was quite a large expanse running alongside a disused railway track and surrounded by a number of well-populated out-of-town districts. It was therefore a favoured place for the people who lived within its vicinity to walk their dogs. From the brief information the police had provided on the phone it appeared the deceased was one such resident, who had been taken ill while walking his dog. The dog had returned home alone a couple of hours later and the wife had reported her husband missing soon after.

When we arrived at the top entrance to the wood – the nearest we could reach by car – the policeman on duty waiting for us completed the story.

'Another man out walking his own dog spotted him about half an hour after the wife phoned us,' said the lean, sinewy constable in a strong valley accent. 'I'm afraid he's quite a way in, boys. If you're ready to go I'll show you the way. CID are with him now.'

Glen and I exchanged glum looks as we gathered our unwieldy removal equipment and followed the policeman into the inky woods. I was extremely glad we had decided to wear Wellington boots. The recent rain had made the earthy track extremely muddy. As I listened to the still hush all around us, disturbed only by the clumping sound of our footsteps, I felt a wave of loneliness blow over me. How awful to die alone out here. It could easily have been a secluded jungle in a distant country as opposed to a wood on the edge of a British suburban sprawl. The same bleak isolation ruled the darkness of night.

After ten minutes of solid walking my brief moment of compassion had drifted away on the biting February winds. The thought we would have to return this way carrying quite possibly a heavy body had muscled its way into my thinking. My sympathy was still in there somewhere, but at times like this selfishness can't help but take over the mind of an already weary body.

A couple of minutes later the almost welcome sight of a portable floodlight up ahead greeted us, as did the presence of three burly looking CID officers. Observing the physique of our policeman friends on these occasions was an important ritual. These looked fine specimens. Surely they would give us a hand with the body? They often did.

One of them stepped forward to greet us as we approached. He looked a little concerned. 'I'm really sorry about this, boys...' he began apologetically.

My heart sank.

'...but the photographer still hasn't shown up. Apparently he's already attending the scene of a suspicious death on the other side of Abertrefil. He's been held up there for a while. The last ETA we had was about one thirty I'm afraid.'

I tipped my head backwards as his words echoed through my brain like the key scene in a drama film. We now had a wait of over an hour in a freezing, pitch-black wood with no guarantee that the photographer would actually turn up at the given time. I closed my eyes and gritted my teeth. Glen was a little more forthcoming.

'Why were we not informed of this earlier?' he growled. I always knew when Glen's mood was rising. He developed an air of portentous superiority.

The officer shrugged. 'Well, we do keep in contact with Control. They should inform you of proceedings. But if you'd already left I suppose there was little they could do.'

Glen turned his attention to the uniformed officer. 'Well couldn't you have told us when we arrived? At least we could have sat in the car and waited.'

The young policeman shuffled uncomfortably in his large black boots, but he remained silent. Glen now entered his 'I don't believe this' mode. It was an extremely impressive facial expression that was accompanied by a cringingly sarcastic smile and topped off by a stance that any actor would have been proud of: left arm on hip and the thumb and forefinger of the right hand thoughtfully holding a pouting chin.

The CID officer broke the brief silence. 'You're welcome to go back and sit in your car until he arrives, mate. But don't forget we're stuck out here as well.'

'Yes. And getting paid more than me in the process.'

Although Glen was now probably pushing his luck, a sore point amongst all funeral directors motivated such a comment. Being salaried meant they didn't get paid a penny for any work done outside of office hours, including call outs such as this. The salary itself certainly didn't match the hours they put in and it was a very serious flaw in the wage structure of many funeral companies. Those working under a contract – whose key words consisted of 'working whatever hours are deemed necessary' – could literally be asked to work 24/7 and there was nothing whatsoever they could do about it. The drivers who were paid on a weekly basis received a minimum of two hours at time-and-a-half for each call out; double time on a Sunday. But without the overtime – and overtime, of course, could never be guaranteed – the driver's wage bordered on the poverty line. Checkout staff working in supermarkets were on better basic money and without being disrespectful to the world's wonderful checkout boys and girls, I defy anyone to compare the merits of scanning a tin of baked beans with picking up corpses from the middle of a freezing cold wood in the pun-friendly dead of night.

The argument, nevertheless, was a serious one. Most tradesmen I know would refuse point black to get out of a comfortable bed for the money a funeral driver would make from a call out. They would expect at least double the amount, if not more. And that would just be the call out fee. A great deal more would be charged when the job had been completed. People stared at me as if I'd just flown in from Pluto when I told them funeral directors effectively did it all for nothing. And not only that, the CID officer's claim that they were in the same boat wasn't entirely true. They worked shifts and he would be tucked up in bed when we were already well into another full day of stressful, sleep-deprived work.

With Glen having potentially blown any chance of sociability, at least for the time being, I fought my own despondency at the situation and tried to strike up a more congenial conversation.

'So is the death suspicious?'

'We're not sure. We thought it might just be a heart attack but the doctor wasn't entirely convinced. Of course, we then have to consider all possibilities.'

'That explains the photographer then.'

'Fraid so. I'm sorry about the inconvenience. I'm a bit brassed off myself. We should have all been long gone from here by now.'

'Don't worry, it's not your fault,' I said. 'Any chance of starting a bonfire here though? It's freezing!'

He laughed and rubbed his balding head. 'You're not wrong there.'

Having determined that we were all in the same proverbial boat we struck up a conversation quite readily after that. Even Glen joined in, although the chastened uniformed policeman had to leave us to return to his post at the entrance to the woods to await the photographer's arrival. The conversation was actually quite stimulating as we stood waiting in the eerie stillness. We swapped stories and anecdotes about each other's jobs and despite the adverse circumstances the mood became quite a jovial one. Then at a quarter past one we had a pleasant surprise – the earlier than expected arrival of the police photographer.

'I'm really sorry, boys. It's been one of those nights.' Looking flustered and fed up he placed his silver metallic camera case on the ground and opened the lid carefully, revealing an impressive array of camera equipment. He removed a camera with a lens the length of a relay baton and proceeded to bend, stoop, and kneel all around the body in an effort to obtain views from every conceivable angle. The body lay cold and motionless in the dark mud and the whole procedure seemed so callous, an intrusion both undignified and unavoidable. Soon Glen and I were lifting the body onto the stretcher and fastening the buckles. We placed the stretcher cover on top and were ready to leave.

'I assume you'd like a hand,' teased John, the CID officer who had first spoken to us.

'As many hands as possible,' I grinned back.

John and one of his colleagues took a corner each and with Glen and myself on the other end we finally set off on the long journey back to the car. The body was heavy but I was just grateful that Glen and I didn't have to cope on our own. After five minutes of trudging and stumbling along, however, I was exhausted. Deprived of sleep, my body was beginning to protest quite forcibly and doubts began to creep into my mind as to whether I was going to make it. After ten minutes I was convinced I was on the verge of total collapse. The journey was taking an age. Had it really been this far? I now had aches and pains breaking out all over my body and my breathing was coming in short, sharp wheezes. Somebody had moved the car, surely. How much further? Please don't let it be much further.

Then in the distance a light. It was the policeman's torch. The small things in life can often be the most enjoyable and that pinprick of light was worth more than the cost of a spaceship at that moment in time. I virtually staggered the last hundred metres or so. Glen was visibly struggling and John, with his slightly rotund figure, had suffered too. But irritatingly his athletic looking partner had barely broken sweat. Was I that unfit?

After we heaved the stretcher onto the estate car I groaned and leaned weakly against the tailgate. My arms felt as though they would now actually fit the jacket I'd received as part of my initial clothing issue. My head pounded and my mouth was dry. It was several seconds before I felt able to speak and when I did, my vocal chords were incapable of producing anything intelligible. I had never felt this bad before, not even after playing football.

Glen looked equally washed out. In fact he looked positively ill. But at least I had the comfort of knowing there would be a few extra pounds in my wage packet for my efforts. All Glen would have is another tale of hardship and endurance to tell in the morning. And then a funeral to arrange with the widow of the man who took their dog for a walk and never came home.

In the cold light of day, neither of us had really suffered that much in comparison.

Of the many coroners' removals I attended from that day forward, John's was a regular face at most of them. We seemed to catch each other virtually every time we attended the scene of a sudden death and it became something of a standing joke between us. One of those unusual professional relationships grew from this continual crossing of paths, one where we greeted each other like old friends, yet remained strangers in reality. I never even knew John's surname and I'm pretty sure he was equally unaware of mine. It never mattered though. Wherever we happened to meet – in a block of flats or on the beach, a farmer's field or the science laboratory of the local university – we always greeted each other with a knowing grin and an amiable muttering of 'here we go again', whatever the circumstances. Our banter made an often difficult part of the job just a touch more bearable.

Although coroner's removals often provided an interesting and varied break from the average working day, most of us dreaded having to attend them. Many could be extremely difficult and distressing. Even worse were the instances where a body had been dead for some time.

It is not my intention to indulge in the gory details of these occasions. It is neither necessary nor ethical and is certainly not the reason that prompted me to write this book. Far better suited to describe this aspect of death are the amazing people who train with admirable dedication to become mortuary technicians and forensic scientists. It suffices me to say that many of the scenes I witnessed at coroner's removals were gruesome, grisly, or just downright unbearable. I have seen suicides by all manner of methods – overdoses, hangings, exhaust fumes from cars, and leaps from tall buildings. I have moved bodies from murder scenes and prison cells and helped pull them from harbours and beaches. I have watched as firemen winch bodies from water filled ditches and road accidents. I have attended scenes where death was discovered weeks – sometimes months – after it had taken place. With a sickening sense of horror and revulsion I have literally picked up the pieces following railway line suicides.

I do not mention any of these to shock or to sensationalise. I call guarded attention to them simply because, in my experience, the general public have no idea that undertakers are involved to such an extent in this unpleasant side of death. Like I once thought myself – if I ever even gave it a thought – I was under the misguided impression that the first time the undertaker saw any body was when he collected it, washed and cleaned, from the hospital at the conclusion of the post mortem. Nothing could be further from the truth. Ambulances rarely pick up a dead body. The police never will, nor, in fairness, do they have the means by which to do so. It is the undertaker every time that collects and transports the deceased, no matter what the circumstances. It is part of the job.

The coroner only becomes involved if the doctor is unsure or unhappy about what he believes to be the cause of death. The first person who must attend any death, wherever it has taken place, is a doctor. Without his declaration of life extinct nothing can happen. If he can provide the reason why the person died then the undertaker can be called. If not, he will ring the police who must then attend first as a matter of course. The involvement of the police can seem a little baffling to the general public. In effect they are there as representatives of the coroner to gather information which may be of use to him when deciding whether a post mortem is required, and if so, to determine the cause of death.

It can be very disconcerting and distressing when an elderly relative has died suddenly – very probably of old age – and the police turn up on the doorstep. It is more often than not a case of red tape and many such incidents are invariably straightforward, not even resulting in a post mortem at all. But all avenues have to be covered; every possibility must be checked out. Very occasionally, that simple, apparently routine death may harbour something just a little more sinister. And the system doesn't always work. Dr Harold Shipman literally got away with murder for several years without being detected.

CID puts in an appearance when the death appears potentially suspicious from the start. Bodies found in odd places or after a long amount of time are guaranteed to attract their attention. It was an interesting aspect of the job to be involved in such cases. I just wished that some of the locations weren't so awkward and that once in a while everything could be left until the morning.

24

No matter how many drivers were required each day, we never seemed to be able to call on enough staff to comfortably cover our funerals. It was a continual battle to put bums on car seats. I know, because for several years I was responsible for writing the driver's orders.

Fleeting the following day's funerals was an absorbing job. It involved looking over the day sheet to see how many drivers were needed for funerals – plus any other requirements – and then literally filling in the blanks. It sounds easy but believe me it could be one of the most frustrating tasks known to man. Occasionally everything would all slot neatly into place, but this was a rare luxury. More often than not I would be staring insanely for ages at each day sheet and steadily gaining a headache at the impossibility of the job in hand.

The first names to go alongside each hearse and limousine were the drivers, both full-time and casual. I would then look to see if any of the funeral directors were free to drive. With the additional expectations and responsibilities making up their working day, it was unusual if they were available. Any funeral director not actually conducting funerals ideally needed to be standing by to arrange funerals as they came in. There were also other factors to be taken into consideration. Someone was usually always on holiday or sick leave, the various offices and chapels of rest around the town all needed to be staffed, and someone had to be available to carry out removals and furnish coffins. I constantly found myself having to 'borrow' staff from other departments to drive on funerals but this then meant their work was being neglected.

Desperation for the services of the casual drivers was such that most of them tended to be in every day anyway. Even then we were often still too short. It was nerve wracking to still be frantically ringing around at half past three in the afternoon leaving messages with the wives, girlfriends, and children of the casual drivers in the hope they were available to drive the following day. Stress levels can rise alarmingly under such pressure and provide the grounds for irrational behaviour...

Panic was setting in on one such day. I was still a driver short for the following morning and I had been trying to get hold of my last hope for hours, a casual driver by the name of Ben Daxon. Ben was an insurance salesman who drove the odd funeral for us whenever he had a spare couple of hours.

It was ten to five when I drove down to Dean Street to go through the orders with Paul. I had been staring at them for most of the day and I was sick of the sight of them. In such situations two heads were often better than one and I hoped that a fresh perspective might come up with a bright idea. I parked my car at the back of Stapleton Road and began walking up the lane when I suddenly saw the elusive Ben Daxon getting into his car outside the Dean Street office. I broke into a run but as I emerged from the lane he was already pulling away. I tried waving and shouting but he couldn't see me and continued on down the street.

Now most people would probably have left it at that and tried phoning again later in the evening. But not me. Oh no. I had been slaving away at these orders all afternoon. I had been ringing Ben for almost as long, cursing the monotonous ring tone and even Ben himself. This was grossly unfair on my part. He had a proper full-time job to do and continually did us favours by helping out whenever he could. But I'd had enough. I wanted to be able to go home in five minutes time and forget all about the blasted orders. I wanted to tie everything up and be finished with it.

I have always considered myself something of a fast runner. Rarely out of the top three sprinters in my year at school, my speed over the first twenty-five metres from a standing start was also well known within my footballing circles. But as I set off down Dean Street in pursuit of Ben's beloved Triumph Herald, I was aware of a hitherto unknown optimism of paranormal proportions that I could actually catch him. I was hoping that by the time I had hit my peak of speed, Ben would have noticed me tearing manically after him in his rear view mirror. But to my dismay he never once looked and my chase developed into a much longer one than expected.

After about ten miles – roughly translated in reality to a hundred and fifty metres – I began to catch him. Much as I would like to claim that this was due to my athletic prowess, it actually had everything to do with Ben slowing down to allow a car to pull out a short distance ahead. It was the break I needed. I drew up alongside him and tapped on the window.

This was a mistake. When you are at the wheel of a vehicle in motion at any speed, you do not expect to see a sweating, leering face peering in at you from outside. Ben, who had clearly been in a world of his own for the past minute, jumped violently and his hands involuntarily swung to the left, causing the car to lurch in the same direction. Thankfully, his slow speed enabled him to brake just before he hit a row of parked cars. Judging by the alarmed expression on his normally unruffled features, he was clearly now expecting some sort of significant announcement from me. It all felt embarrassingly anti-climatic as he wound down his window and I panted hopefully at him.

'Any chance of you driving for us in the morning, Ben?'

As I walked back along Dean Street to the office a few seconds later, I was vaguely aware of a handful of staring faces. However I didn't care. I had my final name and the orders were complete. I wasn't entirely convinced that Ben had been planning on making himself available to drive the following day. But after my determined efforts to ask him I don't think he dared refuse.

The constant battle to come up with drivers and solutions for the following day's work often led to other problems – knock-on effects that would only become apparent as the day progressed. One such incident took place on a particularly hectic day when everyone was trying to do more than they should.

One trick we often used to 'create' extra drivers was to allow the hearse driver and the driver of the limousine to return to base in the hearse as soon as the coffin had been taken into the crematorium. The funeral director would then take the family back home after the funeral, thus enabling the two drivers to go straight onto another funeral that may be about to start. It involved a lot of dashing about but at least it alleviated the immediate problems caused by a lack of staff. Cutting such a fine line, however, could be asking for trouble.

Chris and I were driving on a funeral with Paul and I had arranged such a scenario. It was incredibly tight but I was confident we could make it in time to go onto another funeral.

I parked the limousine round the side of the crematorium while Chris removed the floral tributes from the hearse and placed them in the nearby flower bay. I raised my thumb to Paul who was standing in the window of the crematorium office and leapt into the hearse alongside Chris. We were away. I looked at the digital clock on the dashboard. We had just over twenty minutes to get back to Stapleton Road and load up the coffin for the next funeral. So much could go wrong on these forced manoeuvres – traffic hold-ups or delays at the crematorium – but everything had gone smoothly so far on this occasion and I figured we'd be fine.

As I sat back in the passenger seat and relaxed, I remembered a television interview I had seen a couple of nights previously with one of my comedy heroes, Spike Milligan. Someone had asked him what he would like inscribed on his tombstone when he died. "I told you I was ill" was Spike's now famous response! I had been chuckling about this ever since. This was my kind of humour and it also found favour with Chris as well. Inspired by Mr Milligan's gem we launched into our own tombstone inscription routine, speculating on the tributes that might be etched in stone at the passing of several of our colleagues.

'I've got one for Gareth,' said Chris immediately. "Here Lies Gareth Price Who Worried Himself To Death."

It didn't take me long to respond: 'Robbie the Robot could have "Rust in Peace".'

Much laughter was followed by a few seconds of intense thought. Chris was first again. 'I've got a great one for Denzil: "This Is A Grave Mistake: I'm In The One Three Doors Down".'

This was getting good. Now it was my turn again. "Here Lies Angus The Paperboy, Frightened To Death By Tomato Sauce".'

We continued like this all the way to Stapleton Road, covering the vast majority of our workmates and several others whom we both knew and dealt with on a daily basis. Not even Basil Pemberthy, the bell ringer at St. Stephens, escaped unscathed. "In Life He Was A Bell Ringer – Now He's Just A Dead Ringer." Reg Bowen simply had "Tut Tut Tut" on his in big gold letters. We were still laughing when Chris pulled into the back of the Stapleton Road office.

As we were about to load the next coffin onto the hearse, a panic-stricken Jill came running down the lane towards me.

'Tom...Tom...ring Paul at the crem straight away. It's urgent!'

'Aw, what does he want now,' I sighed, rolling my eyes. 'He knows we're in a hurry.'

'Er... he's stranded there with the family. You took the limousine key with you...'

As that ridiculously hectic day drew to a close and calm had descended once more, I apologised profusely to Paul for leaving him in the lurch outside Westport crematorium. Although naturally annoyed at the time, he knew only too well how much pressure we were all under, rushing around with little time to stop or think. His response reflected his understanding.

'These things happen,' he shrugged. 'I should have asked you for the key. The trouble is there are too few trying to do too much. That's where the real problem lies.'

Unfortunately but predictably, Stewart didn't see it quite the same way. Just as I was about to head for home he called me into his office and gave me the usual lecture. In some ways it was justified – I was guilty of carelessness – but Paul had already dealt with the matter in a far more perceptive manner. I wouldn't have minded so much but the previous day, one of Stewart's more 'favoured' members of staff had been sleeping off a hangover all morning in the back of one of the limousines. Nothing whatsoever had been said about that.

As I left Stewart's office, Chris was hovering around outside waiting for me. He raised his eyebrows. 'Okay?'

'Nah, not really,' I muttered. Then after a pause: 'I've just thought of an inscription for Stewart Lewis's gravestone though.'

'Oh yeah?' he grinned. 'Go on.'

'Underneath This Sod There Lies Another.'

25

When Glen announced he was leaving I was over the moon.

For several months I'd wished I hadn't been so conservative when moving into Stapleton Road. I was given the choice of the two empty flats at the time, but I chose the smaller, single bedroom option thinking it would be the perfect bachelor pad. I considered the three-bedroom monster next door with its enormous living room to be far too extravagant for a single person. I had also figured it would cost a small fortune to furnish it. I was more than content with my choice – until Glen and his girlfriend moved in next door that is. It was then that I realised what a golden opportunity I'd passed up. Fully furnished and decorated the place looked like a penthouse suite and I regretted my failure to see its potential.

Celebrations aside, of course, I was sorry to see Glen go. His decision to leave was clearly prompted by the hassle that had become a resident hindrance to working in Westport. But it may also have been the opportunity for him to return closer to his roots in Tremorlais that finally persuaded him to leave. We'd enjoyed some great times together and although very occasionally we hadn't always seen eye to eye, he was very definitely a soul mate within the climate we worked. I would certainly miss the fun of trying to scare him witless at nights.

Glen first mentioned he was seriously considering a move several months earlier and I had taken the opportunity then to officially register my interest in his flat in the event of him leaving. To my initial surprise Stewart agreed. But I soon realised that in his sheer joy of possibly ridding himself of the person who he considered to be his personal enemy number one at that time, he would probably have allowed Jack The Ripper to set up home there in his place, so jovial was his mood.

When Glen's transfer was eventually finalised I received confirmation that the flat was mine. But it wasn't that simple.

Although the move had been cleared between Stewart and Bilko, Doberman in the middle claimed to know nothing of the arrangement. Normally this would not have caused a problem – Bilko was, after all, senior to Doberman – but with Bilko now on his summer holiday in an exotic, faraway location, Doberman decided to block the move.

One could possibly imagine my anger and frustration at being told the news upon my return from my own holiday. My mood was further intensified by the discovery I had been burgled whilst I was away. Thankfully little had been taken, but as anyone who has had their home broken into knows, it is the violation of privacy that leaves the bigger scar. The break-in created an even greater urgency to move into my new flat as soon as possible so I could attend to matters of security. But Doberman was having none of it. He couldn't possibly allow me to move in until he had confirmed the arrangement with Mr Allen first, this despite an assurance by Stewart that it was a done deal.

I was pleasantly surprised by Stewart's support over the matter. It was never easy to tell which direction Stewart was coming from. He was well known for running with the foxes and hunting with the hounds, but I did get the impression he was genuinely on my side on this occasion. There was, however, another reason, the substance of which I was soon to discover.

I eventually got the green light to move into Glen's old flat nearly three weeks later – a couple of days after Bilko's return from holiday. It may not seem a great inconvenience now but the whole incident left a very bitter taste in my mouth at the time. If I wasn't aware of it already, I certainly knew now that I worked for an organisation that, despite all its pretences and claims, had little or no interest whatsoever in the welfare of its employees. Doberman's obstinate stance was an all too familiar example of the posturing management style sweeping through the company. It was also an example of a glaring lack of man-management skills, an issue that was becoming a matter of great concern to us all. But little did we know that changes were just around the corner…

Gwynfor Evans eased himself into the dark red velvet armchair and grimaced slightly.

'Jiw Jiw, boys bach,' he exclaimed with a shake of the head. 'Business is very slow. Very slow indeed.'

Paul, Chris, and I nodded in agreement. Things had been very quiet. In fact, it was the quietest period I'd known – six funerals last week, five this, and only two booked so far for next week. It was actually rather pleasant not to be rushing everywhere with one eye on the clock. For the first time in my almost four and a half years in Westport I was glancing at my watch for different reasons – willing the hands around the face towards five o'clock so I could go home.

There had been no funerals at all today so Chris and I had spent the whole morning and early afternoon washing and vacuuming the entire fleet down at the garage. It had been an enjoyable few hours actually. No interruptions, no urgent phone calls telling us to drop everything: just a nice steady pace until we finished at about twenty to three. There was little else we could do so we decided to call up to the Dean Street office to have a chat with Paul. Throughout the previous couple of days we had heard nothing but rumours and speculation about big changes taking place in Westport. As Paul was now Stewart's deputy, we thought he might be willing and able to fill us in with a few of the juicy details.

We had been sitting comfortably in the middle office about to interrogate Paul when the front door opened and in sauntered Gwynfor Evans, independent funeral director, to pay his coffin bill. After issuing him with his receipt, Paul invited him into our midst for a cup of tea. Gwynfor was never one to pass up an invitation for a chat and he accepted readily with a grin of delight.

Gwynfor was a lanky, ungainly man in his mid to late fifties, yet he was one of those types who always seemed to look a little older. His leathery brown skin and lazy eyelids gave him a well-worn appearance, but he was an amusing conversationalist and always in possession of a good story to tell.

'Yes indeed,' he continued, smoothing down a stray clump of jet-black hair with the palm of his hand until it finally lay unresisting with the rest of his more obedient mop. 'There is only one thing for it.'

'What's that, Mr Evans?' asked Paul, aware of his role as the straight man.

'We must all ring The Samaritans from different phones and jam their switchboard, boys bach.'

Through the peals of laughter that followed I suddenly had the horrible thought that somewhere deep in the bowels of our company, a seedy, sinister chief accountant was, at this very moment, composing a memo for the attention of all branch managers to this effect. We were very quiet, after all. Profits must be plundering by the minute.

'How's the new chapel of rest coming on, Mr Evans?' inquired Paul. We always liked to keep an eye on the opposition although, to be honest, there was little competition between Gwynfor Evans and ourselves: he pretty much had the small town of Pentre sewn up. We had no branch there and Gwynfor had refused point blank to sell the business to us, or any other conglomerate for that matter, despite several advances.

'Nearly finished now, bach. Another couple of weeks and it should be ready.'

'Excellent. Well done.'

'Thank you, bach. Yes, I'm in the process of organising a tidy little grand opening – local dignitaries and all that.' He scratched his nose and continued with a straight face. 'Mind you, if business carries on like this I'll be making it a 'Bring-a-Body party.'

We roared with laughter again. It wasn't so much the fact that Gwynfor's remarks were funny. They just somehow always seemed unexpected. His permanently doleful expression rarely hinted at the wonderful comments that sprang forth with great regularity, and when they did, his timing was impeccable – that of a seasoned comic. It was when the corners of his mouth finally broke rank and turned upwards into a cheeky smile that we knew a funeral story was on its way. None of them were genuine as far as we knew. But Gwynfor Evans made them sound as though they'd actually happened and in the end we were never entirely sure if they had or not.

'Jiw, boys, I had a girl-and-a-half to deal with last week. 'Tight as a bolt she was. I reckon she was loaded see, but couldn't bear to part with a penny, not even to bury her husband of forty-two years. Well, I thought, I'm not going to be selling a solid oak coffin by yer. Anyway, I was going through the obituary notice with her for the paper and she says to me all she wants to put is *Dafydd Wallace, dead*. "Mrs Wallace, bach," I said, "you can't leave it at that. I know notices in the paper can be expensive, but you need to put a little bit more than *Dafydd Wallace, dead*.' Gwynfor paused to take a sip of tea. It was the perfect punch-line builder. 'So she turned to me with a face as straight as a plank of wood. "Okay, Mr Evans" she says. "Put this then please – *Dafydd Wallace, dead. Ford Fiesta for sale*."

This time we laughed so loud Jill came in from the back office to admonish us because she was talking to a client on the phone.

'Brilliant!' muttered Chris, shaking his head in sheer delight.

Gwynfor drained the contents of his cup and stood up to leave. 'Well, I must be going, boys. Thank you for the tea.'

'A pleasure, Mr Evans,' said Paul as he went to open the door for him. 'You're always welcome anytime.'

He held up his hand and was gone, like a comedian triumphantly exiting the stage. Ten minutes spent with the likes of Gwynfor Evans could boost even the gloomiest of souls.

Following Gwynfor's departure it was several minutes before we were able to rid ourselves of the giggles in order for myself and Chris to quiz Paul about the company's grand plans for the future. He was reluctant at first, having been all but sworn to supposed secrecy. But we were relentless and we played on the obvious fact he was dying to tell someone.

'We won't say a word, honest,' pleaded Chris.

Paul finally surrendered. 'All right, all right. But if anyone finds out, you haven't heard it from me, okay?'

We nodded eagerly on the edge of our seats.

'As of Monday, Stewart will no longer be manager of Westport.'

'*What?*'

'He and Peter Raymond have fallen out big time over the past few months. Bryan Stockton has never had a lot of time for Stewart, but because Doberman always put in a good word he basically tolerated him as a manager.'

'But now Doberman's stuck the knife in,' breathed Chris gleefully.

141

'That's about it. From Monday, Stewart will be based in Abertrefil and demoted to senior funeral director.'

So that was why Stewart had suddenly taken my side over flat-gate. His bromance with Doberman had collapsed. I tried to remain circumspect about this amazing piece of news but it was difficult to hide my joy. Stewart had often made life very unpleasant for me since taking over from Arnold James. Now I felt like a huge coffin had been lifted from my shoulders. I took little satisfaction in the news of a fellow man's downfall, however, and in a strange way I felt sorry for him. But there was a hint of justice about the whole matter and now I felt a kind of liberation, a freedom that would allow me to look forward instead of continually backwards over my weight-free shoulder.

There was one more important issue remaining of course. Even as I asked the question I knew the answer.

'So who's the new gaffer?'

Paul smiled self-consciously.

'Congratulations mate,' I said, offering my hand.

The day just got better and better.

26

It was a beautiful late summer's evening, certainly one too good to waste. I turned off the television, put on my jacket, and walked down the stairs to the front door. An unusually warm sun embraced my face as I stepped outside and I savoured it, eyes closed, for several seconds before turning and locking the door behind me. It had felt warm all day, but in a dark suit and restricted by the necessities of work it had been impossible to enjoy. I set off briskly for the place where I often walked in the evenings, Westport sea front. I enjoyed the peace and the solitude it afforded and the beauty of the rolling blue sea.

My love of the sea originates from my childhood in Brixham. For ten years the sweeping oceans that guarded the South Devon coastline were an influential and significant part of my life. On an evening like this, Mum and Dad would take me down to Breakwater Beach to watch the tide come ambling home, like a parent returning from a day at the office. To many this may sound boring, but it was during my childhood in Brixham that I discovered the calming, soothing qualities of the sea. In no greater place have I experienced this than on Berry Head, the country park jutting out into the English Channel that was barely a ten-minute walk from where we lived. As a result, Berry Head is one of my favourite locations of all time. It is a graceful place embracing windswept cliffs, an awe-inspiring expanse of shimmering ocean, and lovely panoramic views. It was a place to go to be inspired, a place for reflection, a place to ponder, a place to seek peace.

As I now approached the promenade overlooking Westport Bay I realised how much I often missed that safe, innocent cocoon of childhood. Why do we only truly appreciate our youth when it is too late? Is it because adulthood gives us a comparison? Is it because maturity breeds complexity? Far greater minds than mine have studied and researched such themes, but as I reached the railings and stared silently out to sea, I doubted whether they had reached any conclusions more advanced than mine.

The waves lapped gently at the thin strip of sand beneath me and once again I could feel the powerful ocean blue working that old magic again. Although this was a different location to those precious scenes from my childhood, here too was a place to unwind and a place to muse. And I had much to think about. It seemed incredible to me that Westport had been my home for almost five years now. Yet it never really felt like home. Despite the fact that Mum and Dad had now also moved to the area in their retirement, I still felt like a visitor temporarily plying my trade. I knew one day I would move on.

I had already tried. A job interview in London; another in Suffolk – both the result of my growing disillusionment at life and attitudes in my present situation. But maybe things were changing now. As I watched the tide creep slowly closer across the beach, maybe the tide was also turning at work. Stewart had been pushed sideways where he could no longer bother me and Paul had taken his place, a man I admired and respected: a man without apparent bias or devious approach.

Paul had been in charge for a couple of months now. Already the changes had been many, mostly for the better. Lines of communication had been opened and the handling of staff had improved beyond recognition. Everyone was appreciated for what they did and for what their potential could be. It was a whole new atmosphere and a completely contrasting environment in which to work. Six months ago I was on the verge of quitting. Now things had never felt more positive. I still had much to consider but now it was for entirely different reasons. Although the recent changes had been the most influential to date, I had grown used to continual upheaval over the years, most of it concerning colleagues moving on. In the space of five years the personnel in Westport had changed almost beyond recognition. Rhys Parry and Arnold James had started the trend of course. Gareth Price, the funeral director who had stepped in for the 'forgotten funeral' on my very first day, finally decided to try his luck by going it alone, successfully too, much to the company's disgust. He was condemned as some sort of traitor for leaving but his departure came as a direct result of their dismissive and patronising attitude. They had backed Gareth into a corner and so he jumped, taking a frightening number of clients with him.

Bill Travers had been the next to go, deciding to take an early retirement. Then Nigel Prosser left. He'd had enough of the on call – it was too restricting. I knew what he meant. His first love had always been tinkering with cars so it was almost predictable that he left to become a full-time mechanic at a garage on the outskirts of town.

Mark Grainger's departure came as a shock at first, but on reflection it was no real surprise. My friend from Yorkshire had been promoted to the position of funeral director some eighteen months previously, but was then made an offer he probably couldn't refuse from a rival funeral home in town. Although I admired Mark for his move and wished him well, it was, for me, yet another working friendship that had been curtailed prematurely.

Others came and went, including Glen of course. Gilbert Rees transferred his passion for walking in front of the hearse to an undertaker down on his native west coast, and continual changes to casual and clerical staff maintained this unusually high turnover in personnel. But it was the sudden resignation of Denzil Jenkins that was to have the biggest impact on my own career. I was now the senior driver down at Tessum Street garage. I was also next in line for promotion to the position of funeral director. Paul had already told me I could do the job and I felt reasonably confident too. The question was, did I want it?

I stopped walking for a moment and stared thoughtfully across the sweep of the bay. The sea, edging ever closer across the sand towards the tall stone wall beneath me, twinkled and shimmered in the soft glow of a fading evening sun. I followed the coastline from where I stood, right around the curving semi-circle past the imposing block that was Sandacre Hospital and then right to the end where the charming village of Penderi nestled serenely some five miles away. Visibility was perfect and I could even make out the tiny specks that were boats and yachts on the Penderi village waterfront. A stiff breeze was beginning to drift in from off the sea, pulling playfully at my hair and the lapels of my jacket. And teasing my mind in similar vein was the burning question as to whether I should accept Paul's offer to become a funeral director. Yes? No? Maybe...

By now I had already arranged and conducted a handful of funerals for friends who had asked me to look after matters for them personally. I had enjoyed the responsibility, especially the chance to deal with families on a more intimate level. I honestly felt I was doing something worthwhile with my life. There was a great deal more to learn of course, not least the mountain of paperwork required, both official and internal. But it was not the job itself that was causing the doubt in my mind.

Denzil had resigned because he cracked under the pressure. The working environment in which the funeral directors operated was intense and not conducive to the best interests of the families they were looking after, and certainly not the funeral directors themselves. It was okay to have three, maybe four funerals on the go at the same time. But when that number becomes eight or nine it could create all manner of problems. I was often alarmed at the amount of funerals I saw the funeral directors taking on at any one time. It was asking for trouble and the mistake count often told its own story – forgotten cars, mislaid forms, wrong information on paperwork, flowers not taken to the right funeral, and many similar errors became common place. Most of these were happening as a direct result of the pressure of the workload, as the funeral directors struggled to maintain the service expected of them. Thankfully, most slip-ups were of the minor variety and could often be rectified without the family's knowledge that something had gone wrong. But as any undertaker will tell you, mistakes made in the funeral profession can often be blown completely out of all proportion because of the understandably sensitive nature of the job.

It was this pressure and these working conditions that caused me so much apprehension. I was by now in my late twenties and had developed a pretty good idea of what my capabilities were, but equally so my limitations as well. I have never been a confident person. In fact, I would go as far as to say I am at totally the opposite end of the spectrum as far as self-assuredness is concerned. What I have been able to create throughout life however, is a front – a façade if you like – that helps me to hide my lack of confidence behind a wall of pseudo self-assurance. Coming from a theatrical family this wasn't all that hard for me to achieve. I'd clearly inherited some of the acting genes so prominent in both my parents and I moulded myself a superficial confidence, an outward, extroverted demeanour that succeeded in getting me through most situations that life tossed in my direction.

My fear though was whether this act would get me through the roller-coaster ride of being a funeral director. One factor in my favour was that I would not be going into the job blind: I'd had almost five years to build up a detailed knowledge of what was involved. But I had also seen the stress levels rising, the pressures of reaching figures and targets, and the constant rushing around against the clock. Denzil's resignation was now cold proof of one person's struggle with the work load and although others hadn't given up like him, there was enough evidence to suggest they too struggled for much of the time. And on top of all this was the overarching task that most people outside the profession consider the most difficult of all – that of dealing with the grieving and the bereaved.

My walk had now taken me to the harbour, an impressive development area that had been completely transformed in recent years. Westport harbour had once been a shabby, run-down district. But now, with its splendid blocks of classy apartments, substantial marina, and sprinkling of well-themed shops and bars, it had become one of the town's prime locations.

I sat down on a vacant wooden bench overlooking the colourful array of yachts and boats. Yet again my thoughts drifted back to my beloved Brixham, with its own quaint and bustling harbour. There I would sit as a young boy on a similar wooden seat at the top of the harbour steps, gazing fondly at the tightly moored rows of boats below and listening to their masts clinking in the breeze. A glance upwards and I would stare with a child's fascination at the higgledy-piggledy banks of coloured houses and cottages overlooking the harbour like spectators at a sporting event. A group of artists would sit near the railings down by the quayside and paint these scenes over and over again for the hoards of holiday-makers who invade Brixham in their thousands during the summer months. I would watch them with the bright, inquisitive eyes of youth, marvelling at how a few apparently random brushstrokes could suddenly give birth to a boat, a person, someone's house, and then eventually a beautiful painting of a complete scene.

As I smiled at the remembrance of these wonderful memories, Paul's words from earlier in the day interrupted my reverie: "You could be an excellent funeral director, Tom. The job is yours, if you want it." I'd voiced my concerns, not in any great detail, but enough for him to try and put such fears to rest. "Everyone feels daunted with the responsibility when they first become a funeral director," he had told me. "If they don't, they're probably lying – or just plain foolish. But once you get used to it and build up some experience, you'll be fine."

I had looked at Paul, smart and impressive in his dark blue suit, and realised that had he not been sitting behind that desk there would be no decision to make. Never in a million years would Stewart Lewis have offered me the same opportunity. And it was because Paul had taken over the running of the Westport branch that I was seriously considering the promotion he now proposed. We had got on well from the day I first started and although his rise had partly been brought about by the departure of others, he had undoubtedly reached the position of manager on merit. I was probably the only one who questioned my ability to take on this new responsibility but Paul's confidence in me, and the confidence of many around me, was a real boost as I now contemplated my decision.

The stiffening breeze carried a pair of seagulls above the boats for a few seconds until, back under their own power, they swooped and dived playfully before disappearing noisily between two of the apartment blocks behind. I listened nostalgically to the sounds of maritime life around me – that familiar jingling of masts and chains, the creaking of ropes and whipping of sails in the breeze, the gentle chug of a motorboat heading out to sea for a spot of fishing. It could so easily have been twenty years ago back in Brixham. A time when life was less complicated, when decisions were simple and straightforward.

An old man with thin, pointed features and the obligatory lilting Welsh accent approached slowly and sat next to me on the bench. We struck up conversation in almost a matter of fact way. I have always possessed the ability to talk to people, young or old

148

and from any walk of life. I guess to some extent it was all part of the act. But it certainly wasn't the whole story.

Several minutes later the old man stood to leave and declared what a pleasure it had been to talk with me. I felt good. As I watched him shuffle away across the small bridge that connected one side of the harbour with the other, I knew exactly what my answer to Paul was going to be in the morning.

I would give it a go. I would become a funeral director.

27

The first thing I noticed following my promotion was that I did not have to wash vehicles every day. And it was heaven.

If I was to be perfectly honest I had grown to detest washing funeral vehicles. For starters they were so damned long. They took twice the time to wash compared to any normal car and washing them day in, day out, over and over again soon lost its appeal, if indeed any appeal had ever existed in the first place. As time went by my colleagues soon began to realise they had a mutineer in their midst where washing cars was concerned. It wasn't so much that I tried to get out of it: I just lost my enthusiasm. In my defence I think we washed them far too often. There was one particular phase where we had some real fanatics in the ranks and it was they who turned me off the whole process as much as anything else. The times were frequent when a vehicle would return in the afternoon of a beautifully sunny day, still looking as spotless as when it left the garage. On such occasions any normal person could see that just a quick wipe down with a damp chamois leather would suffice. But oh no. Out came the buckets and sponges and the soap addicts would launch into the task with the demented fervour of a bunch of schoolboys who'd just discovered a 'buy one, get one free' offer at the school tuck shop. In my eyes such obsessive behaviour was unhealthy.

Becoming a funeral director was a very shrewd move on my part. Funeral directors were still expected to wash the odd vehicle now and then, particularly the estate cars, which they drove more than anyone else. But it was not high on the list of priorities and this suited me fine, especially as I appeared to have some kind of psychological allergy to car shampoo. I would often drive past the garage on my way to arrange a funeral and glance in on the boys hard at work in their shirtsleeves and Wellington boots. Doing so gave me a blissful feeling of relief that I was no longer involved in such tedious labour. The pleasure was always spoiled somewhat by the fact that the majority of them appeared to be in raptures about what they were doing, but each to their own I guess. Of course, those same bucket boys looked upon me as something of a lazy git who didn't like getting his hands wet. It would be churlish not to concede that, based on unavoidable evidence, they had a very strong argument and were probably just as glad to get rid of me as I was to go.

On one such afternoon I drove along Tessum Street and gave the lads a cheery toot on the horn before making my way to the northern end of town where I had a funeral to arrange on the Grafog estate. The call had only come in half an hour or so ago but the family wanted to see a funeral director straight away to make the arrangements, after which we would remove the body to our chapel of rest. I had organised for one of the drivers, therefore, to meet me at the house in about an hour's time. This was actually only my third funeral arrangement and my first going to the residence. Over the years I grew to prefer arranging funerals in the home as opposed to the office. I found families were far more relaxed in their own surroundings and for me, it was a relief to get away from the distraction of the telephone ringing and the general hustle and bustle of office life.

I pulled up outside the small, pale green terraced house and quickly checked my briefcase to make sure I had everything I might need. It was a futile exercise – there was little I could do if I had forgotten something – yet I always went through the same ritual thereafter.

I was invited into the house with sombre dignity and as there was no hallway, I stepped off the street and straight into the living room. I was immediately taken aback by the amount of people crammed into the tiny space. Every available seat except one was occupied and there were three more people sitting on the floor: another woman was even perched on her husband's lap. I didn't take a head count but there must have been at least thirteen family members in a room where six or seven would have been a crowd.

My initial thought was how we were going to bring the deceased down the open plan staircase in the corner when the time came without causing the family distress. We always preferred to carry out the removal after having asked the family members to wait in another room. Here, there appeared to be nowhere else for them to go. Oh well, I'd worry about that later.

Mr Jack Jefferson, the son of the deceased with whom I had spoken on the phone, ushered me over to the one vacant seat in the room on a small, two-seater sofa next to an old gent, whom I acknowledged as I sat down. I lifted my briefcase onto my lap and opened the lid. The murmur of voices suddenly ceased and for the first of what would be many an occasion, I became aware of the expectant hush that greeted this significant event.

Because people generally have no idea of the processes involved in arranging a funeral, the black briefcase carried by the funeral director takes on an air of total mystery. I could almost hear people thinking as the lid slowly rose upwards: *what is in that briefcase?* Disappointing though it will probably be to the morbid of this world, there is very little inside the briefcase of a funeral director to get excited about. There will be a pad of arrangement sheets on which all the relevant details of the deceased and the funeral itself are recorded, a wad of council forms for the local cemeteries and crematorium, further pads of estimate and newspaper notice forms, various brochures of coffins, floral tributes, and monumental products, samples of service sheets and floral tribute cards, a boring assortment of stationary items, and last, but not least, the obligatory tape measure.

I cannot deny that on this occasion I felt incredibly nervous. Being so new to the role of funeral director I had anticipated this would be the case and decided to employ a tactic that Rhys Parry taught me all those years ago when I first started. He said: "If you ever become a funeral director and you go to the house to arrange a funeral, walk in, sit down, and don't mention the funeral at all for the first five to ten minutes". It seemed a touch illogical to me at first. Then he explained: "Talk to the family. Don't worry about getting information for those first few minutes. Just engage in quiet, friendly conversation. Build up a brief picture of the person whose funeral you are about to arrange. Don't forget, ninety-nine times out of a hundred you've probably never met them before. Find out about the deceased first and you create yourself a platform from which to make the arrangement more personal".

Throughout my career as a funeral director, Rhys's advice stayed with me and rarely did I arrange a funeral anywhere, whether it was in the office or in the home, without using those first few minutes in the way he suggested. It was a wonderfully beneficial way to begin a funeral arrangement for two very good reasons.

Firstly, I discovered it was the perfect way to build up trust. The initial minutes of any new association are important and first impressions rarely disappear from our minds. Arranging a funeral can be an incredibly intense and emotional occasion and the importance of developing a rapport as soon as possible is of paramount importance. It is extremely difficult to win back approval after a bad start.

The second advantage was for my benefit. In my years as a driver I had taken the opportunity, not always deliberately, to observe the styles and techniques of the different funeral directors with whom I worked. I learned a great deal from watching the way they went about their business and made a mental note of the aspects I considered to be of value. One particular talent I noticed among the better funeral directors, the ones who really knew their job, was the ability to weigh up each individual situation within those vital first few minutes. No matter how many people were present during a funeral arrangement, there would almost certainly be one family member who stood out from the rest. He or she would be the one who appeared to be in control, to be organised. They would become my go-to person, the one to whom I would address the difficult, sensitive questions if things became awkward. A good funeral director should also be able to gauge the moods and capabilities of the others in the room too and deal suitably with each and every one of them.

Everyone reacts differently to grief. Some are tearful, others hysterical. Many people will talk constantly while others will remain silent, responding only if spoken to directly. There will usually always be someone present who is slightly suspicious of the whole funeral process. They will want to know every detail of what is being discussed. Each one of these reactions is normal and often an extension of that person's character.

There is no right or wrong way to grieve. I have watched a little old lady respond with steely, dignified determination at the loss of her husband after fifty-two years of marriage. I have seen a grown man built like a brick wall shed a fountain of tears at the loss of his mother. I have witnessed, with tears in my own eyes, the sheer tenacity of a couple who had lost their young daughter to a fatal illness: quite simply they refused to falter under an almost overwhelming weight of grief. I have listened with great unease to the hysterical screaming of a daughter as her father was taken to the graveside and the coffin lowered slowly into the grave. We are all different. We all react to adversity in our own way and in our own time. As I say, there is no right or wrong way to grieve.

Some funeral arrangements need the funeral director to be firm and businesslike while others require gentle persuasion in the right directions. On other occasions the soft, relaxed approach is the best tactic. The common denominator running through all of these is the consistent need of the funeral director to be a good communicator and an exceptional listener. And the foundation of all of this lay in those first few minutes right at the very beginning. To me, that bonding time was the most important thing I did throughout the whole funeral process. With all sincerity I hope I succeeded in achieving these aspirations on most occasions during my funeral directing career.

Of course, there were always the occasional exceptions – the person or family who did not respond to any approach whatsoever. Denzil's friend, Mr Gripton springs to mind. In such cases there is little one can do except gather the information needed as best as possible. But today, as I sat in the home of the late Mr George Jefferson, there were no problems at all. Jack Jefferson, the eldest son, was clearly in charge and he was a joy to deal with, particularly for an inexperienced young funeral director like myself. Other members of the family were also friendly and spoke whenever necessary, but most in that crowded front room remained silent throughout, including the old gent sitting next to me.

I always tried to maintain eye contact with everyone in turn when arranging a funeral. It makes people feel a part of the proceedings, even if they have chosen to stay in the background. Because I was leaning forward slightly in order to write on my briefcase, it wasn't always possible for me to look in the old man's direction. I managed the occasional glance but he didn't really appear to be that interested so I more or less gave up.

When I had finished the arrangement and completed the paperwork I looked at my watch. It was twenty-five past three. Perfect. The driver would be here in five minutes so I thought I'd pop upstairs to measure Mr Jefferson, check for any jewellery, and clear any obstacles that might hinder us when we brought the body down the stairs. I closed my briefcase with a click and smiled gently at everyone in the room before addressing the son once more.

'My colleague will be here shortly, Mr Jefferson. If you could just take me upstairs and show me where Dad is, I'll start getting everything ready.'

A slight frown broke out across his face. 'Er...Dad isn't upstairs,' he said.

'He isn't?'

'No. He's sitting next to you.'

With this incident still very much in my mind, I found myself in what appeared to be an alarmingly similar situation just a few months later. The only major difference here was that the deceased appeared to be sitting alone in a well-worn chair by the fireplace. It wasn't a pleasant sight and he looked far worse than the late Mr Jefferson had. His mouth was a wide-open cavern in a head tilting awkwardly backwards and his facial features bore that same drawn look I knew only too well.

I settled uneasily into one of the armchairs opposite in the busily decorated lounge. I was about to start proceedings but it was no use – I had to ask. I looked at Mrs Davies, a plump and cheery lady in her early fifties, and motioned hesitatingly to the figure sprawled in front of me.

'Is... that Dad sitting there...?

'Oh good gracious no! Dad's in the bedroom upstairs. That,' she said rolling her eyes suddenly, 'is Uncle Bryn, Dad's younger brother.'

'Right.' I was grateful for the confirmation and breathed a private sigh of relief. And as if to confirm Mrs Davies's explanation, Uncle Bryn woke up at that point and mumbled an incomprehensible greeting. He was asleep again within seconds. I figured he must be quite sick – he certainly didn't look well. Mrs Davies read my thoughts.

'Don't worry. He's not ill or anything,' she whispered. 'He's actually a pain in the backside. He won't lift a finger to help but he's quite capable. He's only sixty-eight, eight years younger than Dad.'

With hindsight I should have kept quiet about Uncle Bryn. I certainly should never have allowed his constant snoring to distract me from my task, but in my defence it was one of those snores that would register on the Richter scale – growling, prolonged, and extremely difficult to ignore. My sudden pauses and lapses in concentration must have been obvious despite my genuine attempts to disguise them because Mr Davies, sitting smouldering in the corner of the room was almost ready to explode.

As I was about to explain the questions listed on the Application for Cremation form, Uncle Bryn awoke with a sudden snort. He immediately launched into a coughing fit in a feeble attempt to disguise his snoring and pretend he had never been asleep at all. Why people do this is a constant source of mystery to me. It's like the person who trips over a paving stone while walking down the street and immediately breaks into a jog to try and pretend the trip had never actually happened. Who are they trying to kid?

Following his attempted cover-up, Uncle Bryn stayed awake for a whole three minutes, even contributing to the arrangement with a couple of surprisingly intelligent comments. But his efforts were doomed to failure. The eyelids closed, the head tilted backwards, the mouth fell open, and the dreaded snoring returned. This time it sounded even louder.

I didn't mean to but at that moment I happened to glance despairingly at Mr Davies. It was the signal he had been waiting for. He leapt from his chair like a tiger unleashed. 'Bryn, why don't you bugger off upstairs and have a proper sleep so we can do this in peace!'

Uncle Bryn jumped like a jack-in-the-box. 'I'm not asleep,' he protested croakily. 'I'm listening to every word...'

'Bryn, you've done nothing but sleep all the way through. We can hear you. It's like sitting in the middle of a flaming pig sty!'

I sat horrified as a full-scale argument developed before Mrs Davies, her jolly disposition temporarily abandoned, called for order in no uncertain terms. Finally I was able to finish arranging her father's funeral and Uncle Bryn stayed awake, mostly with indignation, until the very end.

I drove past Tessum Street on the way back to the office about half an hour later and looked in on the boys as they scurried happily around the vehicles with their bright yellow sponges. Just for a second I wondered whether washing cars was the safer option.

28

The trouble with the Reverend Peter Morgan was that he could have giggled for Britain. I know, because I am exactly the same. My first funeral with Peter set the tone for the next fifteen years and it meant that eye contact between us on a funeral was to be avoided at all costs. Even the most fleeting of mutual glances could set us off on an irreversible road to shame and disrepute.

It all started in the ice and snow of my first winter in Westport. Ice can be treacherous in any situation but on a funeral it can lead to sheer anarchy, as Stewart Lewis had discovered to his complete humiliation. And unfortunately for gigglers like the Reverend Morgan and me, the slippery stuff became hazardous for similar reasons.

As we drove into Cwmfach Cemetery on that bitter cold morning I had a slight inkling there may be problems ahead. A blanket of crisp, sparkling snow lay over the whole cemetery and some of the narrow roads that wove in and around the grave sections were still glistening dangerously in the pale sunshine. It was typical that on such a morning we were burying in a rarely used part of the cemetery, which was more than a little difficult to reach. Cwmfach was quite hilly in places and, of course, we had a nice juicy slope with a ridiculously sharp left hand bend to negotiate at the bottom. As we inched down together I left an exaggerated distance between myself and Mark Grainger and Gareth Price in the hearse. It was a good job too because I went into a lovely skid as I approached the bend, at which point Peter began chuckling quietly to himself in the passenger seat.

A snow scene on an early winter's morning such as this somehow creates an almost unreal silence that is beautiful in itself. There was no wind to ruffle the branches of the trees and no sound of traffic in the distance, for the cemetery lay high up above the village of Penderi. There was just a still, reflective quiet that welcomed us as we carefully carried the coffin across to the freshly opened grave. Then with cold, part-working hands we lowered the deceased to her final resting place.

Gingerly, Gareth joined Peter Morgan on the slippery planks and I could see that he looked a little precarious on his feet as he leaned forward during the committal to throw a handful of soil onto the coffin. I swear the sound of a pin falling would have been audible as Peter delivered a calm and soothing graveside service, so tranquil were the surroundings. Which is why the Reverend's sudden exclamation as he slipped while descending from the planks at the end was so painfully out of place.

'Whoaaa!'

It was clearly an involuntary remark borne out of sheer surprise, but if someone had smashed a plate glass window it would not have come close to registering the same devastating impact. The trouble is it didn't really end there. In his spontaneous panic Peter grabbed at Gareth's arm, who was by no means looking any steadier himself, and there followed the wonderful spectacle of swaying bodies and an assortment of arms and legs flailing in all directions like a frenzied windmill. Any dignity present had disappeared by this stage: safety was paramount and balance had to be regained. Sadly I failed to witness the remainder of the show. Feeling an uncontrollable laughter bubbling rapidly to the surface, I turned and fled the shattered scene so I could hide behind a snow-laden tree and giggle in peace.

From this moment forward, Peter and I found it incredibly difficult to do funerals together. However, his parish was a key catchment area of ours so he was one of the ministers we worked with the most. And the problem was that fate seemed to deliberately intervene and cause normal, everyday funerals to throw up giggle-inducing events on a regular basis.

Take the White funeral for instance, my second with Peter as a funeral director. The main service was taking place in Peter's church – St. David's – in the heart of the parish. St. David's wasn't a traditional looking church in the Anglican sense. It was more modern in its design, especially inside where there were no traditional dark wooden pews, just rows of collapsible pine coloured chairs. There were also several pictures on the walls, mostly modern interpretations of biblical themes, and as I stood

159

quietly at the rear of the church with my colleagues while Peter delivered the service in his droll, ponderous voice, I could see to my right a portrait of Christ speaking with his apostles that was hanging a little askew.

I have a certain kind of obsessive anxiety when it comes to things like this so I casually tiptoed over to the wall and stretched out my hand to straighten it. But the moment my hand touched the beechwood frame it inexplicably dropped towards the floor. Horrified, I closed my eyes as a sickening crash echoed intrusively around the church, drawing a startled pause from Peter. I could feel the eyes of the congregation burning into me as they stared disgustedly at the wicked perpetrator of this untimely interruption.

My eyes began to drift uncontrollably in Peter's direction. I tried to stop them but it was some kind of force I couldn't control. Unfortunately his did the same and our eyes met for one of those fatal split seconds. Even from that distance I could see the familiar twinkle in his eyes and the desperate attempt to stop the corners of his mouth from turning upwards into his irrepressible grin. I felt enormous sympathy for him. He was the one in the public eye who had to overcome this. Somehow he managed to continue with the service, but the first few post-interruption sentences contained that slightly strangled quality that probably only I would recognise.

With the service over and having apologised profusely amidst the giggles, one would have thought that would be it for the day. But the funeral gods had other ideas and once again I would be the one to deliver the crushing blow to the Reverend Morgan's eminence within the community.

We were ready to leave and commence with our journey to the crematorium. My hearse driver and the three limousine drivers were all seated and the vast array of private cars were waiting to follow on behind. I nodded my head and began slowly walking the funeral away from the church, allowing plenty of time for everyone to take their place in the cortege. After a few seconds I quickly glanced behind and saw the impressive line of vehicles stretching way back. I continued paging down the road for about a minute before I looked back again to check everything was in order before getting back into the hearse. It was a blessing I did.

Suddenly emerging from the church way back in the distance was the Reverend Peter Morgan, loping frantically down the road in order to try and catch up with us. I closed my eyes with a self-recriminating sigh. I had completely forgotten to make sure the vicar was seated in the limousine before setting off. He must have been locking up the church.

I'm not one to outwardly panic in these situations – I think such a reaction only draws more attention to one's mistakes – but it must have been fairly obvious to those present that something was amiss when I slowed the cortege to a literal crawl. The next time I looked back Peter had managed to reach the first of the private cars in the cortege. Then when he finally drew alongside the first limousine I stopped to allow us both time to get into our respective vehicles, although not before our eyes met once more and the inevitable giggling began.

I could see Peter's face in the wing mirror of the hearse all the way to the crematorium and I shook my head in dismay. Here was one of my best acquaintances in the business and I had done nothing but inflict serious mental abuse on him for the last half hour. Thank goodness he was so easy going. I could think of many of his colleagues who would have broken the sixth commandment at receiving such treatment.

The process of arranging a funeral is like assembling a piece of machinery, with all manner of nuts, bolts, and cogs needing to be in place before it all comes together and functions properly. Therefore, our relationships with the various parties we dealt with outside of our company were of vital importance as we endeavoured to provide a smooth and trouble-free service to our clientele.

The associations were many. Ministers, crematorium and cemetery staff, the local newspaper advertising department, florists, printers, mortuary attendants, nursing home staff, and doctors were the most frequently used. And with the odd exception we got on very well with the vast majority of these. At least personally. As representatives of a large funeral company we often found resentment and suspicion from some quarters. We learned to expect it of course. But although such attitudes were understandable it could be very tiresome at times. Many of us were no great converts to the 'big is best' philosophy of our employers, myself especially. However, no matter how disenchanted I felt, I rarely allowed my objections to go outside the internal zone of the company.

We found the better we became known as individuals the more we were accepted, not least because we could be seen as just normal people endeavouring to do our best rather than the smug face of a disliked, corporate organisation. It was this ability to form good professional working relationships that matched our proficiency in looking after our clients. This is where business succeeds. It is not with the high-ranking officers who never climb down the ladder to see the reality of life, nor is it with the smarmy, cliché-ridden pep-talking of its managers. It is on the shop floor and the front line – in our case the living rooms and the gravesides – where the work was actually done. Personality will always prove more effective than smart-alec sales techniques.

Some of our biggest critics were the various ministers of religion we dealt with. A handful of these were extremely vociferous in their condemnation of the exploitive funeral big boys. Little any of us could say or do would change the minds of such die-hards, nor the opinions of others working in nursing homes, in florists, or digging graves. As I say, I tried to remain loyal during the criticism but it wasn't easy.

Doctors were probably the most detached of those we dealt with. They were frequent visitors to our chapel of rest in Stapleton Road to complete either the first or second part of a cremation form. It was always on these occasions that I wish I had chosen to go through medical school. Admittedly the interest in such a career has never existed, but it may well have been ignited had I known that doctors were eligible for several perks in addition to an extremely comfortable wage. The fee for taking ten minutes to fill out a cremation form is generous to say the least – two a week over twelve months would pay for a nice exotic holiday each year for doctor, Mrs Doctor, and any little doctors in tow. Of course, it was their expertise and seven years hard graft in qualifying that justified the fee, but it was a cushy little number nevertheless.

Two doctors must both sign a form before a cremation can take place. The first part – the more involved of the two – is completed by the deceased's own doctor who treated them during their last illness prior to death. The second part is completed by a nominated doctor from a different practice. The second signature is to back up the first doctor's diagnosis of the cause of death. Because a cremation is so final, the paperwork has to be correct beforehand. Where a burial is concerned the body can always be exhumed in the unlikely event that a problem becomes apparent at a later date. This is extremely rare but in my seventeen years of experience I knew of two such instances.

Doctor's fees were one of many that could not be blamed on the funeral director. Disbursements are always paid for by the undertaker on behalf of the family and then included on the invoice sent out after the funeral. These costs would amount to somewhere between twenty-five and forty per cent of the total funeral bill. For a cremation the fees would include the cost of the cremation, the doctor's form, and the disposal of the ashes afterwards. For a burial there would be the cost of the burial plot – increasingly expensive in this day and age – the grave digging fees, and the removal of any existing memorial to allow the burial to take place. Then in addition to these there is the expense of a newspaper notice, floral tributes, and service sheets. All these can add up to a fairly hefty bill by themselves, but they are charges totally beyond the control of the undertaker.

In some ways the condemnation aimed at funeral directors is a little unfair. The disbursements represent a large chunk of the funeral bill but are rarely questioned or criticised. Where the problem lies as far as Joe Public is concerned is the fee the undertaker charges for their services. I have already stated that I believe funerals are far too expensive. This includes the charges made by undertakers, local councils, newspapers, florists, and many of the other periphery organisations relied upon to put a funeral arrangement together. I was appalled by the pricing policies engaged by my employers, which, in my view, often abused the people we were relying on for business, who in turn were putting their trust in us. But what I can offer in defence of funeral companies is the lack of comparisons made with other industries that regularly charge extortionate amounts for their respective services. Most notably these could include solicitors, estate agents, builders, and architects, along with everyday necessities such as garage repairs, plumbers, and electricians.

In this respect the funeral industry is a victim of its own position in life, and death. The sensitive nature of funerals will always evoke strong feelings when linked with money. Other industries escape public scrutiny simply because human emotions do not run quite so high when their services are engaged. Yet despite accepting the fact that overheads, running costs, staff wages, and a worthwhile profit have to be considered, it was the brazen attitude of my company when it came to money that left me feeling cold. They did themselves no favours and it became increasingly difficult to defend their corner in the face of such public indignation.

As I said, of all the professional parties with whom we dealt, doctors were the most non-committal as far as commenting on such issues were concerned. Their ethics didn't really allow them the luxury. I also found them to be a pretty indifferent bunch to deal with. They rarely made conversation, sometimes appearing to be aloof and always in too much of a hurry to show any interest in us or our methods of working. There were notable exceptions of course, especially Dr Patel, who was a particularly habitual caller to our premises.

Ravinder Patel was a jovial, happy-go-lucky character, squat and round faced with sharp, smiling eyes, quite unlike the more austere exterior displayed by the majority of his colleagues. He was always ready for a laugh and a joke and was often the provider of such during his visits. At Christmas he would drop a dozen bottles of wine into the office for us to share amongst each other. Being a non-drinker I sadly never benefited from his generosity (I never quite got round to asking if he could throw in a bottle of grape juice for me) but I still greatly appreciated the gesture. However I did personally witness his experience with our temperamental office chair, which was worth far more than any act of benevolence on his part. To be blunt, it was entirely our fault. We had known about the chair's ability to suddenly descend for several months but had done nothing about it. When Dr Patel came bustling in one day to fill out a cremation form, the chair had actually behaved itself for several weeks and we had forgotten all about its fickle nature.

Ravi went out to the cold room to check the body in question and then returned to sit on the offending chair in order to write out the form. He was about halfway through when it happened. There he was, merrily writing away when suddenly the chair collapsed and Dr Patel, already a man of limited height, plunged even further down until his chin hovered precariously an inch or two above the desk. Thankfully he took it well, despite looking like an extra from *The Hobbit*. But somewhere in Westport's Registry Office there lies a doctor's cremation form with a line of black ink rising in an upwardly diagonal direction from the middle.

Dr Patel's response to such a situation was in stark contrast to Dr Brown's about a month later: thankfully it didn't involve the office chair. Dr Michael Brown was the complete opposite of Ravi – tall, impassive, and silent. He called into the Dean Street office one day and asked to see Mrs Rees. Sian, one of the new receptionists at the time, dealt with him and explained that Mrs Rees would probably be across the road in the Stapleton Road chapel of rest. He disappeared, only to return a few minutes later looking irritated. He spoke abruptly.

'I have been to your office across the road and they insist Mrs Rees is here.'

'Well I assure you she isn't, doctor,' replied Sian haughtily. 'We don't keep dead bodies at this office.'

'My dear, I have no wish to see a dead body. I have come to see Mrs Connie Rees, whom I believe to be very much alive.'

I had heard some of the conversation from the middle office and I stepped in quickly. 'Mrs Rees is in the flat upstairs, doctor. Let me show you the way.' I took him to Connie's flat door and tried to pass the incident off with a light joke. But it was lost on the tall, detached figure, who, having stooped slightly in the doorway, was already on his way up to see the live Mrs Rees.

Later that afternoon Connie wheezed her way into the back office at ten to five. She always came downstairs about that time to get a first look at the evening paper. 'I didn't like that new doctor from my surgery,' she tutted. 'Excellent at his job but he never smiled the whole time he was with me. It doesn't cost anything to smile.

It doesn't cost anything to have a sense of humour either, I thought. He was probably in a bad mood because there are very few doctors who visit a funeral home and leave empty-handed.

Amongst our closest associates were the many florists in the Westport area. This was no real surprise as we were certainly in a position to put a great deal of business their way. They too could often put in a favourable word on our behalf.

As with any business there were good florists and there were bad. Each individual funeral director had his favourites – tried and trusted concerns who would always come up with the goods. We could never risk promoting a florist whose product was not up to scratch because any comebacks would inevitably be directed at us.

It didn't take me long to organise my own personal favourites in the area and I settled on two florists at opposite ends of the town. The first was situated in the centre of Westport, a cheerful, well-run establishment called The Friendly Bunch. In all the years I dealt with them they never let me down. The second was in a district north of the town and, despite the rumours, my reasons were in no way influenced by the owner's foxy daughter, who I dated for a while. I chose to use Flower Power long before I ever met the lovely Bekki!

I did have mixed feelings at times about trying to sell flowers during a funeral arrangement, but we were heavily encouraged to do so. The discounts negotiated with florists meant a significant rise in the profit margin for each funeral where flowers were sold. Several families appreciated me taking charge of ordering floral tributes for them and that was fine. But in my experience, going to the florist was one of the tasks that many families wanted to do themselves. It was something positive, something personal that they could become involved in and I encouraged them to do this whenever I felt it was best. There is a danger that funeral directors can be too intrusive and literally do too much. Sometimes it is good for a grieving family to take on a little bit of responsibility and feel useful. I never pushed the sale of flowers for this reason alone. Mind you, selling flowers could have unforeseen advantages...

Miss Borthwick approached me at the end of her sister's funeral, a broad smile lighting up her wrinkled, bird-like features.

'Mr Eldwin, thank you so much for all you've done. Emily would have been absolutely thrilled with the way everything has gone today.'

166

'I'm glad you're happy, Miss Borthwick,' I replied, taking hold of the bony hand held out in front of me. 'The vicar gave a lovely service didn't he?'

'Oh he did indeed. Everything was wonderful. And the flowers! Oh, they are so beautiful.'

'Yes, they are nice aren't they? I'm very pleased with them. The flor...'

'You really do have a talent you know.'

'I'm sorry?'

'Not only are you a splendid funeral director and carpenter, but your flower arranging skills are second to none!'

'Oh right... I think you might be mistaken actually, Miss Borthwick. When I said I'd take care of everything, I didn't actually mean...'

'Oh come now, don't be so modest, Mr Eldwin!' she chuckled, cocking her head to one side. 'You've done a wonderful all round job. Well done!'

I opened my mouth to protest but closed it again and smiled sweetly at the aged, yet still attractive face. I didn't want to shatter the illusion, you see.

29

As Mr Woodford read silently through the obituary notice I had written, I stared out through the living room window to the small garden outside. It had stopped raining now and an army of crows were inching their way across the grass in an organised quest for lunch. They looked like a police unit sweep-searching a field for clues to some unsolved mystery.

I turned away and found myself looking once more at the photograph of Stacey Woodford on top of the television set. Bright, beautiful, and vivacious, Stacey smiled back at me from her hotel room in Spain. She was having the time of her life, her fresh, happy face radiant and untroubled. The photo had been taken in the early summer. Now, in blustery mid autumn a handful of months on, her teenage smile was frozen in time, never again to be repeated, never again to bring happiness to others. Three evenings ago Stacey had been knocked down by a car while crossing the road, a tragic accident with devastating consequences. Somehow she survived for a couple of hours but her injury-ravaged body gave up the fight as a team of medics at Sandacre Hospital tried desperately to save her life.

Stacey's death had stunned the community in which she lived and the sheer trauma the event had caused her family was heart-breaking to witness. The arrival of the funeral director on such occasions always brings a wretched sting of finality and having greeted me with initial bravery, Mrs Woodford left the room within minutes, apologising through a flood of tears. Her son, Trevor, Stacey's older brother, went with her and I faced a one to one with Mr Woodford to arrange his daughter's funeral. The tension in that small room was overpowering and the silence between questions deafening. Mr Woodford offered little more than the information I needed and for once I had not pursued conversation like I normally would. Somehow it seemed out of place, intrusive even in a situation like this.

Finally he nodded his head and handed the obituary notice back to me. 'That's fine.' His voice was barely audible, even though the silence hung in the air like invisible ice. His charcoal eyes bore the distant gaze that would become so familiar to me over time. As I tucked the notice inside a polythene folder with all the other paperwork I was collating for Stacey's funeral, I continued to harbour serious doubts about producing my coffin brochure. This, along with going through the wording for the obituary, was usually the most distressing part of a funeral arrangement. I saw no reason to cause further anguish now: I would explain verbally the choices we offered.

Back in the day many people were initially surprised, shocked even, that we showed pictures of coffins at all. Personally, I think it is one of the more astute innovations of modern funeral directing. People have a right to know what is available to them and the costs involved. I knew of many funeral directors who would assume the need of their client. They would choose a cheap, basic coffin when the family may have wanted something a little better; or an expensive solid oak coffin when a less ostentatious option would have been preferred. Painful though it could be, I always believed in people being presented with a choice. It is a long time to regret a wrong or uninformed decision after the funeral has taken place.

Some clients will still leave the final decision to the funeral director and that is okay, as long as it is their wish to do so after having viewed, or had explained, the options available to them. The problem such a decision creates for the funeral director is one of integrity. For us there was intense pressure from above to sell 'up market' coffins and many of my colleagues, whose sales of the basic coffin in the range far outweighed the more expensive ones, often found themselves in the manager's office. It was an ethical dilemma that most of us abhorred. If ever such a decision was left up to me I always offered the coffin next up from the basic. That way I (just about) satisfied the figure-happy area managers and, more importantly, my conscience. I hadn't chosen the cheapest coffin, which, depending on your outlook, could appear disrespectful to the deceased. But I had also refrained from insidiously encouraging my client to spend far more money than they needed to.

But right now I was a long way from reaching that stage. I still had to broach the subject of a coffin and when I did so, Mr Woodford visibly grimaced. For a few brief seconds his weary eyes closed as he realised the task ahead of him. I immediately offered to briefly describe what was available but he stopped me, took a deep breath as he ran his fingers through his short dark hair, and spoke quietly but firmly.

'No, it's got to be done. I'd like to see the coffins please.'

I passed over the brochure, full of admiration for his courage and determination. I witnessed countless such examples over the years in my work. Hardship so often reveals an inner strength that lies dormant until needed. It never ceases to amaze me just how well the human race responds to adversity. Wars, disasters, death – they all somehow bring out the best in us, particularly in the way we treat and respond to each other. Selfishness and pride take a back seat as more positive feelings of care and concern come to the fore. From my brief conversation with Mr Woodford I had learned how overwhelmed he and his family were by the kindness shown to them by friends and neighbours, some of whom they had never really spoken to before. It seemed to prove my theory that tragedy brings people together. It bonds communities, strangers become friends for life, and people actually show they do care about each other. I've even wondered at times if this is one of the reasons why awful things sometimes happen.

Mr Woodford flicked through the pages and once over the initial fear he began to study the pictures and their descriptions more fully. He was a robust man in his early forties with a rugged face that bore the suffering of the past few days. After a while he looked up. 'I know this will sound strange,' he began hesitantly, 'but I'd really like my wife and son to be involved with this.'

'If you think that's okay, by all means, Mr Woodford.'

'You see, Beth really wanted to be a part of arranging Stacey's funeral, but I think she knew deep down she wouldn't be up to it when the time came. I know choosing the coffin is one of the hardest things to do but I really think it would help, knowing she managed to do something positive.'

I smiled understandingly. 'I'm sure you're right. Your wife does need to be included and this is probably as good a way as any.'

'Yes...'

For a minute I thought he was going to open up. I had sensed from the beginning that his troubled mind was almost full to overflowing with thoughts and things he wanted to say; things he *needed* to say. But like so many men in situations like this he remembered his so-called role within the home, within society. He reverted back to tortured silence once again. 'I won't be long,' he muttered.

'Take your time, Mr Woodford. There's no hurry.'

He closed the door quietly behind him and I was alone in a room heavy with the burden of tragedy. Until an hour ago I had never met the Woodford family. Now I felt an integral part of their lives. I looked at the photo on the television set again as I waited for Mr Woodford to return, and then the pine display cabinet opposite. There were more photographs there of Stacey and Trevor through childhood. Stacey smiled sweetly in every one.

Why?

Even to a person with some kind of belief, these events are impossible to understand. But sometimes we have to take responsibility for our actions. If someone chooses to drive while under the influence of alcohol then he must suffer the consequences. Regrettably, innocent victims also pay the price as a result of such selfishness. Stacey had simply been crossing the road, something we all do day and night. She was hit by a man so drunk he could barely string a sentence together when the police arrived. It was his choice. Now it was his nightmare. Along with Stacey's family and friends, he and his wife would also suffer for entirely different reasons. Two families destroyed by one man's foolish decision.

After several minutes Mr Woodford returned and handed me the brochure, pointing silently to the coffin they had chosen. As he sat down I could see the red stains around his eyes.

Soon after, I was ready to leave. Although my presence there had been a necessity, I couldn't help feeling I was an intruder during a time of private heartbreak. I collected together the paperwork and placed it in my briefcase. Back at the office I would then work my way methodically through every piece of information I had gathered in order to organise Stacey's funeral. First of all there would be numerous phone calls. I would speak to the minister to go through the arrangements with him and give him some background details for when he visited with the family. I would contact the burials and cremations office to book a time for the cremation and then get back to the minister to confirm that time with him. This could often become a complicated process when the times that were available at the crematorium didn't match up with the minister's schedule. I would then confirm all the timings with the family before phoning the obituary notice into *The Westport Chronicle*.

The next step would be to order the coffin and it's accessories from our coffin workshop. I would organise the removal of Stacey's body from Sandacre Hospital as soon as the coroner's officer gave the necessary clearance. Depending on the arrangement there would also be other details to coordinate such as ordering flowers and service sheets. Finally, I would enter all the arrangements into the office diary and then over the next few days I would check and double check, making sure everything was in order and going to plan. It could be a long, intricate process – a process the public never sees.

I shook hands solemnly with Mr Woodford and whispered a quiet farewell to his wife in the kitchen. Her face was swollen red with the tears of despair that had clearly flowed throughout every minute I had been there. She barely had the mental strength to muster a response.

As I drove away I let out a huge sigh of relief. The hardest part, for me, was over. Ever since the call had first come in late the previous day I had been quietly dreading arranging such an intensely tragic funeral. As I pulled up outside the house my whole body had physically trembled at the task awaiting me. This was partly due to the fact I had not yet completed my first month as a funeral director – I was still feeling my way in this most testing of professions. Experience brought me more confidence and fortitude over time, but I always felt a surge of nervousness before arranging funerals in such distressing circumstances. I'm sure I'm not alone.

The following week I conducted Stacey's funeral in the rain. The grey, oppressive skies reflected the melancholic mood of the mourners as we moved from private service at the house to public service at St Steven's Church and then finally the short service of committal at the crematorium. Everything went well professionally as far as I was concerned but it was a strained atmosphere, silent and subdued. The whole occasion reminded me greatly of Donny Hughes's funeral some years earlier. But this time I was the funeral director, the person responsible for all that happened during the two hours it took. I bore it with a mixture of pride and trepidation.

I arrived back at the office feeling drained. On my desk was a piece of paper. It was details of an arrangement for me to do that afternoon. I didn't notice the deceased's age until after I'd had a quick lunch break.

'Douglas Wright – aged forty-five.'

I turned to Sian. 'Do we know what Mr Wright died of?'

'I think it was the story on the local news a couple of nights ago. He was driving a minibus and got killed in a head on collision down West Wales somewhere.'

I puffed out my cheeks with a heavy acceptance. I had been so on edge about Stacey's funeral that I'd taken little notice of any current news stories. 'Oh boy,' I breathed to myself. 'Here we go again.'

The same tingling sensation crawled over my body as I turned into Bryce Terrace in the outer district of Cefn Bach. I figured I was a little unlucky to be faced with two such difficult funerals one after the other. But that was the nature of the job. Although every death brings its own sadness I had long realised that not every funeral would involve little old ladies in their eighties who had passed away peacefully of natural causes after a full and well-lived life. The funeral arrangements of Stacey Woodford and now Douglas Wright were certainly testament to that.

Mrs Wright greeted me at the door of her attractive, spacious house with the same stunned silence as that of Mr Woodford a week and a half ago. She managed a small but tired smile as I stepped inside, my shoes clicking on the polished wooden floor of the hallway. She was an ample lady, big boned with large features and a soft, pleasant face that also bore the strain of recent events.

I was ushered into the gracefully decorated front room and I sat down on a soft, cream leather sofa. As I did so I found myself once again looking at family photographs around the room. In the one above the mantelpiece, two radiant young faces beamed down at us.

'Are they your children?' I asked.

'Yes, that's Ben and Samantha,' she replied, her voice quavering ever so slightly.

'How old are they?'

'Ben is thirteen, Samantha eleven.'

I swallowed a lump in my throat. 'How are they coping?'

She gave a tearful smile. 'Ben's been wonderful, quite the man of the house. Samantha's the opposite – very quiet, hardly says a word. It's difficult to know what she's thinking. She shut herself in her bedroom for a couple of hours when I told her what had happened. They're with my brother and his family right now.'

My heart ached. I was there to do a job in a professional capacity but from somewhere deep inside I could sense a need. We must have talked for over half an hour before I finally brought the conversation round to the funeral arrangements. I could tell that it did Mrs Wright a world of good.

My more experienced colleagues had told me that the bereaved would frequently open up and talk to the funeral director, often divulging personal and sensitive information. Grief can purge the soul of many a secret and it went without saying that confidentiality was of prime importance: anything we were told went no further. Nothing Mrs Wright said that day was particularly sensitive, but the need to talk to someone independent and detached from her tragic circumstances was very real and one which, thankfully, I was able to recognise. As our conversation progressed my thoughts returned to the scene of ten days ago when I sat facing Mr Woodford. It had seemed to me that he too desperately wanted to talk. But tradition and self-consciousness probably conspired to keep him silent. The two comparisons said much about society and its perceived expectations: women talk, men don't.

I spent about two hours with Mrs Wright in the end and I really felt I'd achieved something as I bade her farewell. She had chosen to make her husband's funeral arrangements alone without the input of her family and I discerned she was actually the type of person who preferred it that way. She had struck me as a very private and independent individual who saw no reason to change her ways in the face of personal sadness. I admired such resolve and felt uplifted that she had responded to me so positively.

My bubble of achievement soon burst upon returning to the office at quarter to five. Doberman was there in the back office with Paul. He didn't look particularly happy although I'd never really seen him sport any other expression on that hangdog face of his. I often wondered whether the man had been cursed with perpetual misery.

'Where have you been?' he grunted as I placed my briefcase on the desk.

'Arranging a funeral,' I replied, not that I really saw it was any business of his.

'Paul says you left the office at quarter to two?'

'Yes.'

'So how many funerals have you arranged?'

'Just the one, Mr Raymond,' I retorted, trying my best to remain civil.

He shook his head a few times and then completely ignored me. 'Right, I'll be on my way,' he said, referring this remark towards Paul. 'I'll leave it in your hands.' As he marched pompously out of the office with Paul following him, I opened my briefcase and began organising my paperwork for Douglas Wright's funeral. But I couldn't concentrate. My temperature was rising and when Paul returned I rounded on him.

'Okay, so what's the problem?'

'He thinks taking three hours to arrange one funeral is a bit excessive,' he explained hesitantly.

'Oh well, he's the expert isn't he?' I responded sarcastically. 'How many funerals is it he's arranged again? Oh that's right. None.'

'He doesn't think it's a very cost effective use of manpower.'

I rolled my eyes. 'Oh for goodness' sake. You'll have me in tears in a minute.'

'Well… you were gone quite a long time.'

'Yes I was. Apart from the hour long round trip, I was sitting with a widow who has just lost her husband in a road accident. Sometimes it takes a while.'

One of my colleagues spoke up jovially from the middle office. 'I was in and out of a house in twenty-five minutes the other day!' His remark was clearly intended to ease the strained atmosphere. It didn't work.

'Well congratulations,' I snapped. 'If you feel okay about that, it's your call. But either you let me do this job the way I think it should be done or I don't do it at all.'

Six weeks later word filtered down the line that Doberman had left the company under something of a cloud. Nobody I can think of was unhappy at the news. I never set eyes on the man again and that in itself was reason enough for rejoicing. I've met some obnoxious people in my life but Peter Raymond won the gold medal by a length.

We heard a couple of years later that, bizarrely, he was running a stall selling ladies underwear at local markets in the region. His demise could not have had a better ending had I written it myself.

30

If there was great rejoicing at the sudden disappearing act performed by Peter Raymond, the same certainly could not have been said following the departure of Denzil Jenkins a few months earlier. From an entertainment point of view we missed him a great deal. But we needn't have worried. Trevor Davies was a more than adequate replacement. Trevor and Denzil were poles apart as far as personalities go, but they both possessed the wonderful gift of not saying quite what they meant. Denzil had gone down in company folklore with his array of verbal gaffes. In time, Trevor would rival him with his own impressive repertoire of sayings and, in addition, wild claims.

Trevor came to us in his early fifties, a much-travelled man with a mountain of experience behind him in all aspects of life. Or so he said. That was the problem with Trevor Davies – no one really knew if he was telling the truth or not. When he first joined us as a driver we all believed him and his amazing stories. But as time wore on and the rumours from outside sources multiplied, it became increasingly obvious that things were not quite the way Trevor would have us believe. Many were the times when he dug himself into an enormous hole and it never ceased to amaze me how oblivious to it he could be. Like the time he went to India on holiday. On his return one of the questions he was asked was whether he had tried Bombay duck while he was there.

'Yes, yes, of course,' he replied in his imperious, nasal tone. 'Beautiful it was too. Much nicer than the duck you get over here. Not as greasy. Tasted just like tender chicken it did.'

Then there was the day he covered for Reg Bowen on the judge's car. It was during one of two occasions a year when the judge sat in the town of Llangethin about thirty miles west of Westport. Paul went to great pains to ensure Trevor knew where he was going and what he had to do so there would be no mistakes. Trevor was having none of it.

'I know Llangethin like the back of my hand. Been going there for years. Lovely place.'

When the news filtered back a few hours later that Trevor had taken a wrong turn and driven a less-than-amused judge around Asda's car park and out again, there was much hilarity and jovial back-slapping amongst us all. The judge's contract was much more than just driving the judge around in a nice car. It was a high security operation and any employee nominated to drive had to be vetted by the police first. In addition, all routes had been secretly planned beforehand and were never the same two days running. Trevor's unexpected jaunt to the supermarket, therefore, would have caused a security alert of ample proportions.

Reg Bowen in particular enjoyed Trevor's public blunder. There was no love lost between Reg and Trevor. When they worked together they were civil enough, but the moment one of them was out of earshot the other would launch into the most graphic character assassination you could ever wish to hear. Meanwhile Trevor denied everything of course. He said it was the other judge's car in the area that had taken the wrong turning and the judge was rightly furious. The problem was we all knew there was only one judge's car – we had the sole contract.

If you had never visited the moon you could guarantee Trevor had been there. If you *had* visited the moon then Trevor would have been there twice with knobs on. If you owned an elephant, Trevor would also own one, plus a bag to put it in. Trying to get the better of him was a futile exercise because in his mind he was superior to everyone and anything they had ever done. Even when there was physical proof of something he would still argue black was white. It could often be infuriating and when someone like Chris Littlehales – who could never be described as the most tolerant of people – was involved, sparks would inevitably fly.

It was late 1994 when Chris brought into work a beautifully bound book that had recently been presented to him. The book had been published to commemorate the fiftieth anniversary of D-Day and we all took turns to look at this impressive volume before carefully handing it on. But Trevor was pompously dismissive and waved it away. 'I've already got one of those', he said 'I was given it about ten years ago by the rugby club.'

Chris looked at him with raised eyebrows. 'I doubt that very much, Trev.'

'Yes yes, I've got it in the house,' came the assured reply.

'Trev, you haven't got a copy of this book.'

'Yes I have.'

'No you haven't.'

'I'm telling you I was given this book ten years ago.'

I could see Chris's hackles rising, although to be fair it would not have taken a nuclear physicist to notice. He snatched the book from Dai Proctor who was casually glancing through it at the time and held it up in front of Trevor's face.

'Right,' he snapped. 'What does it say on the front of the book?'

'1944-1994: 50th Anniversary of D-Day,' read Trevor.

'So, fifty years on from 1944 would be 1994 – this year, yeah?'

'Yes.'

Chris was building things up beautifully. 'Okay. So it's fifty years since D-Day, hence the 50th Anniversary this year.'

'Of course,' nodded Trevor.

'So how can you have been given a copy of *this* book ten years ago?'

'Well I assure you I was. It's in the house...'

'Trevor, you plank!' shouted Chris. 'If such a book existed it would have been a *fortieth* anniversary, not a fiftieth!'

'Hmm. You could be right I suppose,' Trevor mused, clearly not convinced.

And that wasn't the end of it. A couple of days later he was still insisting to anyone who would listen that he'd been given a copy of the book ten years ago and that Chris didn't have a clue what he was talking about.

Trevor was a short, neat man with a habit of rocking back on his heels when he spoke, usually during the middle of yet another tall story. He also possessed the loudest nasal whine of a voice I've ever heard in my life. I do not wish to sound unkind but it was a cross between the bleating of a goat and a foghorn. In fact, it was so penetrating he was actually banned from going around the back of the crematorium during services because both mourners and vicars complained they could hear his voice resonating through the walls.

Regarded whimsically by Chris as 'a legend in his own lunchtime,' Trevor could be an exasperating man to work with. Over the years most of us developed a system by which we could cope. Firstly we tried not to spend too much time with him in one go. This could be difficult, especially for the poor souls who worked with him down at the garage. The second tactic was to never believe a single word he said. Our standing joke about Trevor was the perfect epitome: Question – how do you know when Trevor's lying? Answer – his lips move. But if Trevor's bragging often drove us to the brink of despair, no one could deny that his ability to confuse words and sentences caused great amusement around the workplace. As was the case with Denzil, many of these have since become celebrated catchphrases in the Westport funeral industry.

Very few people know that the official name for the structure at the crematorium on which the coffin is placed during the service is a 'catafalque.' Originating from Italian it is a strange word at the best of times. But Trevor's instructions when explaining to the family bearers that after carrying the coffin on their shoulders down the crematorium aisle they must then 'place the coffin on the catapult' often caused greater confusion. It also created a certain amount of alarm. I swear I could see utter disbelief on the faces of the bearers at the thought of the coffin being fired into the air towards the furnaces by some ancient mediaeval contraption.

Then there was the time Trevor was talking to a couple of women at the end of a funeral. This in itself was a regular occurrence. Trev fancied himself as a ladies' man and if the tales of his many exploits were to be believed, there would be very few members of Westport's female population he hadn't 'taken out' at some time. Because of his connections with local clubs and previous jobs, Trevor wasn't short of an acquaintance or two. But he often liked to read more into these than was clearly the case – like the two women on this occasion from one of the nursing homes we regularly attended. We all knew them to say a friendly 'hello' to but Trevor always thought he was onto something in these situations. When they invited him to call by for a coffee next time he was passing – a friendly offer we all received from time to time – he was like a bull in a field of cows.

I think I'm in there, Tom my boy.'

Having long tired of arguing with him over such matters, I simply nodded my head and egged him on. We had all learned this was far more fun. 'Yes, go for it Trev. The blonde one certainly had a twinkle in her eye when you were talking to her.'

Trevor puffed out his chest and rocked back on his heels with visible swagger. 'Aye,' he grinned, 'she did, didn't she? I've known her for years. Always had a bit of a thing for me. I'll call in one day for that coffee. I've never been one to look a gift horse in the house.'

Mixed up words aside, it was always sheer bluster and pretence of course. His wife, Jill, would have thrown him out onto the streets if she'd had the least inkling he was flirting, let alone anything else. Jill was lovely – dusky, attractive, and, in our eyes, incredibly long-suffering.

On another day, one of the boys down at the garage was concerned about his wife, who had just been informed she needed to undergo a hysterectomy. Trev was full of advice as usual.

'Now don't worry about it,' he reassured. 'It's nowhere near as bad as they make out. My Jill had an x-directory last year. She took a couple of painkillers and was back in work the following day.

It was a busy day and not just for us. Every funeral we were doing seemed to have attracted a multitude of flowers and the florists had been back and forth the chapel of rest all morning.

Such scenarios can be a nightmare for all concerned. At times, I have found myself wading through so many flowers and wreaths strewn around the chapel floor while I sorted them all out that I began to wonder whether I had been mysteriously transported to the New Covent Garden flower market. The headache worsens upon the discovery that the card bearing the message from the sender does not have the name of the deceased written on the reverse. Many of the smaller, less conscientious florists often did this and with more than one funeral a day it could be virtually impossible to discern which funeral they were for. On one occasion I actually took the same bunch of flowers on two separate funerals. It was the safe option, but one of those families must be wondering to this day who on earth 'Bernard and Ada' were.

But hectic days like these were a worry for the florists themselves too. Making up quality wreaths and bouquets is an intricate, painstaking art and certainly not one to be rushed. It was to the credit of the florists we had chosen to use that they rarely, if ever, let us down. I don't remember a single situation arising where either of my two chosen florists, The Friendly Bunch or Flower Power, delivered me a sub-standard floral tribute.

Anyway, Chris and I were slowly booking in all the flowers we had received for my next funeral at our chapel of rest in Penderi Village one day. We had already listed more than thirty tributes as they lay on the floor in the front garage and the task was never ending. Typically there seemed to be between five and ten names per card too. We always supplied the family with a full list of every tribute sent so every name on each card needed to be listed. Apart from being a keepsake for the family, it was also our record of having received that particular tribute in the event of any problem later. A wreath not turning up on time, or even not turning up at all, was an occasional and potentially distressing occurrence.

I muttered to myself as I tried to read the spidery scrawl of one particular florist's handwriting. It could have been any one of 'Mary,' 'Mave,' 'Mark,' or 'Mack.' In the end I shrugged my shoulders. 'Just put Mary down,' I told Chris. 'If it's wrong, it's wrong. There's not a lot else we can do.'

Not for the first time in my undertaking career did I curse flowers. I had no problem with tributes from immediate family members, but any more was a waste in my eyes. There was irony in the fact that all this money was being spent on the deceased and they themselves were unable to appreciate it. I understand why people send flowers. It is the last thing they can physically do for the deceased, a public obligation that is very visible in its intentions. This was proved to me time and again when many families sensibly requested 'family flowers only but donations in lieu to charity' at the end of the obituary notice. With the anonymity of sending a cheque comes a very lukewarm response and I often believed that people felt they were off the hook when they saw a request for donations.

I closed my eyes and sighed disbelievingly as I heard another florist's van pull up across the front of the premises and a young man leaping out of the driver's seat.

'More flowers for the Morgan funeral,' I heard him call.

Trevor was giving the hearse a quick swill at the front of the garage and he went forward to take them. From the back I could see the driver handing him another two tributes, a large oasis and a bunch of lilies. Within seconds the lad was back in the van and making to pull away.

'I'm sorry I can't stop,' he shouted through the open window. 'Things are crazy today. The writing on the cards is a bit rushed too but if there's any problem, just give us a ring.'

I could see Trevor was a touch bemused. Because they were so busy the florist in question had hired in an additional van – this one had no livery on it.

'Well which florist shall I say you are?' he retorted.

'The Friendly Bunch', yelled the driver as he disappeared down the street.

Trevor looked back at us with a look of disbelief on his face. 'Well that was a stupid thing to say. I don't want to know if they're friendly or not; just the name of the florist.

31

It was just one of those funerals.

Every so often in the life of an undertaker a funeral comes along where things habitually go wrong. Nothing that would make the evening news; just continual irritations that test the funeral director's dignity to the limit. These funerals were predestined to happen and there was nothing the funeral director could do to alter the course of events. The Griffiths funeral was one such occasion. It had all started so perfectly. The arrangement was a huge success and I had built up a wonderful rapport with the family of the late Myfanwy Griffiths. At that stage nothing led me to believe that by the end I would be wishing a grave-sized hole would open up into which I could completely disappear.

The first sign of trouble manifested itself when we took the late Mrs Griffiths home. The coffin had gone into the front room quite smoothly and we hadn't needed to tilt it, as could often be the case. The doorway and front hallway were all generous enough to allow the coffin to be negotiated around the corners in a level position and we placed it neatly on the chrome trestles in the middle of the room with the minimum of fuss.

With the coffin in place I excused the two drivers who had assisted me – they had followed me to the house on their way to Sandacre Hospital to carry out removals. I then set about the task of checking the body to make sure nothing had been disturbed during transit before allowing the family into the room to view their mother. It was from this moment on that things started to go awry. I undid the screws and lifted up the lid, but I hadn't noticed the glass chandelier directly above me. With a sickening crash I caught it with the top of the lid and the whole thing shattered into pieces, most of which rained down inside the open coffin.

For a few seconds I froze, waiting for someone to dash in and catch me in my horrified stupor. But no one came. As the blood finally began to pump back around my now shaking body I tried to analyse the situation. But no matter which way I looked at it, I was in trouble. I glanced down reluctantly at Mrs Griffiths and for a split second thought how extravagant she looked as she lay peacefully in her coffin, lavishly covered in sparkling diamonds. Except they weren't diamonds. They were extremely sharp shards of glass and with a hint of panic I began picking them from off the cream-coloured coffin gown in which we had dressed her only an hour earlier. Inevitably, several fragments had slipped down the sides and these were extremely difficult to locate, not to say treacherous to remove.

I picked up the remainder of the glass that had landed on the floor around the coffin and added it to the impressive pile I'd made on the nearby coffee table. After a very long ten minutes I had finally cleared all traces of my vandalism. But now came the hard part. With the sorry remains of a once beautiful chandelier hanging limply above my head, I had little choice but to own up. In the back of my mind, however, was the thought that in the adjacent room were three daughters and a son waiting quietly to see their mother resting peacefully in her coffin. They were not expecting to see a gibbering funeral director confessing to the destruction of their light fittings.

It actually made me feel a lot worse when the family were so nice about it all. One of the daughters even apologised for the positioning of the chandelier, saying it 'was a touch awkward where it was.' Up until then I had always considered the middle of a room to be the perfect place for a light fitting. But right now I longed to agree with her. I honestly think if I'd accidentally bulldozed the whole property down to the ground, the Griffiths family would have just smiled and said that they'd never really liked the house anyway.

Apart from losing the burial form and only finding it at the eleventh hour, everything else went fairly smoothly in the run up to the funeral. Then all hell broke loose.

The first incident happened just as we were getting ready to leave Stapleton Road. A wreath had been delivered there by mistake instead of going straight to the residence and I had left it in the middle of the garage floor so there was no way I could forget to take it with us. My forgetfulness was famous amongst my colleagues and I often had to resort to such extreme measures at times in order to remember things. The problem was that while it may have been a good idea theoretically, in reality it was an unbelievably half-witted thing to do. The thought never entered my head that Andy Morris, my hearse driver, would probably reverse into the garage to wait for me when he drove up from Tessum Street and not notice it. When I walked over from the Dean Street office in my stripes and tailcoat I was confronted by the sight of Andy looking down forlornly at the wreath like someone who had just run over a cat. Although I risk the wrath of animal lovers the world over, at that particular moment in time I would have much preferred it if he had.

'Sorry Tom,' shrugged Andy ruefully. 'Didn't see it there.'

I puffed air into my cheeks and wiggled it around my mouth. There wasn't a great deal we could do – we were due at the house in ten minutes. I bent down and desperately tried to raise some of the stems to recreate a semblance of shape to the flowers. After a couple of minutes it did look slightly better. But the damage, and the obvious tyre mark that had caused it, was still very much apparent.

'Was Mrs Griffiths into motor racing by any chance?' asked Andy casually.

'No. I don't think so.'

'Pity. You could have said the flowers were from Michelin.'

I couldn't help but smile. Andy was one of the most laid back characters I knew. He had only recently come to us after we had taken over the small family funeral business he worked for. He had his own style of doing things and he certainly wasn't going to change just because a larger company now employed him.

Lean, handsome, and always ready to break into a smile, Andy had one speed while working – leisurely. It was a joy to watch and I should have taken more notice. While everyone else was all huff and puff like the hare, Andy drifted along in his relaxed, unflappable way and like the tortoise, still got the job done with the least amount of effort. He never seemed intimidated by anyone around or above him, a quality I would have happily paid good money for.

We had to go. There was nothing more we could do. I gave up on the wreath from Michelin and just hoped that no one would take too close a look.

Halfway through the service at St George's Church in Brynmawr, the verger sat on a wasp. It caused quite a commotion to say the least and shattered the tranquil silence that had been prominent during the prayers. Benjamin Mills, the verger in question, was a large man and not one to do things by halves. He leapt around with surprising agility and for several seconds there was a distinct uneasiness in the air until the cause of the spectacle had been established. After all, it would take an extremely peculiar individual to start leaping around in the middle of a funeral service for no reason.

I sympathised greatly with Benjamin Mills, as I'm sure did many of the mourners. Having been the recipient of a wasp's capabilities myself, I was well aware of the discomfort their sting can cause. But as the verger was lead away grimacing by one of the churchwardens, it occurred to me that although the pain would soon wear off, the poor man's embarrassment of his ill-timed misfortune would probably take much longer to heal. It was about this time too that I realised the funeral was doomed. The light fitting, the flowers, and now the verger. I was starting to feel uneasy. I didn't have to wait long for mishap number four. Thankfully, once again, it had little to do with me, unless of course my mere presence was some sort of jinx. It was beginning to cross my mind.

St. George's was one of only a handful of churches in the Westport area where church bells were rung before and after a funeral service. Following today, the figure would be reduced by one more. As the Reverend Dennis Sinclair solemnly led the procession out of the church to the sound of a solitary bell, a peace had settled on proceedings once again. Such an atmosphere was generally present at the funerals taken by the Rev Sinclair. He was a wonderful minister, certainly one of the most sincere I would ever meet. His sense of humour was legendary too, as was his joke telling during journeys to the crematorium or the cemetery. Today, however, I am sure he offered up one or two extra prayers of gratitude before retiring to bed for the night, because his life was probably spared for a few more years.

When the procession was about halfway between the church and the hearse, the bell suddenly made a muffled, clunking sound, followed immediately by an almighty thud. I turned around just in time to see a huge metal ball thundering towards the ground having bounced spectacularly off of the church roof. There was no time to even shout out a warning, but miraculously the ball hit the soft turf literally three feet away from the startled vicar. I could hear the gasps and the 'oooh's' coming from behind at the near miss and although Dennis laughed off the incident with a big grin on his heavily side-burned face, I knew he realised he had been blessed with a very lucky escape

As for me, I firmly believed that something big was conspiring against me and I was slowly losing control of the funeral. Conversations about leaping vergers and the vicar's close encounter with the grim reaper were going on around me and I was having great difficulty attracting people's attention back to the matter in hand – that of encouraging them to their cars so that we could set off for the cemetery.

The cemetery.

I swallowed hard. Having now accepted that dark forces were at work, I knew there was plenty of time yet for things to get even worse. The burial part of a funeral always offers opportunities for various tribulations. Things rarely go wrong of course. But on a day like today...

I finally managed to drag the mourners from their assorted speculations on the vicar's charmed life and the state of the verger's ample rear. I refused point blank to perform any sort of walk in front of the hearse other than to see the cortege out onto the main road and throughout the entire thirty-minute crawl to Millfield Cemetery, I nervously tried to anticipate the major pitfalls that lay ahead. Carrying the coffin onto the planks at the graveside, standing on the planks with the vicar while he performed the committal service, and then the family stepping forward one by one to throw a handful of soil down onto the coffin. All were fraught with risk and danger. I noticed Andy behind the wheel grinning at my anxiety. He was enjoying this, as I had often revelled in similar situations when driving on a funeral without the ultimate responsibility. They were happy, carefree days that seemed way too far in the distant past right now.

We reached the cemetery and were directed down one of the narrow roads in between the sections by the gravedigger.

Andy eventually pulled up alongside the trolley that had been put out for us and as I got out of the hearse I could see we had a walk of about twenty metres between headstones until we reached the grave. Most funeral directors will go and have a quick look at the grave upon arriving at a cemetery as a matter of course: the practice had never seemed like a better idea than it did now.

With a feeling of impending gloom I noticed that the recent rain had left the turf a little soggy in places. I had all but convinced myself that one of the bearers was going to slip while carrying the coffin to the graveside. But amazingly, nothing happened. The family bearers all negotiated the awkward route without the hint of a problem. I could have balanced a glass of water on the coffin, so steadily was it lowered into the grave. Perhaps everything was going to be okay.

'Tom.'

I turned around and the Rev Sinclair was at my shoulder.

'I've left the hymn sheets in the limousine,' he whispered. 'The family wanted to sing 'The Lord's My Shepherd' straight after the committal. They phoned me about it last night. I forgot to tell you.'

'But you have got hymn sheets with you?' I asked, my heart racing.

'Oh yes. I did them on the church photocopier this morning. I've just left them in the limo.'

I breathed a sigh of relief. 'No problem, vicar.'

Alan Hodder was driving the limousine and I motioned him over. 'Alan, can you pop back to the car and get the vicar's hymn sheets please.'

As he turned and made his way back to the limousine I had a sudden flashing premonition. Maybe I should have asked Andy, even though he was driving the hearse. Knowing Alan he could easily return with the wrong item, even if the hymn sheets were the only things there. From past experience I knew that despite his best intentions, having Alan Hodder on a funeral was tantamount to being accompanied to an auction by a man with a nervous twitch. Perhaps unfairly, he had always been tainted by having that accident on his first day. I heaved a sigh of relief when I saw him coming towards us clutching a wad of paper hymn sheets. I admonished myself for having such little faith in my driver. Now we were on the final leg. Another few minutes and this funeral would be over.

The reason Alan slipped and gave such a life-like impression of a human star was because he was rushing. The calm, controlled approach of Andy Morris was called for, especially as the grass underfoot was quite greasy. The sight of approximately fifty sheets of white paper flying into the air like a flock of frightened birds just added to the whole effect. They floated back down to earth like glitter in a snow dome as Alan stood up shakily, with a rather unfortunately situated brown streak of mud stretching from his left buttock all the way down to just below the back of his knee.

At the ludicrous sight of mourners breaking rank and moving *en masse* amongst the gravestones in order to retrieve a hymn sheet each, I didn't know whether to laugh, cry, or just run away. Eventually I opted for the former. Both Andy and the vicar were already sporting pastel shades of facial red, but they were pale in comparison to the scarlet tones of poor Alan. He was positively glowing and it was impossible not to break into a grin, even for me in my supposed position of supreme dignity.

Thankfully, the calamities that had plagued the Griffiths funeral throughout had reached their zenith with Alan's gymnastic display. The remaining minutes passed by without further incident and I finally felt able to relax. It is surprising how much sheer relief can cause one to loosen up. As I mingled with the mourners I overheard many snippets of conversation about the morning's capers with an inner amusement that belied my uneasiness during the previous hour or so.

And the events that had taken place successfully diverted people's attention away from the pitiful looking wreath that Andy inadvertently destroyed earlier. No one seemed to notice and nothing was ever said.

A week later I received a neatly addressed pale blue envelope in the post. Inside was an equally neatly written letter from one of the daughters of the late Myfanwy Griffiths. It was a very sincere and honest thank you for my efforts on their behalf in carrying out the funeral arrangements for their dear mother. This was the same funeral director, of course, who had destroyed their chandelier and was responsible for the obliteration of one of the wreaths. The letter even went on to say that their Mum would have been the first to giggle at the various mishaps that took place.

As I read the closing sentence of that letter, where grateful thanks were repeated once more, I was deeply touched. Not only by the words of a family whose humble gratitude for what I had done was so heart-warmingly evident, but also by the irony of life as a funeral director. A couple of weeks earlier I had arranged and conducted a funeral that had been perfect from start to finish, one on which I had worked extremely hard, occasionally in my own time, to ensure everything was in place. Circumstances had necessitated that I spent far more time on this funeral than dealing with the arrangements for the Griffiths family. Yet not one word of thanks or appreciation had ever been uttered in my direction.

I never possessed the arrogance or the egotism to expect praise and gratitude. When it did come along it was always a boost to my spirits, but I always viewed it as a sign that I had achieved exactly what the client wanted and expected of me. Some of my colleagues, especially during my later years in the profession, used such commendation as a yardstick to measure how wonderfully important they were in the undertaking scheme of things. To me, they were in the wrong line of work. The contents of that letter from the Griffiths family went far deeper than the expressions contained within. It was an acknowledgement that I had done my best for them and that I had become a trusted friend in a time of need. It also showed that such appreciation could come when least expected.

Especially when the funeral concerned would not have looked out of place in a *Carry On* film.

32

If every so often a rogue funeral came along, the same could be said for nights on call – the only difference being that the latter were far more frequent.

Like many undertakers I found it almost impossible to sleep when I was on call. I would lie there tossing and turning, waiting for the telephone to ring. At times I would develop a kind of switched on telepathy that allowed me to predict a phone call seconds before it happened. On other occasions I would jump like a jackrabbit at the sudden invasion of its shrill tones.

Over the years I grew to detest Alexander Graham Bell's otherwise wonderful invention. Even now I still marvel at the ability we have to pick up a piece of moulded plastic and listen to someone's voice from anywhere up to twelve thousand miles away. It is an amazing and convenient medium by which we can keep in touch, do our business deals, and make our lives easier. But at night, in the mysterious world of the undertaker, it becomes a tormentor, an irritant, and a heartless piece of technology created only to cause misery and hardship.

Mobile phones have now taken the communication concept to a whole new level. These I hate with a vengeance. People have forgotten how to walk down the street without tapping away at the screen or holding completely meaningless conversations with someone they probably don't even like. Mobile phones are to the new millennium what cigarettes were to the 1950's – blatant fashion accessories until the realisation sinks in as to how anti-social they are. They have their uses of course, but I fail to see how being accessible whilst sitting on the toilet can be considered a major improvement to modern day life.

It didn't take mobile phones to make undertakers any more obtainable than we already were when on call. We needed to be ready to leap into action as soon as the phone rang, whatever we might be doing. In the days before cell phones we carried pagers if we wanted to go out while on duty. But I for one gave up trying to do anything when on call because invariably it would be interrupted. I therefore resigned myself to a night in and hoped that any call outs would take place between the relatively sensible hours of five and eleven o'clock in the evening. Whole weekends on call could be horrendous if things got busy. But at least there were opportunities to catch up on lost sleep on Saturday and Sunday. The worst time to be on call were the weeknights and the one I will never forget as long as I live was the night of the horizontal rain.

Amazingly I had managed to get to sleep. And it was deep, blissful sleep too: rare for me but welcome nevertheless. A jangling noise sounded from somewhere and at first I didn't take a lot of notice – I was probably involved in some absurd incident in one of my frequently bizarre dreams – but the noise was persistent. Slowly I came to and fumbled for the alarm clock. This was unusual for me as well. Being a light sleeper I am usually wide-awake and clear headed within seconds of being roused. But that night I must have been exhausted. I couldn't believe it was morning already.

Despite several prods and pushes at the alarm clock, the damned thing wouldn't switch off. I sat up groggily in the dark and stared at the red numbers. Quarter to two. I'd better get up I suppose and start…

Quarter to two!

The telephone continued its impertinent clamour from the living room and having worked out it wasn't likely to stop until I did something about it, I half stepped, half fell out of bed and staggered blindly towards the wretched noise.

'Come on, come on. Where've you been?'

I just love stupid questions at quarter to two in the morning. 'Where most normal people are,' I muttered stroppily. 'Fast asleep in bed.'

Ceri snorted down the phone. 'You haven't got time for that. Coroner's removal, mate. Have you got your pen?' I could hear the glee in his abrasive Welsh voice.

I noted the details that he hollered down the phone and then he rang off, still chuckling to himself. I replaced the receiver and snarled in the dark. To be plucked from bed to attend a removal in the middle of the night is, as I have already stated, cruel to the point of barbaric. To be plucked from bed for the task by Ceri Williams was nothing short of sadistic.

Ceri was one of the loudest, most intimidating people I have ever met in my life. He could be extremely entertaining and witty when he wanted, but more often than not he enjoyed showing off and took things too far. He was something of the company bad boy and could have wallpapered an entire wall with the numerous written warnings he had received down the years. It was often a topic of conversation as to how he was actually still employed, so often did he stray from company procedure.

Colleagues like Ceri were now on telephone duties because of an intervention by Bilko, one of the last acts he performed before he too rode off into the sunset like his former sidekick, Doberman. He had never been happy that an old woman was still answering the telephones out of hours in this brand new corporate era of funeral directing. He had therefore consigned poor Connie to enforced retirement. Although the change was probably inevitable, it still meant an extra person was required to be on call each night. A new rota was worked out accordingly and senior members of staff such as Paul and Ceri were designated to phone duties. It all meant a bout of musical chairs for the rest of us as we moved around to fit in, but the end result meant we would all be doing slightly more on call than before, despite one of the female receptionists also agreeing to be included on phone duty.

Yawning loudly I stepped outside into the night and became even more depressed by the state of the weather. A torrential rainstorm was belting down from the blackness above and a wind whipped viciously in all directions, taking sheets of rain with it. My chin sank onto my chest at the near Arctic conditions until I finally counted to three and sprinted round to the garage at the back of the building. In just those few seconds I was drenched. A problem with the lock at the time meant the double doors could no longer be opened from inside.

I picked up Chris Littlehales at twenty past two and he looked exactly how I felt. By half past two we were at the residence and, thankfully, the front door of the house opened straight out onto the street. At least we didn't have far to walk. By another stroke of luck, at least as far as we were concerned, the death was fairly straightforward. Within a few minutes we had attended to the removal and the police were accompanying us to the Sandacre Hospital mortuary. It looked as though we might be back home by quarter to four. Maybe, just maybe, I might be able to grab a couple of hours sleep.

Hazel Judd, the mortuary technician on call met us at the mortuary door with an apologetic smile.

'Can you ring Ceri straight away?'

'Aw what? You are joking aren't you?'

'Sorry. It's another coroner's removal.'

I dialled Ceri's home phone number with a sense of blind desperation in my head. It was answered within one ring.

'Ha ha! It's not your night tonight, is it?'

His patronising sarcasm grated on my already frail state of mind but I was determined not to let him get under my skin. 'Another coroners' I believe,' I stated quietly.

'Yes, my friend. You're going to love this one...'

I suddenly saw a way out of speaking to him. 'I can get the details off Hazel,' I interrupted as the technician walked into her office. I raised my eyebrows enquiringly. 'I think the police have already given them to her.'

Hazel nodded and pointed at her writing pad on the desk.

'Oh right, okay then.' He sounded devastated. 'I'll get back to sleep in my nice cosy bed then. Is it still raining out there?'

'No it's just stopped,' I lied, hoping he couldn't hear the wind throwing the rain against the office window. 'I'll see you in the morning.'

I replaced the receiver and gritted my teeth. There had been no reason to ring him. He just wanted to gloat.

I was even less pleased when Hazel informed me that a body had been found by a member of the public somewhere near the docks and that was where we had to go. Chris and I just exchanged pained glances. This was grossly unreasonable. Once again I was convinced that someone somehow had staged all this in order to wind me up. I could picture some fiendish being in a gadget-laden laboratory with the as yet unknown technology to interfere with the lives of poor defenceless mortals like myself. The timing was too uncanny for it to be coincidence surely?

195

We unloaded the first removal and were then ready to leave. 'You can come with us if you want, Haze!' I joked, as Chris and I ventured back out into the pouring rain.

To my surprise, Hazel furrowed her brow and responded pensively. 'I could actually. It would be more exciting than sitting here waiting for you to come back.'

I looked up with an expression that questioned her sanity. In her shoes I would have no hesitation in putting my feet up on the desk and having a nap in the warm, dry office. I certainly wouldn't consider embarking upon an expedition into a vicious storm unless I had to. I was having enough problem motivating myself now when I had no choice. But the mortuary technician is a strange breed. They have to be a couple of wards short of a hospital to do such a grisly job. If anyone thinks undertaking is an odd profession, go and spend a few days working with the technicians at your local hospital mortuary. They are worth every penny they get.

Chris, Hazel, and I set off in our funeral ambulance for Westport docks. It was now almost half past three and there was no sign of a let up in the weather. In fact, it was probably getting worse: when it rains in South Wales it doesn't mess about. We had rough directions of where to go upon reaching the docks but it was a large area and as none of us were too familiar with the landscape, especially in the dark of night, it took a while to locate the exact spot. Even then access wasn't entirely straightforward. We could see a white police van across a raised section of waste ground but there didn't appear to be any direct way to access it. We eventually found a muddy track leading from the gravel road we were on that led towards a small dip. A total of three police vehicles were now visible in the stormy blackness. As we slowly approached the scene I was puzzled to see the police carrier suddenly start up and move away with undue haste. I caught a brief glimpse of a grinning face beneath a helmet as it sped past. I parked the ambulance beside the police photographer's Bedford van and we jumped out. Immediately the ferocious wind ripped powerfully at the doors and then all three of us as we struggled to retain our balance. This particular spot was extremely isolated and vulnerable to the elements, particularly in adverse weather like this.

Because the ground we were standing on was raised we found ourselves looking down a twenty-metre drop to the water's edge. It wasn't just any old drop either. It was thick with shrubbery and undergrowth and at first glance there didn't seem to be any easy way down to the tiny cove below, where three shadowy figures stood hunched over an even darker object on the ground.

I heard Chris swear as he stood alongside me. I felt like joining him. The difficulties we faced were obvious and it seemed the elements and circumstances were conspiring against us by the second.

One of the three detectives saw we had arrived and beckoned us down. I turned to Hazel.

'You'd better stay up here, Haze. It's pointless you getting all messed up.'

'Nah!' she grinned. 'It'll be a laugh!'

She was enjoying every minute of this while my body and spirit craved to be elsewhere. I looked at her and shrugged a smile. Hazel was a pretty girl, early twenties with pale skin and hair as black as the night in which we now stood. Few people would ever guess her choice of career just by looking at her.

Somehow we managed to clamber down through the scrub while carrying our equipment until we stood at the bottom on a small pebbly inlet alongside the men from CID. I was a touch surprised to see that my mate John wasn't in attendance. It was his lucky night. Usually we were sure to meet up in a situation like this. In fact, although I knew the photographer, the other two were completely new faces to me. Not that I was really taking much notice. My attention was being drawn to a far more ominous problem.

'This is him,' said one of the officers. 'Hope you're feeling strong.'

As I stared at the body lying prostrate on the pebbles below, his feet still submerged in the rippling water, I suddenly knew why the police carrier had sped away as we arrived. The deceased was huge, somewhere between eighteen and twenty stone in my estimation. Chris, never being one to hold back with what was on his mind, colourfully questioned how on earth we were going to get the body up the slope to our ambulance.

'We're going to need help on this one,' I conceded.

'We'll give you a hand,' said the officer. 'You got everything you want, Don?'

The photographer nodded. He was already collecting up his armoury of equipment – two steel cases, tripod, and a shoulder bag. He wouldn't be assisting with the lift at any rate, nor should he be expected to.

Hoisting the body onto the stretcher was an effort in itself. There was probably a good deal of water retention – the deceased had apparently been missing for the best part of a week, presumably most of it in the water. This would now increase the already colossal body weight. But the really difficult part was still to come.

Chris and I each took a corner of the stretcher at the head – always the heaviest end – and expected the two CID officers to take the feet. But only the smaller, silent one took a position. His taller, stronger looking colleague picked up two polythene exhibit bags and set off up the slope. Because Hazel was with us he clearly expected her to make up the team. Make no mistake about it, Hazel was a strong girl. I had seen her in action in the mortuary on countless occasions, pulling and lifting bodies of all shapes and sizes around the place. But this was different. I was about to say something when she stepped forward and took hold of the vacant corner.

'Come on then, let's go!' she enthused.

Now I *knew* she was insane.

We set off slowly, almost blindly, as the sheeting rain was now being whipped into our faces by huge gusts of mighty wind. We staggered and rolled up the slope, each one of us stumbling from time to time as we trampled through the sodden overgrowth. The weight of the stretcher was pulling my arms out of their sockets and I began to breathe in short agonising gasps. How Hazel was managing I had no idea. I could barely see her in front of me through the darkness, the rain, and the pain barrier.

All things considered, it wasn't the ideal time for my pager to go off. Unfortunately, or fortunately, whichever way you want to look at it, I had no spare breath with which to scream out my disbelief, but it acted as a spontaneous hint to take a breather. Gasping, I stared upwards into the blinding rain. I was just about all in but we were only two thirds of the way up the slope. As we all stood there panting I heard the voice of the plastic bag-carrying CID officer from the top of the ridge.

'Jiw, boys – look. Horizontal rain. The wind is blowing the rain straight across in a horizontal line.'

That was the moment I lost it. 'Look, mate!' I yelled angrily. 'Instead of poncing around up there with a couple of plastic bags, why don't you come down here and give us a flaming hand! We're funeral directors, not mountain bloody rescue!'

Normally there would probably have been a stunned and silent response. But the howling wind and driving (horizontal) rain completely ruined the effect. My outburst worked though. The officer abandoned his plastic bags and meekly descended back down the slope until he was in between Chris and me at the rear. Together we all lifted and although it was still a struggle of Himalayan proportions, his intervention made a huge difference. Finally we reached the top and seconds later we heaved the stretcher onto the back of the ambulance. The officer retrieved his precious bags and in a mood of tight-lipped silence returned to his car. I was convinced I saw a smile of smug satisfaction on his wheezing colleague's face.

As I stood leaning against the ambulance, my chest still heaving, I remembered my pager had gone off. At approaching half past four in the morning it could only mean one thing – another removal. But by now I really didn't care. I was resigning in the morning anyway. I'd had enough. The pittance of a wage we received just wasn't worth the hassle. Many of my friends only worked nine till five, five days a week – suffering barely half the stress and pressure – yet still earned more. It was ludicrous.

As we drove back to Sandacre Hospital I debated whether to ask Chris to ring Ceri. I wasn't sure I could cope with him again in my delicate state of mind. But on reflection Chris was probably even more likely to explode at any sarcasm our aggravating colleague cared to utter. By the time we pulled into the loading bay of the mortuary I'd cooled down considerably and, resigned to my fate, disappeared into the mortuary office once more and picked up the phone...

'Where the cowin' 'hell have you been?'

'On a coroner's removal, Ceri,' I replied wearily. 'The one you sent us on, remember?'

'I paged you ages ago.'

'Yes, you did. But unfortunately there are no phone boxes down by the docks.'

'I've been lying here trying to stay awake for the last half hour, waiting for you to call back.' He sounded quite fed up himself now. Although it had been a lousy night for Chris and myself, I suddenly realised this hadn't been much fun for Ceri either. Continually being woken from sleep was unpleasant at the best of times, let alone trying to stay awake.

'Sorry, Ceri,' I relented. 'There wasn't a lot we could do.'

'Yeah, I know, he replied, his voice softer. 'Anyway, you've got a removal at The Cedarwood nursing home. They'll give you all the details when you get there.'

'All right. We'll be on our way as soon as we've unloaded here.'

'Okay, mate. If anyone else rings now I'm going to tell them to bugger off until half past eight. You've done enough tonight.' There was a rare tone of magnanimity in his voice and as I put down the receiver I remembered that despite all the differences in personality and temperament that were a part of working life, we were all in this job together, night and day. Undertaking could be a tough ask for everyone at times. The nature of the job itself, the pressure and stress of continually trying to deliver one hundred per cent customer satisfaction in trying circumstances, the awful, often disturbing scenes we witnessed, the lack of understanding from clueless management, and exhausting nights like this – they all added up to a vocation that could test its workforce to the limit.

It was twenty past five when I knocked quietly on the big wooden door of The Cedarwood nursing home. The rain had abated but the wind, still savage and commanding, threatened to play cruel games with our weary bodies. Eventually the door opened and a gaping-mouthed matron stood staring at us for several seconds.

'Hello,' I began. 'We're here to carry out a removal for you.'

A semblance of recognition appeared in her elfin-like features and she invited us into the warm, silent building. It was only then that I appreciated just how dishevelled Chris and I both looked. Our shoes and trouser bottoms were muddy and sodden, our raincoats hung limply like wet towels, and Chris's hair was plastered to his head like a piece of damp carpet. Normally we wouldn't dream of attending any removal in such a sorry looking state but there was nothing we could do about it now.

'Looks like you've had a busy night, boys,' sang the lively little woman as she held open the door to a small, dimly lit room.

'Yes,' I sighed, 'it's certainly been one of the more interesting ones.'

It wasn't long before I was crawling up the stairs towards my flat to enjoy maybe a snippet of precious sleep. But something had been bothering me for the last couple of hours and it wasn't until I collapsed between the sheets that it suddenly occurred to me what it was.

Who on earth goes out walking in the middle of the night in teeming, horizontal rain and discovers a body in a location that is barely accessible?

33

I didn't resign in the morning of course. After grabbing an hours' sleep and turning up for work exactly on time, another torturous night on call was already being consigned to the memory banks. The fact I was now off call for a whole week aided my short memory. Over the years I grew to accept that probably the only positive aspect of being on call was the appreciation it generated of blissful, work-free evenings when the telephone did not dictate my life.

I regularly said I'd had enough and wanted to find a job that was less exacting. I always suffered these moments of crisis when things were getting on top of me – occasions that had now increased since becoming a funeral director. Rarely were such misgivings the result of the work itself. It was usually always the dreadfully high-pressured environment in which we were required to perform, especially working the long hours expected.

Working while tired, especially after a demanding night on call, was the worst aspect of the job. It is not a profession where you can bluff your way through the day or get away with providing a substandard service. Yet for all the downsides that came as a consequence of working for a large company, I loved my job. No matter what was thrown at me in the way of conditions, difficulties, or sheer bad management, I still returned continuously to the reason why I had chosen to become a funeral director: people. I wanted to help people. I wanted to be a small beacon of light at a dark and painful time and feel I was doing something useful with my life in the process. As I have stated before, I have never really been a confident person deep down. But funeral directing, despite its many peripheral problems, was something I knew I could do and hopefully do well. I felt that I had found my niche career-wise and I was reluctant to give up on it for whatever reason.

There is little doubt that the whole process of being on duty out of hours was intrusive as far as having a life was concerned. It was also the major cause of my low periods, probably brought on by sheer exhaustion. But somehow I always survived. Somehow I would endure ordeals like the night of the horizontal rain and always come bouncing back for more. I would tolerate being called out with little more than aggrieved reluctance. But one occasion got to me like no other could. It was the night I was just about to watch a rugby match involving my beloved New Zealand All Blacks...

My father and mother enjoyed a very rewarding and fruitful career in the theatre during the 1940's and early 1950's – Dad as a director, actor, producer, and author; Mum as an actress and costume designer. Repertory theatre rocked in those days, running hand in hand with the cinema as one of the main attractions for entertainment seekers. Sadly this amazing life took place long before mine began, but I grew up in a theatrical environment where those fondly remembered days of my parents were constantly referred to. The stories, the scrapbooks, the photographs, the plays that my father wrote – they have all been a familiar part of my life for as long as I can remember and I have always maintained the greatest admiration and respect for the achievements of my parents in their chosen profession.

During the early 1950's my father was at the pinnacle of his success. But then it all started to go wrong. Television was introduced and although it presented an incredible new concept in entertainment, it also caused a crisis in the world of live drama. People stopped going out to the theatre to watch the plays and productions that had once been so popular. Instead they chose to remain within their own four walls and watch this amazing phenomenon being beamed into their own homes.

Dad understandably resented this new development that had begun to dismantle his beloved world. Defiantly, he and my mother decided to take a gamble and emigrate to the other side of the world – to the rapidly developing country of New Zealand. It was a bold decision but they felt they had little to lose, especially in view of the fact that television would not reach this far corner of the earth for a few more years.

With a young daughter in tow they moved around New Zealand's North Island while Dad continued to work in the world of entertainment. He managed theatres for Kerridge Odeon in Auckland, Hamilton, and Whangarei; became a radio announcer in the east coast town of Napier; and still produced plays, including his own, in various theatres and venues along the way. Dad was able to prolong his career doing the things he loved best and it was a rewarding and worthwhile experience in a beautiful, still relatively unknown country. Then after seven years the time was right to return to the British Isles and retire from the theatre once and for all in order to concentrate on family life.

And they would have their work cut out too, returning with far more than they had arrived. At the beginning of 1963, Mum gave birth to a bouncing baby boy in the Auckland suburb of Howick, six months before the Eldwin family sailed away from the land of the long white cloud forever.

The shrill tone of the alarm clock sounded and I stared groggily at the dial.

3.20am.

I was up and dressed in a flash and with dawn still a couple of hours away I settled down in front of the television with all manner of snacks and drinks around me.

The tingle of anticipation began to reach fever pitch inside my excited body as the men in black ran out onto a sunny Eden Park pitch in Auckland, New Zealand. As they performed the Haka I felt that familiar shiver go down my spine and the hairs on the back of my neck stand upright with respect. The Haka always has that effect on me. There then followed that warm, fiery sensation in the pit of my stomach – a combination of pride, identity, and belonging. This was my team, my nation, my spiritual home. The All Blacks were kicking off. Just seconds to go now until eighty minutes of bliss watching the boys in black go about their business with their usual devastating efficiency. It wasn't just the winning – it was the taking apart.

The New Zealand number ten drew back his foot and the ball sailed high into the pale blue sky where it seemed to hang for an age until the All Black pack arrived to re-gather with an air of inevitability. 'Here we go!' I drooled out loud.

At first I didn't believe it when the phone rang. Then for a split second I tried to ignore it. But it was no use. With a face like an aggravated front row forward I picked up the receiver and snarled into the mouthpiece. Perhaps it was a joke. Everyone in work knew I'd be watching the All Blacks at this time.

It wasn't a joke.

I replaced the receiver in stunned disbelief. My mind flashed back to the seventies and the promotional blurb for the successful sci-fi film, *Alien*. A man with a voice like gravel hauntingly declared: *In space, no one can hear you scream*. No one can hear you scream in an isolated first floor flat in South Wales either so I let out a real spine chiller. I just couldn't believe it. I knew I should have swapped my Friday night on call. But it had been so quiet lately; no middle of the night calls for a couple of weeks. I was sure I'd get away with it. For the umpteenth time in my undertaking life I questioned whether this was all a deliberate set up. The timing was uncanny to the point of downright heartless. Surely there was a regulation somewhere that prohibited calling me out just as an All Black rugby test match kicked off?

The address scribbled angrily on the pad in front of me told me there was no such law. I stormed round the house getting ready to leave and abandon my visual link up with the Southern Hemisphere. Before I left I pressed the record button on my video recorder with unnecessary vigour. Many often questioned why I didn't do this in the first place – I could then watch the match at a more agreeable hour. Such profane suggestions usually came from the mouths of women, a species who just don't understand the essential things in life. If ever the chance arises to watch a sporting event live as opposed to a recording a few hours later, it is no contest in the decision stakes. Live wins every time. I can't explain it – that's just the way it is.

Confirming my suspicions of supernatural interference, the removal that night took just over an hour and twenty minutes – the exact length of a rugby match. I had been like a man with the world on my shoulders throughout, much to the amusement of my colleague, whose knowledge and interest in sport would struggle to cover the head of a coffin screw. It somehow made the whole thing harder for me to stomach. The heathen failed to see the significance of missing a "stupid game of rugby."

From that day – or night – on, I never risked missing a New Zealand rugby test match again. If my on call clashed with an All

Black fixture there was only ever one outcome – I swapped my on call quicker than a Jonah Lomu burst down the left wing.

It may surprise some people that I would support New Zealand at all. I was brought up in England after spending only six months in the land of my birth, certainly not long enough to form any opinions or decide allegiances. But as I grew up I realised that six weeks would have been enough: the fact I was born in New Zealand was the important issue. Maybe it was a case of the distance, the fact I had drawn my first breath in a country so far away. Maybe it was because I was always unique at school when places of birth were discussed. But as time went on I became fiercely proud of my 'Kiwi heritage' and my support of the All Blacks reflected that.

And living in Wales, it was often a relief to be able to claim New Zealand citizenship. It meant I could escape the worst of the tedious Welsh hostility towards the English. Whenever the comments and the abuse began I would immediately declare, in an unmistakably English accent, my allegiance to the silver fern. Even New Zealanders occasionally suffered at the hands of the Welsh though – just ask any of the All Blacks who toured the principality in 1989 – but generally it got me off the hook.

My claim of New Zealand loyalty was genuine of course, but I hadn't spent just over twenty years growing up in England without feeling something for the place. I support every other English sporting team with a passion and the anti-English rants in Wales did strike a raw nerve on more than one occasion. At times the sheer venom of these tirades left me feeling bewildered and saddened. The Welsh have so much more to offer the world than this hatred with which they are readily associated. If only they would just bury the distant past. But although I was rightly generally considered English, once my Welsh colleagues and associates got to know me and realise I wasn't actually one of the Englishmen who personally invaded Wales five hundred years ago or whenever it was, I was pretty much accepted for who I was.

No amount of bigotry, however, could compare with being called out at such an inopportune moment. In my life I have suffered my fair share of bad times – broken relationships, unexpectedly expensive car repairs, and disappointments such as the realisation that Abba were no longer going to record together. But for me, missing a New Zealand rugby test is just about as bad as it gets.

I will never forget Christmas time when I was a child in Brixham. Admittedly a great deal of this was influenced by the anticipation of a big toy haul each year. But the sheer magic of the occasion itself was unforgettable too and these overall memories have outlasted the content of any Christmas stocking by a long way.

My mother and father must take much of the credit for the fond memories I now have of Christmas throughout the seventies. They made it fun. They made it special. They made each Christmas unique to our family. My favourite recollection is of the occasions when Dad would number every single gift laid out under the Christmas tree. We would then draw numbers out of a hat and the numbered present corresponding with the number drawn would be opened by its recipient in front of everyone before drawing the next number. This process meant that opening our presents often took up a couple of hours. But it was so much more fun and civilized than everyone ripping into parcels in just a few minutes and barely appreciating any of them, let alone remembering later who they were from.

After the presents it would of course be time for Christmas dinner. I always looked forward to this part of the day, not least for the food we rarely seemed to have at any other time of the year. Prawn cocktails, chestnut stuffing, bread sauce, sprouts – without which no Christmas dinner in the world would be complete – and all those little 'extras' that could be found in cupboards and on side tables throughout the house. The whole atmosphere of Christmas was one of sheer captivation for me – the carols, the sociability, the twinkling coloured lights across streets and in shop windows on cold, dark, evenings. Then when I was a little older and more perceptive the real meaning of the celebrations became an important addition. Together they all added up to create a setting of beauty and charm unparalleled by any other time of year. Unfortunately, as we grow up and head for adulthood we also forsake the joyous, simple pleasures of being young. Maturity can demand a high price at times. We rarely appreciate the innocence of our former years until we have more complex problems and issues with which to compare them. By then it is too late.

And so it was with Christmas for me. Without really knowing it was happening, Christmas no longer held me in its charm as I progressed through the late teenage years. It never would again. Having children of your own does rekindle some of the magic, but that pure, unexplainable excitement has gone forever. I also feel that the relentless juggernaut of commercialism in recent times has done much to kill the real spirit of Christmas. The true meaning, thankfully, is still there, but it lies hidden behind shelves overloaded with materialism, alcohol, and expensive toys.

Something I always vividly remember thinking about at Christmas as a child was the plight of those people who had to work on Christmas Day. At the time I couldn't think of anything worse: it seemed so unfair. But little did I know I was destined to become one of those unfortunate people myself in my own working life. If I'd had the least inkling as a child that this would be my fate I would have been horrified to the point of disbelief.

Despite the waning excitement in the festive season over the years, the sorry fact that I found myself in a job which necessitated working most Christmases never instilled great enthusiasm in me. I, along with many of my colleagues, would often watch jealously as everyone else seemed to finish on Christmas Eve ready to enjoy the celebrations uninterrupted, while we braced ourselves for one of our busiest times of the year. It was for this reason that I rarely enjoyed the arrival of Christmas. Even on the few occasions I managed to avoid being on call over the holiday period, I always dreaded the return to work afterwards. Unfortunately death is no respecter of holidays and people continue to die on a daily, and nightly, basis. To put it bluntly, extended periods of public holiday – especially when combined with a weekend – meant that the workload piled up (not literally I hasten to add!). We then had to work like crazy to get things back on an even keel. Because December and January are traditionally the most hectic months for an undertaker, this would usually take several weeks.

And so Christmas often used to pass me by with barely a whimper. I didn't lose too much sleep over the fact, but occasionally I would get fed up, particularly on one Christmas morning when I was just preparing to open gifts with my family. The telephone rang out in its usual rude and insensitive way. Paul's cheery Christmas greetings were followed by the news of a nursing home removal. I was on duty with Duncan Forster, an amiable man in his mid-fifties with close-cropped grey hair and a thin, well-used face. He had recently come to us seeking something quiet and uncomplicated to see him through to retirement. He was another under the disillusioned impression that undertaking was undemanding. He seemed to be enjoying his newfound status however and was totally unfazed at being called out on Christmas morning. No doubt he had his eyes on the overtime.

Duncan quickly became known for his rather frugal nature and obtaining money from him for anything was like trying to procure a claim from an insurance company. One of his many money-saving scams was to stuff a small bottle of whisky down his sock at our annual Christmas bash to save paying the extortionate prices at the bar. He often ordered a new suit from his wife's catalogue for the party too, but would usually return it the following week, as long as nothing untoward had happened to it during the festivities. Although I am always careful with money myself, Duncan took miserliness to a new level. Rumour has it that the Welsh Valleys were formed because he once dropped a fifty pence piece down a rabbit hole.

Nursing homes are not the worst places to visit on Christmas Day, even for a removal. I picked Duncan up from his house and we even found room for a few laughs and a joke or two along the way. Such joviality was no doubt induced by the knowledge that this call out would more than likely be a quick one, as nursing home removals were inclined to be. But an additional reason was that the chance of being offered some tasty Christmas fare was pretty high too. We were both enthusiastic members of the 'Free Food Wherever You Can Get It' club.

Fifty per cent of our optimism was justified. A plate of mince pies and some slices of Christmas cake were duly pushed our way by two jolly, high-spirited nurses. But the removal was far from trouble-free. The death itself was not necessarily a sad one as such. There was no immediate family and the old lady had been quite ill for some time. It was this news, especially when we were told she had taken a serious turn for the worse a couple of days before, which was about to exasperate me.

I had a bad feeling as we climbed ominously up the narrow staircase all the way to the second floor. My fears were realised when we entered the room and discovered a huge woman, with rolls of fat the length and breadth of her body, slumped awkwardly on an upright chair. My good nature swept out of me like water down a plughole, while by my side Duncan was impersonating a goldfish. Sheer professionalism prevented me from revealing my innermost thoughts but it was a close call. I felt like saying to the matron that If she was so ill and death clearly so inevitable, why on earth hadn't they transferred her to a room on the ground floor? They had the means – a stair lift with harnesses which could so easily have been utilised while she was alive. In death it was of little use to us, as was the tiny, upright lift. Now we would have to negotiate two very challenging staircases with a large and heavy body on a stretcher.

Most undertakers will identify with me when I say that many nursing homes are not purpose-built. Often they are large converted houses or guesthouses, where extra, profitable bed space takes precedence over reasonable access. This was one such home and to this day I have no idea how we brought that lady down from the second floor. There is little dignity in death and even if there is, it rapidly evaporates in these kinds of situation. Ultimately the body has to be moved somehow: there is no way of avoiding the fact. In most cases this is carried out with the minimum of fuss, but occasionally the removal has to be executed in the best way possible to avoid injury or accident.

In my time I attended numerous courses that dealt with different lifting techniques. But all the examples we were shown took place in nice spacious rooms with perfect conditions. In reality it is nothing like that and I found little on these courses to aid me in the workplace. In fact, when we became bored with the blusterings of the tutor or health and safety officer instructing us, we would start asking withering questions which we knew could not be answered. These included how to lift a body out of a bathtub, how to safely move someone who had died while sitting on the toilet (a regular place of death unfortunately), or how to manoeuvre an extremely weighty body out of a tight space or down a narrow, winding staircase. Such loaded enquiries were either met with nonsensical drivel or stony-faced silence, the latter usually giving way to an eventual sheepish grin which was a crystal clear giveaway that the bearer had been rumbled. The best suggestion any of them could come up with was to send for help when faced with difficulties and get as many people to the scene as possible. But this was as futile as it was useless. I could have summoned the entire population of Manchester to the nursing home where Duncan and I had just struggled to the point of exhaustion. But their only involvement would have been to stand by and cheer us on. Only two people can negotiate a stretcher down a narrow staircase: there is no room for anyone else to assist.

By the time Duncan and I had unloaded the body at our chapel of rest some forty-five minutes later, we were both staggering around like drunken men. My arms and legs were like jelly and I felt physically sick. Poor old Duncan, almost thirty years my senior, was in an even worse state. When I finally got home again at a fraction after eleven o'clock, all I could do was sit quietly and wait for my protesting body to recover while the festivities carried on around me.

It seemed almost criminally unfair that barely ninety minutes later I was on my way out again, summoned not only by Paul, but also those unseen forces that only operated when I was on call. As I changed once again, the glorious aroma of roasting turkey and chestnut stuffing floated teasingly under my nose, reminding me even more of the cruel and inhibiting career I had chosen. I walked dejectedly to the car and drove away, knowing that when I returned I would be eating my Christmas dinner alone from a plate kept warm in the oven...if I was lucky. The way things were going there would be another call out straight after this one. I could probably kiss Christmas goodbye for yet another year.

As I picked Duncan up once more my mood had sunk to a level of sheer misery. This was a crazy, stupid job. What on earth had I been thinking when I decided to try my luck in the funeral profession? The fact that Duncan was counting up his overtime as we drove along didn't help. At least if I'd stayed as a driver there would have been the consolation of a healthy looking wallet come next pay day.

The dashboard clock read twenty past one as we pulled up outside a pretty looking detached bungalow on the outskirts of Westport. I didn't really notice any great detail though. I was too busy wallowing in self-pity, knowing that about ninety-five per cent of the population were, at this very moment, tucking into their delicious Christmas dinners, completely uninterested in the few like myself who were working like it was any normal day. I told Duncan to wait in the car while I went and spoke to the family. I said I would be as quick as possible: after all, there was little I could do on Christmas Day in the way of arranging a funeral.

A tImorous, middle-aged woman with dark wavy hair greeted me at the door. She clutched a handkerchief in her hand and seemed to be in a mild state of shock. She offered a thin but appealing smile and invited me into a beautifully clean and welcoming hallway. The shades on the walls were soft pastel colours, interrupted by a small number of tasteful watercolours and a family portrait.

'My Dad is in the bedroom there,' she pointed as we passed a room with the door half open. I glanced in and saw a still, silent figure in the dim light lying peacefully in bed. 'That's how we found him this morning. It was so unexpected. He... wasn't even ill. We haven't... moved him. Will you see to it all...?' She broke off as the tears trickled down her drawn cheeks.

'Yes of course,' I replied, strangely at a loss as to know what else to say.

'The rest of the family are in here,' she continued. We'd really appreciate your guidance on a few matters. If it's not too much trouble.' She guided me into a spacious and elegant living room where a handful of adults and two teenage children were gathered silently among the golds and the creams of the furnishings. The mournful hush was deafening and the atmosphere a mixture of bewilderment, distress, and unfinished business. The two teenagers, clearly brother and sister, sat huddled together on one of two settees, holding hands and staring into empty space. Only the girl acknowledged me briefly before returning to her state of disbelief. One of the men managed to string a greeting together; the others merely acknowledged me with distracted nods. And still the silence hung heavily in the air.

212

As I gently responded to the family's handful of questions my eyes were continually drawn to a beautiful silver Christmas tree to my left, tall and majestic with its array of decorations and trimmings. Beneath lay a pile of unopened gifts and presents, clearly untouched since the moment they had been placed there. At times the whole scene distracted me and I struggled for the right words while passing on the advice they sought. Not that they noticed. I could have said almost anything to this engaging, soft-mannered family and they would have accepted it. Their uncertainties, borne simply from the inexperience of death and its procedures, were elementary matters for me to explain and I could see the concern lifting from their faces as I spoke.

I had taken the details I needed and with there being little more to discuss at that stage, I excused myself from the room in order to proceed with the removal. But instead of going straight outside to call Duncan in with the stretcher, I stepped quietly into the bedroom and closed the door. I looked down at the gentleman lying in his bed and began to chastise myself for being so selfish. In the other room sat a family whose Christmas had been devastated by the death of someone they clearly adored. They had awoken with the joyous expectation of a family Christmas together, not anticipating for one minute that their whole day was about to be turned upside down. And me? I was moaning because I would be an hour late for my Christmas dinner. The comparison was an uncomfortable one.

When I returned to that sombre living room some ten minutes later to say goodbye, I knew the family had warmed to me. They bid me farewell with handshakes and grateful smiles.

'Thank you so much for coming, Mr Eldwin,' said the daughter. 'You have been wonderful; so very helpful. And we're really sorry to have ruined your Christmas Day.'

'Please call me Tom,' I replied. And you haven't ruined it at all. That's what we're here for. I'm just glad I've been able to be of some help to you.'

And I meant every single word.

34

Although it would be slightly misleading to label late twentieth century Westport a multi-cultural society, there were small pockets of various ethnic communities dotted around the town. As undertakers we dealt with a good many of these and we actually became the official undertaker of choice for the town's Jewish population.

I loved dealing with the Jews. They were a polite, friendly group of people, especially Joseph Mills. Joseph – he insisted I call him this and not Mr Mills – was the member of the local Jewish community responsible for organising their funerals. In simple terms he was a linkman between funeral director and family. Not long after my promotion to funeral director I happened to be involved in a couple of Jewish funerals and from that time on I was given the task of looking after them on a permanent basis. From start to finish it was a pleasure to deal with Joseph. He was a short, orderly man in his early fifties with kind, twinkling eyes and a perennial smile on his rubicund face. Most of his fellow Jews owned several prominent shops and businesses in Westport, but Joseph was quite content earning his keep as a salesman in a local car dealership.

If Joseph had a gloomy side I never saw it. He was always amiable and grateful for what we did. He also never failed to gently press a five-pound note into the hand of anyone who had assisted on the funeral in any way. But quite frankly, we never really did that much. We would provide a hearse and whatever limousines were required; and a coffin, always plain with rope handles, as was the Jewish custom. We would also make arrangements to facilitate the Taharah (the washing of the dead) at our chapel of rest, usually on the first evening following the death. Apart from this we did very little. The Jews undertook virtually everything themselves. They dealt with the funeral arrangements, prepared the body at the Taharah, and acted as bearers and grave fillers at the small Jewish burial section in Cwmfach Cemetery.

The system of having a mediator between the funeral director and the mourners was actually a very good one, although from my point of view it meant very little contact with the family themselves. This enabled me to build up a rapport with Joseph Mills however, and I thoroughly enjoyed the working relationship that evolved as a result. The only difficulty that arose for us as a company was when Joseph first made contact to notify us our services were required. Under Jewish law the body must be laid to rest, if possible, within twenty-four hours of death. In the UK, Jews, along with other religions who embrace a similar doctrine, are allowed to carry out the burial of their dead within this timescale. Normally the paperwork takes longer to process, although burials generally do not present the delays more often associated with cremation. Such short notice could create havoc with our fleeting arrangements; nevertheless we always managed to provide what was required in the way of staff and vehicles, even if it caused mayhem behind the scenes at times.

I was fascinated with the whole process and content of the Jewish funeral. Everything about them was steeped in tradition – practices that had survived thousands of years. I always felt very aware of such time-honoured customs at these funerals and the atmosphere they created. This was never more in evidence that when I listened to the rabbi half sing, half chant parts of the service by the graveside in ancient Hebrew. In the middle of a modern twentieth century town, with all the sounds and the hustle and bustle that life now brings, the contrast was almost breathtaking.

There was a synagogue in Westport, a low, flat, unpretentious building with the Star of David incorporated into the brickwork above the door. The cortege would always pause quietly outside for a few reflective moments on the way to the cemetery. The Jews also owned a small chapel in the grounds of Cwmfach Cemetery where they would hold services prior to the burial. In later years, however, they sold the chapel and just performed a shortened service at the graveside. In many ways this was symptomatic of the Jewish community in Westport. By Joseph Mills's own admission the Jewish population in the area was, literally, dying out. This was almost visibly noticeable over time as the funerals became less frequent and the numbers attending them dwindled.

Not long before Mark Grainger moved on to pastures new he carried out a Russian Orthodox funeral, the first such funeral anyone in our company had ever dealt with. It was an interesting experience, possibly because no one had any idea what shape or form the funeral itself would take.

Because there was no Russian Orthodox minister in the area, Mark had to arrange for one to travel down from Bristol on the day of the funeral to take the service. He met us at the cemetery, a tall, bearded man, imposing in his ministerial robes and headgear, who spoke no English. The service was held by the graveside in front of a handful of people. I had volunteered to drive Mark's hearse that day, mostly out of curiosity. With hindsight, I would have happily remained back at the office and relied on someone telling me all about it.

With the coffin resting on the trolley at the back of the hearse, my colleagues and I took hold of the webs and threaded them through the handles of the coffin and underneath – these are the long cloth tapes undertakers use to lower a coffin into the grave. We also used them to carry the coffin across the grass to the grave and this we did today as usual. Normally we would lower the coffin as soon as we were standing on the planks. Only for a Catholic funeral would we wait a few seconds while the priest blessed the grave. Because of his inability to communicate with the minister (very few British funeral directors are fluent in Russian as far as I am aware!), Mark had not been able to establish exactly what we were to do at this point.

We stepped onto the planks and paused, waiting for this large man to give us some indication of what he wanted us to do, but his face bore a remote, impassive expression. After what seemed an age of inactivity we decided to proceed with lowering the coffin into the grave. This jerked the minister into action and with a stern shake of his head he raised his hand slowly and commandingly into the air. We froze in our tracks and waited once again. And waited. And waited some more. The minister seemed to have disappeared into a completely different zone to that of everyone else. Then suddenly he launched into a tangle of complicated Russian words, his voice booming like a rampant thunderstorm. Standing next to him, as was my misfortune, surely broke every health and safety regulation on noise emission that has ever been written.

After five minutes my arms began to ache. The deceased was reasonably lightweight but as we held the coffin there in mid air, it became heavier to us by the minute. The glances exchanged between us told me I wasn't the only one struggling. We continually stared at Mark, our expressions urging him to do something. But I could tell he was in trouble. Like the rest of us he had no idea which part of the service we had reached, nor when the coffin could be lowered.

Another couple of minutes passed and I began to fear the long-term effect on my shoulder joints. I had reached the stage where I couldn't care less when the right time to lower a coffin at a Russian Orthodox funeral was: if something didn't happen soon it would be descending at a rate of knots, possibly with my aching arms still attached. Unfortunately, Mark was one of life's perfectionists who continually desired to get things exactly right. Most of the time I am too, but not when something akin to a fourteenth century torture technique is in progress.

Finally, blissfully, Mark looked at us. His face was a mixture of desperation and embarrassment. Goodness only knows what our expressions must have looked like but he was clearly prompted into assertiveness by what he saw. The minister had been in full flow for a while now and nothing short of a nuclear explosion was going to stop him. Mark motioned for us to lay the coffin down at an angle across the planks. This we did and the small congregation of mourners would surely have heard our sighs of relief had it not been for the thundering, chanting voice of Rasputin to my right.

Forty-five minutes later the service finally drew to a close. We lowered the coffin almost anti-climatically into the grave and muttered private gratitude at Mark's inspired intervention. We just wished he'd done it a bit sooner.

Although this was the sole Russian Orthodox funeral our company had ever been involved with, we handled a number of funerals for other eastern European minorities established in the

Westport area during my time. These included the Latvians, who had a small community spread across the east side of the town.

The Latvian funeral that will always stick in my mind was the one where the funeral director took photographs at the request of the family. He used up a whole roll of film photographing the deceased in his coffin at the chapel of rest, the floral tributes, the mourners, and finally the coffin resting in the grave. These photographs were then sent to his family in Riga, none of whom he had seen since immigrating to Wales in the early sixties to try and earn desperately needed money to send back home. Financial hardship and political complications prevented them from ever visiting each other and the tragedy of this man's life stayed with me for several weeks following his funeral.

And so from time to time we carried out a funeral for someone who belonged to a culture or religion that, to us, was a step outside of our usual square. They always added a little extra colour and intrigue to the working day. And very occasionally complete mayhem.

Whether the members of Westport's Chinese community lived exceptionally long lives or they just went to another funeral director or not I have no idea. But they were certainly a rarity. Then suddenly, for no apparent reason, we had a run of three in a short space of time. And because Andy Morris – who had now also been promoted to the position of funeral director – happened to deal with the first, he was immediately designated our resident Chinese undertaker. Andy handled all three with his usual casual competence and clearly made a lasting impression, for his name was bandied about with great respect throughout the Chinese community thereafter.

Following the professional success of the first two funerals, Andy was oozing confidence when the Wu family turned up at the Dean Street office late one afternoon asking for Andy personally (*It has to be Andy, he very good*). It was a very commendable accomplishment to have built up such a strong trust in a relatively short space of time. But following Chinese funeral number three, I got the distinct impression that my usually unflappable colleague wished he had not gained quite such a meritorious reputation.

To be honest, the Wu family were completely crazy. But it was a nice crazy, at least to those of us who watched with amusement as Andy desperately tried to hold everything together. They meant no harm – in fact they loved him to bits – but with their many visits, phone calls, and hustle and bustle, they became the only people I'd ever known to drive mild-mannered Andy to the brink of destruction. It was a tribute to his temperament that he didn't topple over the edge.

It all reached a peak with the Wu family's confusion over the set up of our company. I, for one, did not blame them for this at all. By now we were fronting fifteen different funeral directors within a thirty-mile radius and on occasions it was hard enough even for us to remember who we were working for at any given time so we could hardly expect Joe Public to understand the intricacies of takeovers and retaining old company names. It was also confusing when the names of the original undertakers displayed proudly above the shop fronts had long since passed on. For example, our Stapleton Road office (where I lived) was known as DB Evans, but the last in a steady line of funeral directing Evans's had been dead now for nearly thirty years. Our branch in Millfield went under the long established name of T Griffith Morgan, but to our knowledge the one and only Mr Morgan had gone the way of his many clients more than sixty years ago. Then there was BJ Thomas & Son of Dean Street, the office at the heart of our vast emporium. Three generations of the Thomas family had proudly taken care of the local dead for decades, but Bryn Thomas, great-grandson and last in the well known Thomas funeral directing clan, had been twiddling his thumbs in the funeral-free sky on high for well over twenty-five years. And it was BJ Thomas & Son who now provided the Wu family with the source of their perplexity.

One morning Paul entered the Dean Street office with a huge grin on his face. He didn't say a word for several minutes but it was clear something had greatly amused him. For some reason Paul always arrived at work in a state of half dress. The only funeral attire he wore was an open-necked white shirt with his black tie draped casually round his neck. The remainder of his clothing usually consisted of tracksuit bottoms and trainers. There were a few theories bandied about as to why he chose to arrive like this, even when he was the manager. The most plausible was that being the bearer of a well-earned reputation for exhibitionism, he quite enjoyed going through the routine of getting changed in front of those who were unlucky enough to be in the vicinity. All the funeral directors kept their morning suits, overcoats, raincoats, etc in a large wardrobe in the back office. Paul took up most of the space in this and his section resembled a miniature menswear department, complete with an array of after-shaves, deodorants, and shampoos stacked high and wide across the upper shelf. He was one of the most immaculately presented men I have ever met. Anyway, while Paul was adorning himself on this particular morning, someone eventually asked him the reason for his unwavering smile. After a few seconds he finally spoke.

'I had the Wu family on the phone again last night.'

Andy sat bolt upright in his chair, a pale shade of horror on his face. 'Aw come on, you're joking,' he groaned.

'Fraid not. They asked for you straight away.'

Andy rubbed an anxious hand across his forehead. 'What do they want now?' There was desperation in his voice.

We all felt for Andy in an entertaining sort of way. The Wu's had not left him alone since their first meeting and there were still two days to go until the funeral.

'I didn't ask to be honest,' said Paul, tucking his shirt into his trousers. 'I told them you were off duty last night but would give them a ring sometime this morning.'

'Cheers, Paul,' replied Andy gratefully.

There was a brief silence until Paul spoke again. 'They really like you, don't they?'

'Uh?'

'The Wu's. You've got a real fan club there.'

'Don't be dull.'

'I'm serious,' said Paul. 'You should've heard them last night.'

Andy was now looking at our manager with an expression that combined both anxiety and suspicion.

Paul continued. 'When Mr Wu rang last night he asked to speak to Mr Thomas. I said we don't actually have a Mr Thomas working for us. "Yes, yes, Mr Thomas the owner," he insisted. So I told him that unfortunately, Mr Thomas was dead. Well, he almost exploded with grief. (Now Paul assumed the voice of a very emotional Mr Wu.) "Aw no. Andy is dead? But we speak only to him this morning. Aw no! This is so bad. What has happened to our Andy?"

By now we were all in hysterics, except of course for Andy, whose hand covered his weary face.

'Make no mistake about it,' Paul continued. 'You're an honorary son of the Wu family.'

And he remained so right through to the funeral. In the eyes of his adopted family Andy could do no wrong, although this was hardly surprising considering his recent rise from the dead. It was almost as though roles had been reversed, for the Wu's now seemed to be far more concerned about pleasing 'their Andy' than vice versa. This Utopian relationship was tested to the limit, however, when the Wu's almost set fire to the chapel of rest on the day of the funeral. Only Andy could have got away with rebuking them the following day and still emerge as their hero.

At many Chinese funerals it is customary for the family to burn clothing and other personal items that belonged to the deceased. As it appeared we may need to be prepared to cater for Chinese funerals in the future, we invested in a metallic dustbin which the Wu family told Andy would be perfect for this purpose. The bin was placed just outside the sliding door of the chapel of rest and, as with the Jews, we basically allowed them to carry on with their practices and customs. I happened to be based at the chapel of rest that day and I was pleased – it was always interesting to witness something new. It was also enjoyable to smell the rich, scented aroma of joss sticks that had been lit around the coffin.

It was possibly because of the joss sticks that I failed to notice the slightly harder scent of singeing wood and burning carpet. I didn't even notice it until the cortege was on its way to the cemetery. I went into the chapel area to tidy up when I saw the dark scorch marks on both the altar table and the deep red carpet beneath my feet. I was a little dumbstruck at first and didn't quite know what to do. The table was easy enough – we usually covered it with a tablecloth anyway – but the carpet was a different matter. Thankfully this was replaced a couple of years later during one of the company's rare refurbishment drives.

I picked up the still warm, smouldering dustbin and carefully carried it out to the back of the building. I smiled. The Wu funeral had provided many highlights over the past few days, but it was this humble, silver dustbin that would provide me with my favourite.

While the Wu funeral was taking place, Andy had wandered around the outside of the building to where the dustbin was situated on the pavement. With the sliding doors that led into the chapel area open, the members of the family were drifting back and forth as they carried out their rituals. It was here that the damage to the altar and carpet had occurred and with hindsight, I figured it had certainly been a sensible decision not to allow the bin to be placed alongside the coffin in the chapel itself, as had been requested by the excitable Wu's the day before: the damage could have reached epic proportions. But by this stage Andy could have probably talked the Wu's into having an all-night disco complete with a Bee Gees tribute band instead of a funeral so they readily agreed to his compromise, thinking it was a marvellous idea.

Even though we had never embraced anything like this before, Andy was not unduly worried by the thought of a bonfire outside the chapel of rest. However, he strolled around outside on the day just to make sure everything was under control while the rest of us remained in the small office chatting quietly. A few minutes later I heard the sound of running feet and a woman emerged into view from around the corner. Her hand was clasped to her mouth and what remained visible of her face was a healthy shade of red. I only caught a glimpse of her eyes as she shot past the window but there was an expression of deep horror in them. My first inkling was that she had been walking past the sliding doors and had casually glanced inside, catching a glimpse somehow of the late Mr Wu in his open coffin. Maybe all this dustbin business in a residential area had not been such a good idea after all.

Andy sauntered into the office a few seconds later with his usual *sang-froid*, a huge grin on his tanned, fine-looking face. 'You didn't just happen to see a woman sprinting past the window did you?' he asked matter-of-factly.

'Yes, I did,' I nodded. 'What was all that about?'

'Well, I was standing beside the smoking dustbin with Mr Wu's two sons when she came walking down the hill and said,

"Ooh, I'll have two pieces of toast and a cup of coffee, please," as she walked past.

I nearly fell off my chair. 'What did you say to her?'

'Oh nothing much. I just told her that this was a funeral service and could she show a little more respect. I think she was a bit embarrassed.'

35

As I stood at the back of the crematorium chapel, I watched the Gerston family with a smile as they bade their mother farewell. The funeral of Camilla Edith Gerston was probably the most unconventional I had ever arranged, yet arguably it was one of the most engaging.

Just as we were expected to deal with all manner of religions and beliefs when arranging funerals, we also needed to accommodate those with no belief at all. Funerals can so often be the scene of mild hypocrisy. I have never ceased to be amazed by the number of people who claim to have little or no belief whatsoever in God, yet turn with great haste to a minister of religion when a christening, marriage, or funeral is pending.

Surprisingly to some, in view of my own faith, I had the utmost respect for atheists who stuck to their non-beliefs right to the end. "We'd better have a minister otherwise everyone will think it odd," was a phrase I often heard when arranging a funeral. It was a trap many supposed religious sceptics succumbed to and I occasionally wondered just how firm their principles were when it came to the crunch. These days, atheist and non-religious funeral ceremonies are far more commonplace, but in eighties and nineties Westport there were only a handful of funerals where a minister of religion wasn't involved.

One family who had no intention of forsaking their way of thinking, however, were the Gerstons and I really admired them for it. Neither the son or daughter of the deceased had any belief in God and they wanted a funeral for their mother, also an atheist, without any religious involvement whatsoever. I suggested maybe one of them, or a friend of the family, could stand and say a few words in the absence of a minister. I told the Gerstons to think along those lines and let me know when they had decided.

It wasn't until the morning of the funeral that I finally gleaned from daughter, Rosie what shape the funeral would take. She rang just as I had decided I probably wasn't going to find out until I arrived at the crematorium. I was grateful for the warning though because it gave me time to get my head around the idea they had come up with and find out if it was allowed.

'Tom,' said the gravelly Welsh voice, 'we've decided not to have anyone speak at the funeral. What we thought we'd do was take a few bottles of wine and some glasses to the crematorium and just toast Mam farewell.'

My speechless response prompted Rosie to check I was still on the line.

'Do you think that will be okay?

'I... er... yeah... I think so.' To be honest I wasn't entirely sure. I knew that the drinking of alcohol was prohibited in and around the crematorium but I figured something like this might be okay. 'It... will be just a few bottles, won't it? Nothing else?'

Rosie cackled. 'Oh no, we won't be getting plastered. Don't worry!'

I laughed. 'I will just need to check with the crematorium but I can't see there being a problem.'

And there wasn't. Daryl Jenkins, the crematorium superintendent, was, like myself, a trifle wary at first, but once I assured him the funeral wouldn't turn into some sort of lager frenzy he was fine. Of course, I was relying heavily on the Gerstons not to let me down here, but as Daryl joined me quietly at the back of the chapel, we witnessed one of the more unusual send-offs in Westport funeral history.

Mrs Gerston's son, thin and with long dark hair, handed out a glass to each of the mourners, an offbeat collection of characters numbering about twenty. Then together with his sister they casually strolled amongst them, pouring a measure into each glass from four dark-coloured bottles. Finally, he stood facing the small gathering, raised his glass towards the coffin and simply said: 'Cheers, Mum.' And that was it.

Daryl and I walked down the aisle soon after and he waited to open the doors while I stepped up to the vacant lectern. I pressed the button below the microphone and the coffin descended slowly out of view. I can still see the image now. The coffin was bedecked not with a spray of flowers but by a huge basket of apples, pears, oranges, bananas, kiwifruit, plums, and grapes. To someone conditioned to only seeing wreaths sitting on top of the coffin it was an amazingly surreal sight.

'Mam liked to see flowers growing in the garden, not dying in a vase,' Rosie told me afterwards. 'But she loved fruit of all kinds. It just seems to be more in keeping with her character to say it with fruit.' I could find no reason to disagree. And despite the rather eccentric nature of the whole funeral, the lack of religious input, and to me, the carefree, almost blasé farewell, there was something refreshingly appealing about Mam Gerston's simple, uncomplicated, and principled send-off.

I would not have been unduly concerned had funeral tradition been turned on its head and all floral tributes became of the fruit rather than the flowery kind. This has nothing to do with my aforementioned apathy towards the vast quantities of flowers I dealt with on a daily basis. It is because I suffer from hay fever.

Ever since I was old enough to sneeze I have been debilitated every summer by hay fever. My fellow victims, who, like me, endure this lousy, unpleasant condition year after year will already know how much of an affliction it can be. A streaming nose and merciless itching of the eyes and throat has long blighted my enjoyment of summer and all its fringe benefits. How careless of me, then, to choose a career where pollen-bearing, sneeze-inducing objects of nature were rarely more than a few feet away. Yet on one memorable occasion they inadvertently caused me to become an unrivalled hero.

I was conducting the funeral of the late Mr Samuel Atkinson, one of those nice, quiet funerals that every funeral director craves. Everything was going beautifully on a warm and dusty June morning until at the crematorium a small but solvable problem arose. My two drivers were acting as bearers, but only one member of the small gathering was willing to assist. It was no big deal – I would act as the fourth bearer.

Very few funeral directors like to bear the coffin when conducting a funeral because he wants, quite correctly, to be looking after the family: it is difficult to do this effectively while balancing a coffin on one's shoulders. But on this occasion it was a minor inconvenience and after instructing the family to follow on behind as we shouldered the coffin down the crematorium aisle, I hoisted the coffin upwards with my fellow bearers. I immediately realised I had taken up completely the wrong position. As I stood at the back with the head of the coffin resting on my left shoulder, my face was being invaded by a particularly dense, overlapping section of the enormous wreath on top of the coffin. As we set off after the minister I knew I was in big trouble. Sure enough, ten seconds down the aisle my nose began twitching. After twenty seconds I had sneezed four times and by the time we had placed the coffin onto the catafalque, my eyes were streaming like rivers.

While my colleagues disappeared out of the side door, I remained at the top of the aisle showing the oncoming congregation to their seats. I had already extracted my white handkerchief from the top pocket of my tailcoat and began attending to my nose before it took on its usual impersonation of a dripping tap following such an attack. My eyes now felt like golf balls and I dabbed gently at them as the unbearable itching began to kick in. I felt relieved that the funeral was a relatively small one and this enabled me to retreat hastily to the rear of the chapel where I could suffer in peace away from the public eye.

By the time the service finished my symptoms had died down and my eyes and nose were no longer trying to emulate the Niagara Falls. I was able to mill around outside with the mourners feeling a little less self-conscious about any afflicted appearance. Thankfully it was the hearse driver's task to collect the wreath from the back of the crematorium and bring it round to the flower bay for everyone to see. I wanted nothing more to do with the malicious monstrosity and told him to place it as far away from me as possible.

I took up an unassuming position just by the side door of the crematorium and out of sight of the mourners as I waited for everyone to disperse, catching snippets of conversation here and there. Families rarely get together between funerals and weddings and it was often amusing to hear the various comments and updates between relatives. Mr Atkinson's family was no exception:

'Well, well! You've grown into a beautiful young woman, Lauren. I remember when you were just a little girl!'

'Hello, Bryn. You haven't changed a bit!'

'Good grief, John, how the devil are you, bach?'

'...and Derek's in the police force now. Last time you saw him he was still in school...'

Then there would be the comments about the deceased and the funeral itself:

'He'd been ill for a while, poor bugger. He's in the best place now.'

'Sam and I go back years. We used to go down the club together every Friday night without fail.'

'He was a wonderful man was Sam. Always ready with a smile and a wave, see.'

'It was a lovely service. The vicar did him proud. And the flowers. Weren't they gorgeous?'

No, I snapped to myself. They were sinister and evil, sent to prey on poor, suffering funeral... My thoughts were interrupted by a conversation to my right. A stout, heavily made-up woman was speaking in an animated Welsh accent to her friend:

'...and the funeral director – did you see him, Mave? Tears pouring down his cheeks as he showed us to our seats. I never knew they got so involved you know. Now that is what I call real service.'

It was about a fortnight later when I saw the Atkinson family again. It was also a situation that caused me further embarrassment and this time there was no escape.

The disposal of the ashes following a cremation can take on many forms. It can also grow into a very pricey addition to the expense of the funeral if taken to the extreme. Several town and city councils are now providing special sections within their cemeteries where ashes can be buried. These involve buying a small plot and then the compulsory purchase of an engraved tablet, the cost of which can run into hundreds of pounds. If people want to go to all this extra trouble and expense to bury the ashes of a loved one it is their decision. But it begs the question in me as to why they don't just opt for a burial in the first place.

Others will choose to bury the ashes in a family grave where there may have been no more room for a full burial to take place. Another option is to use a church garden of remembrance, although the condition for this is usually that the deceased was an active member of that church, or that one of the family members regularly attends. But the majority of clients would simply have them scattered in the gardens of Westport Crematorium. There was no extra charge for this, which made it a popular option and one that Daryl Jenkins carried out with painstaking finesse. A short, round man with a waddle rather than a walk, Daryl took his role of chief ashes-scatterer very seriously indeed. Every morning before the crematorium opened he would make large, extravagant crosses on the grass with his many pots of ashes. If ever the family wished to attend this fleeting ceremony – and occasionally they did – he would revel in his role and make the whole event a tasteful extravaganza.

But the Atkinson family wanted something a little more personal and so they chose to scatter their father's ashes over the Starton Cliffs, a bleak and expansive section of nearby coastline. When he had been alive Mr Atkinson loved to walk here and watch the shimmering ocean below so the connection provided the perfect way for his family to now say their final farewell.

I was certainly not adverse to such requests. Only a few weeks previously I had scattered the ashes of a football fan on the pitch of his beloved Westport United. Then a few months earlier I had carried out two similar scatterings, one on a bowling green for the club's late president, and another in a local public garden near Penderi. Permission had to be sought for requests on private property but they were rarely, if ever, refused. Local authorities also liked to be informed of any intended scatterings of ashes in a public place, but as long as everything was done discreetly and with dignity there was never a problem.

I met the Atkinson family in the small car park near the edge of Starton Cliffs and together we walked up the slope to the cliff top itself. It was a beautiful summer's day and the view across the aqua blue ocean was stunning. We all stood quietly for a couple of minutes, absorbing the peace and the majesty of the panorama before us. In the midst of such beauty it was so easy to forget, even if just for a fleeting fragment of time, the ills and worries of the world.

A standing joke in our company was that if ever a funeral director wanted to 'disappear' for an hour or two he would always claim he had to go and dispose of some ashes somewhere. It was the perfect excuse to legitimately escape the hurly burly of the office and the constant hazard of being drawn into something else simply by being available at the time. A couple of my colleagues actively encouraged such scatterings in remote, obscure locations so they could disappear for a whole afternoon. When Duncan Forster became a funeral director he could have scattered ashes for Britain. He disappeared three or four times a week to dispose of the cremated remains from various funerals he had arranged. This became something of a mystery during periods when he was carrying out more burials than cremations. To this day I am convinced he scattered one particular client's ashes on at least three separate occasions. Suspicions were also aroused when Westport's High Street apparently became a popular location to scatter the remains of a loved one. Duncan was often spotted there after leaving the office with a bronze coloured urn in a brown paper carrier bag.

I now held a similar urn in my hands and as I unscrewed the lid I motioned the gathered family to step forward a little closer to the edge of the precipice. I stretched out my arm and slowly tipped the urn in a downward direction…

As I have wended my merry, and not so merry way through life I have often pondered as to why unexpected and humiliating twists of fate strike when they are least wanted. Their timing is a triumph of unearthly precision and I regularly, if not compliantly, conceded to the fact that I was the perfect target for their jokes and their trickery.

The intention was that the ashes of Samuel Atkinson would cascade gently down the cliff and spread evenly over the foaming sea below. It was a romantic notion. But they never made it that far. In fact, it would be no exaggeration to suggest they went nowhere near their intended target at all. At the precise moment I turned the urn upside down, a single gust of wind whipped in from absolutely nowhere and sent a wave of ashes sweeping over me like a grey blanket.

As I brushed Mr Atkinson from my jacket and trousers I could sense the eyes of his nearest and dearest watching me. I was almost purple with embarrassment and could feel the sweat breaking out all over. It was several seconds before I plucked up the courage to look in their direction.

'I'm really sorry,' I stammered.

At least half the faces had muted smiles on them; the rest were looking as horrified as I felt. Judging by the comments made to me as we walked back to the car park however, their concerns, nobly, were for me and not the final resting place of their father. Thankfully I'd had the sense to keep my mouth shut otherwise it could have been far worse. It was bad enough to be brushing ashes from off my clothes in front of the family without having to start spitting them out as well.

The son came over to me as I was about to get into my car with a huge grin that was like balm to my traumatised soul. He helped flick some more ashes from off my shoulders that I'd missed. 'Don't worry,' he said kindly. 'Dad never liked going too close to the edge anyway. He's probably better off scattered up by yer.'

I appreciated the sentiment, but as I undressed later that night and several more specks of gritty, grey dust fell to the floor, I felt a little guilty that not quite all of Mr Atkinson was scattered on Starton Cliffs.

For a period of several months an artificial limb stood in the corner of the fridge room at the Sandacre Hospital mortuary. In fact, it was there so long it became part of the scenery. The leg had been removed from a Mr Wheatley prior to a post mortem examination – and no one had ever bothered to claim it.

In the beginning, before we no longer noticed it was there, I continually teased Hazel and her boss, Colin Ashley, telling them they had to stop messing around pulling people's legs and other similarly infantile comments, the like of which I seem to excel at. Then, as I say, the leg became indistinct by its familiarity. But I soon noticed the day it disappeared.

'The leg! It's gone!'

Colin laughed. He was a small, trim man in his mid-forties, thin faced with a busy, pleasant nature. I always enjoyed dealing with both Hazel and Colin. They were good company and friendly, trustworthy acquaintances.

'Yes, I finally got rid of the leg!' he celebrated. 'I went to the hospital incinerator yesterday. After nine months I can safely say that Mr Wheatley's false leg has finally been cremated!'

And that, so I thought, was that.

Two weeks later on another visit to the mortuary, I found Colin seated behind his desk, an uncharacteristic look on his face that was a toss-up between solemnity and disbelief.

'You okay, Colin?' I frowned.

He looked up and gave a wry smile. 'Yeah, I'm fine,' he replied. 'Sit down a minute and listen to this.'

I perched curiously on an easy chair in his immaculate office.

'You remember the wooden leg I finally incinerated last week?'

'After all this time how could I forget?' I laughed.

Colin continued. 'Well ten minutes before you arrived, Mr Wheatley's son was in here asking if by any chance we still had his father's false leg. I told him it had been incinerated and asked him why.

'Don't tell me he finally wanted it back after all this time?'

'Yes,' Colin nodded, 'but there was a very good reason why he wanted it back. He told me in the months since his father's death they had been trying to sort out his finances but he and the solicitor kept coming up ten thousand pounds short. Then yesterday an old friend of Mr Wheatley's they hadn't seen since the funeral turned up at the house for a chat. Out of the blue he just happened to ask if they found the ten grand the old man kept hidden inside his wooden leg!' Colin shook his head, paused, and looked up. 'I don't know whether it was true or not, but his son looked pretty sick when he left.'

36

If public perception of the funeral business is a little hazy, then its knowledge and understanding of embalming is shrouded in almost complete mystery. It is not, after all, the kind of subject one would choose to open a conversation with around the dinner table. Even people who use the services of an undertaker will usually drift through the whole funeral arranging process without ever knowing about the methods and intricacies of embalming. But this lack of information could often cause problems of an ethical nature.

The larger funeral companies push embalming for the extra revenue. Funeral directors were therefore expected to pursue a one hundred per cent success rate with clients as far as embalming was concerned. Because very few people really want to know what goes on in the embalming theatre – especially when it concerns a loved one – it can be easy for the funeral director to dismiss the procedure in a couple of well chosen sentences. The buzz phrase for embalming is 'hygienic treatment.' It is actually quite a clever marketing tactic for it removes the stigma of the dreaded 'E' word and emphasises the prime reason why it is done in the process. Clients accept the brief explanation that accompanies the introduction of hygienic treatment and are basically happy to leave it at that.

I believe there are actually two reasons for embalming. The main one is to preserve the condition of the body, primarily until the funeral has taken place. This allows the family of the deceased to view their relative in the best possible circumstances. As with all funeral directors, I wanted the final, lasting memory for my clients to be a positive one. But unless the body is placed into cold storage immediately, embalming techniques need to be administered as soon as possible after death occurs. Like any living organism that ceases to exist, it does not take long for the natural process of decomposition to begin. The changes this event can create are often visually dramatic, even horrific at times. Once such a stage is reached it is virtually impossible for even the most experienced of embalmers to rectify. In the world of embalming, prevention rather than cure is the key.

As the reference above may suggest, the second reason for embalming, in my opinion, is for the undertaker. Opponents of embalming rarely give a thought to people working in the funeral profession who are required to deal with unpleasant situations on a daily basis. Embalming eliminates most of the health risks that threaten the funeral worker, as well as the general unpleasantness that can come with death. For this reason alone I was sympathetic towards the pro-embalming argument. I just didn't agree with the pushy sales methods employed to promote it.

We were fortunate in Westport to eventually have the services of a first class embalmer. Having left the building industry in his mid-twenties, Dafydd Phillips started out as a part-time driver with no more ambition than to seek a permanent position. It didn't take long for him to secure one as a full-time driver on the funeral ambulance with Dai Proctor. It took him even less time to discover an interest in what happened on the embalming table. His curiosity soon turned into a wholly unexpected career move and with encouragement from various quarters within the company, he began training to become a fully qualified embalmer.

Dafydd was a pleasure to work with. Dedicated, thorough, and hard grafting, he plunged himself into his new profession with the enthusiasm of a child at Christmas with a new toy. He learned his trade well, but it did set him apart from everyone else. Anyone who takes up the scalpel of an embalmer with such zeal is, of course, a complete fruit loop.

Despite the fact we were in a morbid line of work, the majority of us actually disliked the embalming side of things. Some individuals, especially the more precious funeral directors, would rarely be seen anywhere near a dead body, let alone the embalming theatre. But most of us steered clear simply because we were relatively normal. Dafydd on the other hand loved it. In fact, with all the gossiping and backstabbing that was rife in the Westport branches, he had gone on record as saying he much preferred the company of his clients. There was a great deal of sense and truth hidden away in his statement but it didn't alter the fact that as far as we were concerned he was a couple of handles short of a coffin. And the proof was very much in evidence beyond the white Wellingtons and formaldehyde.

When Dafydd worked on the funeral ambulance he gained himself a bit of a reputation for being gruesome. Most of us needed to be dragged reluctantly to the gory, more incident-packed coroner's removals that often came along. Dafydd, however, would be there like a shot, fascinated with every aspect of the job in hand. But with time I realised he was no more macabre than the rest of us when it came to the unpleasant stuff. It just didn't bother him like it did others. The whole physical process of death genuinely absorbed him. And that captivation would manifest itself later when he pursued his new found interest with equal enthusiasm.

Despite my admiration for Dafydd I did find his behaviour a touch worrying at times. Dai Proctor returned from a particularly nasty coroner's removal one afternoon, shaking his head in disbelief as he made his way to the kitchen to put the kettle on.

'That Dafydd is off his head,' he announced. 'We've just been to one of the most disgusting removals ever – bloke's been dead at least four weeks in a small bed-sitter. The place is buzzing. It then took CID over half an hour to turn up and what does Dafydd do?' Dai wrinkled up his face as he answered his own question. 'He sits on the bed about four feet away from the body and watches TV while we wait.'

Dafydd entered the kitchen a couple of minutes later and rushed towards the kettle where he began making a cup of tea with his usual vigorous haste. Apart from his embalming, which he worked at meticulously, I never saw him do anything slowly. Just going up town with him was tiring. He didn't walk. He galloped along at a pace that wasn't far short of actually running.

'Anything decent on the telly this afternoon?' I called.

Dafydd turned and grinned sheepishly. 'Yeah, a good old black and white film,' he said. 'But CID turned up and I missed the end.'

With his skinny frame and big glasses, Dafydd cut an unusual figure. He certainly never gave the outward appearance that he was actually a highly-skilled person in a bizarre and challenging profession. After buying himself a home haircut set (*why should I line the pockets of hairdressers when I can do it myself*) he regularly shaved his hair to within a centimetre of his head and looked like a young Jim Bowen, the comedian and presenter of TV quiz show, Bullseye. Cries of 'Great! Smashing! Super!' and 'Come and have a look at what you could've embalmed!' regularly rang out when Dafydd was around.

His painfully thin physique was a remarkable achievement because I have rarely seen anyone with an appetite to match that of Dafydd's. He always ate the biggest lunch in work, would then go home and cook a large meal in the evening, and in between he'd always have a 'snack' of some sort, usually what most normal people would consider a meal in itself. How he maintained his lean appearance was one of the great mysteries of life.

Being one of the company's eternal bachelors, Dafydd caused riots of laughter in work one day when he announced he'd just bought himself a dishwasher. He genuinely couldn't see what all the fuss was about, despite admitting he used very few dishes throughout the week. His reason for splashing out was because he liked a bit of luxury in life, he explained.

His taste for the highlife clearly extended to his choice of bed linen too. Often when we removed bodies from hospitals the mortuary staff would leave the hospital bed sheets wrapped around the deceased, which we would dispose of back at the chapel of rest. This was common practice, although maybe local health authorities should take a keener look at their linen expenditure, especially as they are always pleading poverty. Occasionally Dafydd would take home the odd bed sheet for his own use. Understandably he took his fair share of stick for this, but again he remained oblivious to the cries of disapproval. "Put them on boil wash and they're fine," he retorted. "That's all the laundry at the hospital does before using them again." It was hard to argue with his logic. He was actually very choosy about which hospital's bed linen he claimed though. He would only really consider one – The Prince Charles hospital in nearby Bronllan. His reasoning was extremely admirable. He figured the Prince Charles logo stamped in bright red would impress the girls.

Dafydd's amazingly droll sense of humour appealed to me. It was so subtle and unassuming that many people missed it altogether. But the best part about it was that he rarely tried to be funny. His humour was his character and he would regularly crease me up with laughter simply by being himself. Like the many occasions he would turn up for work in a badly creased white shirt, but with the breast pocket neatly ironed. "I like a nice pocket on a shirt," he would declare seriously. His sartorial fastidiousness did not extend to his call-out attire at night though. He usually just put his suit on straight over his pyjamas, resulting in a strange, diluted paisley pattern under his white shirt. It did provide me with the priceless opportunity to coin the phrase 'Embalmers in Pyjamas' though.

And then there was the time he turned up on my doorstep at half past eleven one night in an advanced state of inebriation.

'Tom, my old buddy,' he slurred. 'How the devil are you?'

'I'm... er.... okay, mate. Just off to bed actually.'

'Damned good idea. I'm jusht off myshelf.' He giggled manically. 'When I get home that ish.'

'Great...'

'Now then. The reashon I am calling ish to ashk you if you have any TCP antisheptic liquid?

'TCP Liquid? Don't you think you've had enough to drink?'

Dafydd thought this was hilariously funny and he stood there laughing for several seconds with a strange wheezing sound. 'No, no, no,' he managed finally. 'Itsh not for me, silly. Itsh for a pigeon.'

'A pigeon?'

'Yesh. A little friendly pigeon.'

I waited for the explanation, but Dafydd had suddenly become obsessed with the collar of his jacket, which was sticking out at an angle behind his right ear. He could obviously see it out of the corner of his bleary eye and possibly thinking it was some sort of insect he began swatting wildly, but his attempts were way off the mark. In the end he gave up and leered at me, totally oblivious as to why he was there.

'The pigeon?' I prompted.

'Uh?'

'You wanted TCP Liquid for a pigeon.'

'Ahhh!' He pointed a finger at me as though I'd just discovered the meaning of life. 'Thash right! Do you have any?'

'I think so. But…why?'

'I found a poor little injured pigeon in my garden thish morning. He's hurt hish little foot. I would like to dip hish poor little foot into a beaker of TCP Liquid to make it better.'

I was astonished. 'Do you really think that will help?

He put his arm around my shoulder and pulled me closer before looking around to check that no one was listening. Finally, through breath that could have lit a bonfire from twenty metres, he whispered hoarsely: 'Yesh. But don't tell anyone.'

I found it hard to run back upstairs to my flat. My legs, like the rest of me, were shaking with laughter. As I rummaged in my bathroom cabinet for the miraculous pigeon elixir that was TCP Liquid, I could hear a drunken call floating up the staircase that sounded like a yodelling owl. When I presented Dafydd with the precious bottle a couple of minutes later, tears formed in his eyes. He gave me a manly hug – the type you see in American war movies – and then staggered into the dark night, presumably to return home somehow and attend to his pigeon's poor little foot.

It probably comes as no surprise to learn that Dafydd remembered nothing of his mission of mercy the following day. He did admit to having found a pigeon with a limp, but denied being anywhere near my flat the previous night. He just gave me one of his questioning looks that made me feel like I had made the whole thing up. As for my bottle of TCP Liquid it was never seen again. Goodness knows where that ended up. I just hope it wasn't down Dafydd's throat.

There is no question that Dafydd Phillips was a wonderful character, both to work with and to observe. There was far more to him than just someone to laugh at however: deep down he was a kind and generous human being. But because he could also be shy and moody, many misread him and often failed to give him the credit he deserved. What was never in doubt to anyone though was the fact he was an extremely good embalmer.

As a funeral director I was the grateful recipient of Dafydd's handiwork on many an occasion. I lost count of the number of families who, having come to the chapel of rest for a viewing, commented on how peaceful their loved one looked. Dafydd's presentation of the deceased was superb and it always gave me a buzz when I saw a family so pleased and contented with the final memories they would have. But in all my years of attending to viewings, I never received a response as passionate as that of Mr Evans of Cefn Bach.

Bryan Evans was a big man with lazy hair and a habit of putting his head to one side during a conversation. He didn't strike me as being an animated type and he had handled his wife's premature death at the age of fifty with the philosophical acceptance of one not easily aroused by anything or anyone. It wasn't until a few days later that I found out his marriage had not been an entirely happy one. Nevertheless, he said all the right things and took great care in making sure his wife's wishes were carried out right down to the tiniest detail.

Dafydd had made a wonderful job of embalming Mrs Evans and preparing her for viewing. He had managed to give her face a fresh, natural colour and an expression that conveyed peace and serenity: he had also washed and styled her hair to perfection. It seemed that although Dafydd took great care over each body he embalmed, he often did a little bit more for me. When I mentioned it to him one day he simply said it was because I wasn't arrogant and demanding like some of my more pompous colleagues.

I had arranged to meet Mr Evans at our chapel of rest in Brynmawr one evening so he could come and see his wife. Like all conscientious funeral directors I arrived a little earlier than the agreed time in order to check the coffin and make sure everything was okay. Mrs Evans still looked perfect and I relaxed in the knowledge that her husband was going to be pleased with what we had done. Finally, I lit the two large church candles on the altar and retreated to the office to await his arrival.

A few minutes later the chapel doorbell rang and there stood Mr Evans looking very smart in a light grey suit.

'Hello, Mr Evans,' I greeted. 'Do come in.'

'Thanks, Tom.' Despite his size and bulk he stepped in nimbly and I showed him through into the small office.

'Everything is ready for you,' I explained, beginning the patter I had delivered on so many occasions. 'I'll take you through to see your wife and then I'll leave you to spend some time to yourself. Now you take as long as you want and I'll be waiting here in the office if you need me for anything. Okay?'

'You're very kind, Tom. Thank you.'

Although I'd only known Bryan Evans for a few days, I had realised he was something of a rough diamond. I'd also heard he could be a bit of a 'Jack the Lad' character too. But in my dealings with him to date he had been both placid and polite at all times. His manners were immaculate and I never got the impression that any of this was some kind of act.

We reached the coffin in the viewing area of the chapel and I leaned forward to gently remove the face cloth. I stepped back and allowed Mr Evans to move in closer and see his wife lying there peacefully, silently...

'Flaming heck!'

Bryan Evans's hoarse voice smashed the serenity of the moment and a feeling of sickening horror swept over me. What was wrong? What had happened? I was sure everything had been okay when I checked earlier. I glanced numbly at the huge man who was staring into the coffin in wide-eyed shock.

'That isn't Jean,' he gawped.

My legs turned to jelly. It was the wrong body. We had the wrong body! Rationality returned within seconds. Of course it was the right body. Our whole procedure was based on checking, re-checking, and then checking again. This was what all our laborious paperwork was about. This was what the wrist tags that clearly bore the name of the deceased were for. Everyone who has had anything to do with the body – from the removal right through to the funeral itself – had to check the identity. That was what we all did: it was second nature. Mrs Evans had been no exception. This procedure had been carried out from the beginning right up until now. Of course it was the right body. Wasn't it?

I swallowed hard. 'Is there a problem, Mr Evans?'

'Yeah, there is. She looks absolutely amazing. If I'd known she could look as good as this, I'd have had her done years ago.'

240

37

The one-liners from the likes of Bryan Evans could provide a glint of sunshine during a drab working day. They usually emerged from seemingly innocuous situations; unexpected and improbable but always welcome. Like a BBC comedy they would be repeated over and over again in the weeks that followed and, in time, enter local funeral folklore.

Such priceless comments or reactions barely contained a surrounding story, but I would like to spend this chapter sharing some of these brief anecdotes in the hope I can convey each moment well enough for you to enjoy them as much as I did at the time.

The phone rang early one morning just as Andy Morris and I arrived at Dean Street for work. Andy took the call and came off the phone with his usual relaxed grin.

'Removal,' he announced. 'A Mr Gwilym has died up in Moorlands. That was his wife. She sounds in a terrible state – wants to know if we can go straight away.'

I was perpetually at a loss to understand how Andy could be so calm and collected about these things. Despite all my years working in such an unpredictable profession I still hated the unexpected and being diverted from my plans for the day. This particular morning I had heaps to do but now I was on my way out of the door again and wouldn't be back for over an hour. I knew Andy was equally busy but he was just so irritatingly laid back about it all. Why oh why could I not be more like him?

We set off in the estate car and just under half an hour later pulled up outside a small bungalow in the pleasant and affluent district of Moorlands. The serene hush of morning still hung in the air as we got out of the car in our black suits and made for the small wooden gate at the foot of a neat front garden. Then suddenly there was a commotion at the bungalow. A woman burst out of the front door and came running down the path, waving her arms at us and yelling hysterically.

'You can't repair the boiler today! My husband's just died!'

If you asked five different people to phrase a sentence of your choice on any particular subject, you would more than likely receive five subtly different versions. There is nothing unusual about this. We all think in contrasting ways, therefore the words we decide to use in our conversations will undoubtedly vary from person to person. For example, I might say to someone: "There's a good film on television tonight. I think I'll stay home and watch it." Someone else, however, might say it another way: "There's a film on TV tonight that really looks worth watching." The sentiment is virtually identical but there is a slight variation in the execution.

Despite accepting there are differences in the way we speak, both Duncan Forster and I were completely dumbstruck at the choice of words from one particular gentleman at the conclusion of a funeral late one autumn afternoon. He asked us to attend a wake with a phrase so unbelievable there would surely be no one else on earth that would even think of putting it the way he did, let alone utter it.

We had just dropped the vicar at the family home in the hearse – he had been invited back – and were about to leave when a thin, droopy-eyed man in a black, ill-fitting suit walked out in front of us with his hand held aloft. He ambled round to the driver's side and the next thing we knew he was leering into the open window.

'You the undertakers?' he growled.

Duncan and I glanced uneasily at each other. Sitting in a big black hearse wearing morning suits was clearly not giving the game away too much.

'Yes, we are,' said Duncan.

'Good.' He nodded his head with great satisfaction and then continued. 'The corpse's brother wants you to come in and have a drink.'

We politely declined. After such an eloquent offer we felt unable to fraternise with the corpse's brother and keep a straight face.

When Duncan became a funeral director it didn't take him long to earn a reputation for attracting life's odd balls. There were many occasions when he would wearily return to the office armed with the revelations of the latest in a long line of extremely peculiar clients. Jazz quartets playing outside the crematorium, instructions for the most bizarre of items to be placed in the coffin, neurotic women, and warring families at the graveside: you name it, Duncan dealt with it. He was a magnet for eccentric behaviour and it was all much to the delight of his easily entertained colleagues. There were so many it was hard to keep track of them all. But the one character with whom I will always associate poor old Duncan was the gloriously named and completely barmy Miss Tinkerton.

It had started out as one of those blissfully quiet and uneventful mornings. Which is why it just had to be Duncan who answered the phone when it rang. My hand had been poised over the receiver but my colleague was one of those men who hated hanging around doing nothing.

'It's okay,' he called from his desk. 'I'll get it.'

As the conversation kicked in it became clearly obvious that Duncan was wishing he hadn't been so eager to pick up the phone. His voice became strained and his already pallid features turned even paler. When his rough hand brushed across his forehead and stroked the top of his closely cropped hair, I knew he had landed another of his specialities.

'Why me?' he muttered, replacing the receiver noisily.

'What's up?'

'That was Colin at Sandacre mortuary. He wants me to go down straight away. He's got a woman there whose mother has just died and she wants to see a funeral director immediately.'

'What! In the mortuary?'

'Yes. Apparently she's a total fruitcake.' He burst into his familiar peal of stuttering laughter. This was usually always a nervous reaction with Duncan. In the grinning face there was also a look of desperation.

'Do you want me to come with you?'

'Are you sure?'

'Yeah, I've got nothing to do at the moment. Sounds like you need a bit of moral support.' I'm ashamed to admit that my generosity had little to do with providing professional assistance for my hapless colleague. I just couldn't pass up the opportunity of meeting one of Duncan's nut jobs on the starting line.

When we arrived at the mortuary Colin was both relieved and apologetic. 'I'm really sorry about this, Duncan. She just turned up demanding to see her mother. Then she said she wanted to see a funeral director to arrange the funeral right away. I tried telling her it was more usual to do this at a funeral home, or even in her own home, but she would have none of it. "Mummy needs to hear what's going on, it's her funeral," she said. He shook his head and held out his arms.

At the sight of Duncan's collapsing expression I suppose the noble thing to do would have been to step in and offer to take over. After all, I was more experienced. But I was a coward and a blighter and I allowed the poor man to enter the mortuary viewing room displaying a visible nervousness not unlike that of a teenager arriving home late from a party. I followed him to the doorway of the small mortuary chapel of rest and waited there. In my defence, this particular move was not actually to gain a grandstand seat to proceedings. I genuinely wanted to see how the opening exchanges panned out to ensure things were going to be okay. There had been isolated instances in the past where abnormal behaviour, motivated by grief, had caused an unpleasant scene.

At first I thought Miss Tinkerton had someone with her. She was chattering away in a high-pitched, almost childlike voice. It soon became evident, however, that no one else was in the room. She was talking to her deceased mother who, except for her face, lay covered by a large purple pall in front of the alter.

Talking to the deceased is not unusual. I witnessed it many times over the years and the practice is probably one of the most natural things to do when a loved one dies. I spoke a few words to my own father and mother when saying my final farewells to them. But that was the key – a few words. Miss Tinkerton was jabbering to her mother like nothing had happened.

Surprisingly – and I don't really know why – Miss Tinkerton was an extremely attractive lady. I suppose after having been briefed as to her apparent sanity before actually setting eyes on her, I had built up some sort of picture of a completely wild and dotty-looking woman. Such an assumption could not have been further from the truth. She looked to be in her mid-fifties, although it was difficult to tell. With dark brown hair bunched up fashionably behind her head – highlighted by a red flower delicately perched to one side – and equally deep brown eyes underlining a sultry bronzed complexion, her whole appearance was distinctly Mediterranean. But despite her fetching appearance it was clearly evident that Miss Tinkerton was, albeit in a nice way, barking mad. I watched with both amusement and anticipation as Duncan slowly approached her with a view to introducing himself.

'Good morning,' he began. 'It's Miss Tinkerton isn't it?'

She immediately ceased from her one-sided conversation and looked up. 'Yes, it is. Good morning.' She smiled at her mother and then looked up at Duncan again. 'Excuse me a minute, Mummy. Are you the funeral director?'

'Yes I am,' Duncan replied, extending forth his hand. I could hear the tremble in his voice. 'My name is Duncan Forster of BJ Thomas & Son. I'm very sorry to hear that your mother has passed away.'

'Oh yes I know. Thank you so much. But it isn't really sad because Mummy has been in a lot of pain lately with her illness. Now her suffering is over, isn't it Mummy?'

'Right. Well perhaps you'd like to come down to the office and we can start discussing...'

'Oh, no no no!' cried Miss Tinkerton. 'I must get to know you first. Now then, Duncan, how long have you been a funeral director?'

'Well, about two years now.'

'Ah. Not very long!' she teased. 'And tell me, Duncan, how old are you?'

'Uh? I'm...er... fifty-nine,' he spluttered.

'I see, I see.' Miss Tinkerton placed the back of her hand thoughtfully under her chin and cocked her head to one side. 'You look very good for fifty-nine. Now tell me Duncan, are you married?'

'Ye-ees.'

'Splendid, splendid! Mummy will like that. She always thought there was something highly suspicious about a grown man who was still single, didn't you Mummy?' She gave an appealing little chuckle and Duncan joined in with his nervous laugh.

They seemed to be getting on fine so far and I was a little conscious about eavesdropping, but as Miss Tinkerton had paid no attention to me whatsoever I remained quietly in the doorway witnessing this special bonding of funeral director and client. My only difficulty was going to be suppressing the giggles that were fighting to escape with wicked determination.

'And do you enjoy your job, Duncan?'

'Yes I do,' my colleague answered. It can be a bit difficult at times. But it's always nice to help people, especially someone as delightful as yourself.'

Duncan was in the zone. It was probably nervous energy but he actually seemed to be enjoying his acquaintance with this odd yet somehow captivating woman. There was definitely something alluring about her – the way she stood in her figure-hugging black dress and cone heels, the way she coyly put her head to one side as she spoke, and the manner in which she asked her questions and responded to the answers. I was warming to her myself.

'Why thank you, Duncan! What a charming man you are!' She returned those engaging brown eyes towards mother and addressed her once more in the now familiar gossipy tones. 'Now then, Mummy, this is Duncan. He's the very nice man who is going to make all the arrangements for your funeral. Duncan, I'd like you to meet my dear mother – Grace Perkins.'

And before Duncan stopped to think what he was doing, he stretched forth his hand and responded. 'Hello, Mrs Perkins. And how are you today?'

Although Duncan's *faux pas* caused great mirth amongst his colleagues, the fact he had spoken to the late Mrs Perkins the way he did cemented his relationship with Miss Tinkerton for life. From that moment on he could do no wrong. And to think I'd had the audacity to wonder whether I should step in and take over. My supposedly less experienced colleague had handled the situation far more admirably than I, or anyone else could have done.

According to Duncan the arrangement went like clockwork and notwithstanding the occasional eccentric contribution from Miss Tinkerton, it was one of the best funerals he'd ever arranged. I insisted on driving Duncan's hearse at the funeral and although everything was incident-free as far as the charming Miss Tinkerton was concerned, I wouldn't have missed it for the world. This is mainly because Duncan added to his steadily growing collection of verbal gaffes.

Technically I blamed the minister. He was one we had never dealt with before, but he delivered an uplifting service in our Brynymor chapel of rest, after which he asked the congregation to be upstanding. Usually, following the completion of the service – which would be listened to via the intercom in the office – the funeral director always walked into the chapel and asked the congregation to rise just prior to the coffin being taken outside to the hearse. This was almost second nature to funeral directors and Duncan, nervous in his desire for everything to go as planned that day, was clearly running on autopilot. He marched into the chapel and turned to face the gathered mourners until we, the bearers, were positioned alongside the coffin. Then Duncan made his now legendary announcement:

'Would you all please stand...'

There was an uneasy silence.

'...oh dear! You already are!' Duncan's composure crumpled for a few seconds and with a self-conscious giggle he ushered us out of the door.

Both Chris and I were glad of this because we had turned bright red in our attempts to stifle the escape-seeking laughter bubbling away beneath the surface. Once outside we had time for a quick chuckle before the mourners began to emerge. But Duncan didn't seem to care and he just hovered around, muttering to himself and wearing an enormously screwy grin on his face.

It would seem that Miss Tinkerton had wielded rather a worrying influence on dear old Duncan.

The price of a funeral, as I have already discussed, was a constant topic of conversation amongst the public and undertakers alike. Stories and articles would often frequent the pages of newspapers and magazines and it was always a subject that provoked strong debate and opinion. I doubt this will ever change.

Prompted by the general consensus that funerals were vastly overpriced, many local authorities began to consider starting up their own council-operated funeral service. It was actually quite a noble idea. The thought of cheaper funerals appealed greatly to the likes of pensioners and low-income families who might suddenly be faced with an unexpected and extremely costly funeral bill.

The concept of council funeral homes certainly rattled the cages of the larger concerns in the funeral industry – until it transpired that companies like ours would probably be invited to run them. But this would have given birth to problems far bigger than the average funeral bill. Whether people are affluent or scraping to make ends meet, everyone loves a bargain. The jealousy that could easily occur, therefore, between families having cheaper or more expensive funerals according to status may well have created its own complications, no matter how genuine the intent was in the first place. Being granted such a contract could also have made things extremely difficult for the funeral directors. For example, I could be in the position of arranging a funeral with a hard working family one day and then arranging an almost identical funeral the following week for a family on benefits via the council. The bill for the latter would be anything up to forty per cent less than the former.

This may have been the reason why the various local authorities retreated to discuss the whole concept at length. Presumably this would have included the sensible option of setting up totally independently to any existing funeral company. In the meantime media interest in the story was very keen and several council officials were sought out for their comments on the matter. There was little they could say except that the proposed idea would be examined in great detail to see whether it was feasible or not. At least that's what should have been said. One particular councillor found a rather unfortunate way of putting it:

'Setting up a council run funeral home is certainly something we would like to consider, but there is a great deal that needs to be discussed first. Death is a very sensitive issue and it would be a grave mistake for us to rush things. Therefore, it is our intention to set up a body so we can look at it from every possible angle.'

I didn't enjoy covering the office on a Saturday morning. Being on call was bad enough, but manning a busy office alone with all the phones from every other office in the area diverted through to the one location could be extremely stressful and the stuff from which nightmares are made.

The telephone system in the Dean Street office had three separate lines and this was the root of the problem. It was a frequent hindrance for another line to start ringing while in the middle of a conversation with someone else. It was ludicrous to try and break off a conversation where you were taking the details of a death from a distressed client to answer another line, not to say extremely unprofessional.

This whole scenario made a mockery of the company's demand that all telephone calls must be answered within five rings. Yeah, right. I eagerly anticipated the recruitment drive aimed at far off planets with strange names, inhabited by extra-terrestrials sporting four arms, eight ears, and three mouths dotted all over their little green bodies. Employing such freaks was the only way the phones would get answered within company regulations on a Saturday morning, that's for sure. It could often be equally as difficult during the week, even when manning levels were slightly more realistic. But trying to answer three phone lines was only part of the dilemma facing the Saturday morning one-man band. Heaven help anyone who happened to have a leaky bladder. The toilet was a no-go area because it is a proven scientific fact that the telephone will ring just as you are getting into full flow.

In the end we came up with a simple but effective solution to allow the call of nature to be fulfilled uninterrupted. We would block all three lines by removing the receivers from their hooks and make for the toilet in the blissful knowledge that the phone could not ruin one's moment of relief. Unless, of course, someone came in through the front door.

It was on one such Saturday that the phone never seemed to stop ringing and there was a constant procession of clients paying bills or making general enquiries. It was complete mayhem and I longed for twelve o'clock to come and rescue me. But just around the corner was one of those fleeting moments that raised a smile and armed me with a new tale to tell.

I was in the toilet when the front door opened yet again. Cursing, I rushed to finish my business and made for the front office where there stood a hesitant man about my age in a blue checked shirt. I shook his hand and inquired how I might help him. It was mightily tempting to ask him if he could assist me in answering the telephones afterwards.

'My uncle passed away this morning,' he announced quietly. 'I'm responsible for making the arrangements.'

'No problem, sir. I'm sorry to hear of your loss. If you'd like to take a seat I'll start by taking some details. Would you like a cup of tea or coffee?'

'Oh, no thank you. I was actually wondering if it would be possible for someone to come to the house later this afternoon? You see, I have a few things to take care of in town first.'

I could have hugged him. 'Yes, by all means,' I replied, sitting down behind the desk. 'Where has your uncle passed away?'

'At Millfield Hospice.'

'Okay,' I said. 'We won't be able to move your uncle until after the weekend anyway, but what I'll do is ask you a few questions now and then pass the details onto the funeral director on duty. I'll ask him to call and see you, say about four o'clock?'

'That sounds perfect,' replied the softly spoken man.

I pulled out a 'first call' sheet from the top drawer. 'Now then, can I have your name first?'

'Tony Stempson. S.T.E.M.P.S.O.N.'

'And your address and telephone number, Mr Stempson?' He duly obliged.

'Will the funeral be a burial or a cremation?'

'Cremation.'

'And your uncle's full name?

'Roy Edwin Stiff.'

38

Despite the sensitivity and sobriety of my work as a funeral director, I never missed the chance to introduce a little humour into a funeral arrangement. I guess this came about because of my own fun-loving personality, but I was also clearly influenced by having observed the wonderful, light-hearted effect the likes of Rhys Parry and Islwyn Thomas had upon the families they dealt with too. To the outsider this may seem an inappropriate tool to use at the time of someone's death. I can assure you it was never employed loosely. If the opportunity failed to arise I left well alone: many arrangements were naturally sombre and edgy affairs from start to finish. The utilisation of such a device depended on knowing when the time was right. I believe I had the ability to gauge correctly those particular moments, those windows of opportunity that came along. If so, this ability was one of my positive strengths as a funeral director and I am firmly convinced it worked wonders on the occasions it was applied.

I grew up with humour in the home. My father, a writer of a number of comedy plays during his career in the theatre, had a wonderful sense of humour and could find a joke in almost any situation. I think I have inherited that same capacity to try and seek out laughter where others remain hesitant. But as I have grown older I've come to realise that a sense of humour isn't just a shallow means of entertainment. At times it has been a lifesaver, a remedy, and a safety valve; the means by which sanity could be restored in the face of adversity. There have been countless occasions in my life when something has gone horribly wrong and dark clouds of despair have gathered vulture-like over my head. Yet somehow I have managed to dredge up a joke or a witty line from somewhere and ease the tension in my troubled mind, as well as make someone, somewhere laugh. And because of these experiences it seemed obvious to me that humour could be used effectively in my role as a funeral director.

It is an oft-used, maybe worn-out phrase, but I have no doubt whatsoever in my mind that laughter *is* the best medicine. I have seen the heartening results from a sprinkling of appropriately-timed humour. I have witnessed tears of grief turn to tears of laughter with just a few carefully chosen words. Although from time to time I may have been responsible for planting the seeds, it very often transpired that grieving families themselves were the ones who nurtured and grew the trees of humour during a funeral arrangement.

Laughter breaks the ice in almost any situation I know. It relieves strain and eases anxicty. It has happened for me and I have seen it work for others too. As a funeral director I walked into countless homes where the atmosphere of grief and shock was so tactile it was almost touchable. Yet after a well-measured remark and a friendly smile it could feel like the iceberg had exploded. Witnessing people slowly relax, open up, and start remembering good times with a positive zest was a wonderfully uplifting experience. This was certainly the case with Lydia and Debbie Nording.

I first met the Nordings when husband and father, Raymond passed away after a long illness. I was called to the house at eight o'clock one evening to carry out the removal and from the moment I walked through the door of their modest first floor flat on the perimeter of town, I knew I was going to hit it off with Lydia and Debbie. Within five minutes we were smiling together and as I left the house carrying Mr Nording on a stretcher, I knew the arrangement the following morning would go well.

Life so often throws up opposites – contradictions of situations that would normally be considered against the odds. Here was a sixty-eight year old lady who had just lost her husband and friend of almost fifty years, and a daughter who would never see her beloved father again. Yet in their moment of despair they had found a courage and a reaction that surprised them. Although they didn't actually come out and say it, I could tell that the awful reality of death, the mysteries of the undertaker, and the arranging of a funeral no longer held any fear or trepidation. And the thing that had helped them the most was a portion of well-timed, understated humour. Laughter. It breaks down barriers and apprehensions like nothing else on earth.

Every so often in funeral directing a family will come along where, on a personal level, everything clicks. It happens in life too. It is how we make friendships that last over and above the normal, everyday acquaintances we encounter. When this marriage of personalities takes place at the time of something so intensely affecting as the death of a loved one, it was, for me, in my role as a funeral director, a wonderfully fulfilling experience. And as in the case of any friendship in its embryonic stages, it takes two parties to make the whole thing work. Lydia and Debbie Nording were two of the most friendly, responsive, and likeable individuals I have ever had the pleasure of meeting. When I arrived the following morning, briefcase in hand, it was already like being reunited with old friends. We talked as though we had known each other for years. And in between the chatting and the laughing, we arranged the funeral of the late Raymond Nording.

Dealing with such charming people makes life more bearable. If only the world contained more Lydia's and Debbie's. They weren't glamorous, nor were they ostentatious. In fact, they were very probably the kind of people you would pass on the street each day without ever really noticing them. But they were warm, honest individuals – dependable and welcoming. In many ways they were an odd pair – Mrs Nording, with her soft, northern accent and pencil drawn eyebrows on a bright but pale face, was the epitome of her generation. Upright and prim, her modest home was predictably decorated with china figurines, a tea service clearly of antique value, and paintings and ornaments that proudly declared an allegiance to a bygone age. Daughter, Debbie, was an accountant, and had she chosen not to tell me this I would have guessed anyway. From her dark-rimmed spectacles and curly brown hair – already flecked with tinges of grey – to her modest, unspectacular clothing, she looked every inch the stereotypical image of an accountant. Many of the more fanciful and trendy in society would unfairly label Debbie as plain. But beyond the demure appearance there was a beauty I found captivating. Her personality clearly brought it to the fore and, for me, stood her head and shoulders above the supposedly more attractive of this world.

Wendy Fisher was proof that warmth and glamour could go hand in hand. I first met Wendy in similar circumstances – the sudden death of her husband, Graham. But whereas Raymond Nording was in his early seventies and ailing, Graham was a vibrant, active man of fifty-one. His death rocked the world of Wendy and her two daughters and over time I saw firsthand the devastation that this particular loss created.

The funeral of Graham Fisher was one of the largest I ever conducted. He was an incredibly popular man with many associations and as time passed I became genuinely sorry that I never had the opportunity of meeting him myself. Funeral directors always meet families less one member and this fact became even more regretful as my friendship with the remaining Fishers developed beyond the funeral. The service took place at St. Michael's Church in the heart of Westport's town centre, followed by a burial at Millfield Cemetery. It was a moving occasion made all the more poignant by the hundreds of mourners who turned out to pay their last respects. Most funeral directors will admit to being a little nervous prior to conducting a funeral of this magnitude and I willingly confess I felt quite intimidated, overawed even, on this particular occasion. But I coped and it was an immense feeling of satisfaction and relief that engulfed me as we drove away from the graveside that day. Professionally it was a job well done.

But for Wendy, like everyone else who loses their partner or loved one in such tragic circumstances, the anguish and the dull pain of loneliness were only just beginning. The passage of time between death and the funeral is when most friends make contact with the bereaved, either through a visit, a telephone call, or by sending a card or an email. But it is not always this period of limbo when the contact is required: it is needed at the conclusion of the funeral when the hollow void of despair sets in, when everyone else has resumed their lives and their commitments. That is the hardest time of all. I was very much aware of this when I continued to keep in touch with Wendy following the funeral. One by one the visits and the phone calls from friends and relatives dwindled until she was left too soon in almost comparative isolation to pick up the pieces of her broken life.

Funeral directors are professional people and we were regularly told, quite rightly, that becoming emotionally involved with clients was not advisable. For starters, it is physically impossible to go the extra mile with every family that comes your way. Also, the job could be mentally draining enough without taking on the added burden of unofficial bereavement counsellor. As I have said, every so often a client comes along with whom a rapport is so strong it naturally develops into friendship. But out of the many hundreds of funerals I arranged, it has only been Wendy I have remained in touch with.

Compared to the more decorous Nording mother and daughter, Wendy was openly different – a very stylish and confident woman. Or at least it was clear she used to be. The sudden death of her beloved Graham shook Wendy to the core and it took a very long time for her to recover, if indeed anyone ever does fully recuperate from such a life-changing event. Throughout the whole arrangement and beyond I rarely saw Wendy remove her large-framed dark glasses, even for the funeral itself. It was as though they were a hiding place, a shield from the prying eyes of a world that will stare and scrutinise those who are the victims of tragedy. When I did finally glimpse those tired, tearful eyes they were as dark and deep as space itself, matching her black, bobbed hair to perfection. She was a short and vivacious woman and despite being entrenched in middle age, she exuded charm and beauty. There was also something faintly exotic about Wendy's appearance. Nothing overtly obvious: it was just there, maybe exaggerated by her animated mannerisms and rapid, precise speech.

The years have helped dull the pain for Wendy Fisher, but time will never take it away completely. And I think it would probably be wrong if it did. Surely there is little point building up relationships as close as husband and wife, child and parent, or brother and sister, simply for the memories to fade with time. True love is too strong to allow that to happen. With my own parents both now passed on there will always be an emptiness where they used to be. But I wouldn't have it any other way. That is *their* space. It belongs to them. I don't ever want it to be replaced by anything or anyone else. I want their love, their character, and their humour to live on in that space for the rest of my own days.

I am grateful that I was allowed the opportunity to build up a rapport with the likes of the Nordings and Wendy during my funeral directing career, together with the countless other people I met along the way. The same person arranging and conducting a funeral is, for me, the only way to do the job properly. These days so many undertaking companies split the process into two – those who arrange the funeral and those who conduct the funeral on the day. In my eyes this is so wrong. Whenever I am dealing with any business for whatever reason, I am keen to see the same person from start to finish. People like continuity. It is the way trust and understanding is built up between two parties. With something as sensitive and bewildering as arranging a funeral, the fact that the client can see the same familiar face on the difficult day of the funeral as they did when making the arrangements brings a great deal of stability and reassurance. Too many times I have seen the funeral director turn up at the funeral and having to ask who the relatives or main mourners are because they've never met the family. It is bad practice and I'm thankful I never had to be a part of it. Barring extenuating circumstances I always arranged and conducted my funerals: hopefully, if applicable, I had attended the house removal beforehand too. Continuity was one of the most important aspects of my work and I am perpetually surprised that so many funeral companies ignore it completely.

Such continuity is impossible at times for perfectly acceptable reasons. But there was one occasion when I was glad I had to step into another funeral directors shoes, although not, I must admit, at first.

All children can at some stage expect to farewell their parents or guardians from this life. It is an unavoidable event that escapes no one. But when the situation is reversed it is an event of immense tragedy. Children's funerals are a stark contrast to the normal day-to-day world of the funeral director. The whole atmosphere is highly charged in a silent, heart-breaking way.

In the funeral profession there is always an element of personal satisfaction in arranging funerals and assisting the bereaved. But I failed to meet a single funeral director who enjoyed dealing with the funeral of a child. In Westport, as with undertakers the world over, we would all baulk at the news of a child's death. Then quietly one of us would take up the summons with grim fortitude and set about trying to relieve a fraction of the traumatic mountain a family somewhere were about to climb. Children's funerals, thankfully, were rare and I considered myself fortunate that in all my time as a funeral director I was involved in only a mere handful. But the one in particular I will never forget was a funeral I hadn't actually arranged.

Little Christopher Morgan was only eight years old when he died of cancer. One of my colleagues had dealt with the arrangements so apart from knowing that we had a very sad funeral taking place, I knew little of the actual details. It was a few days after Christopher's funeral that I received a message from my colleague, asking if I could call round to see the parents and arrange with them a 'Thanks For Sympathy' notice to put into the *Westport Chronicle*. The colleague in question had already been on sick leave for a couple of days and looked like being off for a while longer. Understandably he didn't want to leave the family waiting too long. Although I readily agreed I was extremely apprehensive about going. Nobody liked making cold visits to another funeral director's family because they had had the time to build up the trust and the bond I have previously spoken about. Somehow it seemed a touch invasive for a stranger to suddenly take over proceedings and this occasion would be even more difficult because of the circumstances.

My heart pounded as I rang the bell of Mr and Mrs Morgan's three-story house high up on Crompton's Hill overlooking the town of Westport. I had rehearsed my opening lines over and over again in the car on the way. Beyond that I barely knew what to say.

A friendly looking man about my age opened the door. He was tall with wavy, sandy-coloured hair and pale blue eyes that narrowed to slits as he greeted me with a warm smile. 'You must be Tom. Please, come in.'

I hadn't expected such an upbeat welcome. 'It's nice to meet you,' I replied, stepping into the busy looking house. 'I've heard a great deal about you.'

'Oh dear!' laughed Mr Morgan. 'I hope it was mostly good!' He owned one of those sparkly Welsh accents that can be so pleasant on the ears.

'Oh it was much better than that!' I winked, immediately warming to this amiable man.

257

At that moment his wife entered the room, a tiny blonde woman with a kindly face that hinted vaguely at the terrible trauma of the previous few weeks. Like her husband, she smiled sweetly and together they ushered me to the dark wood chair beneath the front window. They sat down side by side on the pastel sofa opposite, clutching hands tightly. It was the first revealed sign of the pain they must be going through.

We talked for several minutes before I began to go through the wording for a 'Thanks For Sympathy' notice with them. It wasn't a difficult task. They had jotted down most of the things they wanted to say. All I needed to do was collate them into a readable paragraph and put the finishing touches. It was completed in no time.

Throughout the conversation my eyes were continually drawn to a small, framed photograph standing almost discreetly on top of the teak bookcase just to my left. In it, a young boy stood beside a water fountain carrying an expensive looking camcorder. As I placed the completed notice for the newspaper into my pocket, I nodded my head towards the photo. 'Is that Christopher there?' I asked.

'Yes, it is,' said his mother with a sad smile. Her accent was even more musical than her husband's. 'That picture was taken just two months before he passed away. He loved his camcorder, see. It was a gift from the local steam train association. They presented it to him on his seventh birthday.'

Mr Morgan took up the story. 'They were wonderful. They really took Chris to their hearts. He was such a talkative little chap that when he visited them at the train station he completely won them over. They invited him to all sorts of events and gatherings after that.'

'These are the photos we took that day,' continued his wife. She handed me a small, pale blue photo album bearing the cartoon characters Sylvester and Tweetie on the cover. I flicked through the album and saw several photographs of Christopher at the train station, including one of him sitting proudly in the driver's seat of a large steam locomotive. The excited expression on his young, pale face was beautiful. The final photograph in the album showed a train driver in full vintage uniform presenting Christopher with his camcorder.

40

'Do you fancy a trip to Ireland?'

I thought he was joking.

Paul repeated the question and added a little extra spice. 'Do you fancy an all expenses paid trip to Ireland on the ferry?'

'Are you serious?'

'Of course I'm serious.'

'Well, yeah. You know I would. When is it?'

Paul rummaged through some papers on his desk and then pulled a folder out. 'We've got a coffin to go to Ireland next Wednesday,' he said, referring to an official-looking document. 'The ferry leaves at 9.00pm in the evening and arrives in Ireland at 7.00am the following morning. You'll meet a funeral director from Slattery's Funeral Service at the docks, transfer the coffin from the estate to his vehicle, and then sail back overnight at 9.00pm.' He looked up. 'That means you've also got the whole day in Ireland to do whatever you want.'

'Great! I'm going!'

Paul grinned. 'I knew you would! No one else is interested.'

When I first started working in Wales all those years ago, I would have been surprised at such a statement. Now I just expected it. The apparent higher-than-average reluctance of the Welsh to travel never ceased to amaze me. I thought at first I was just working with a bunch of shallow, unadventurous 'stay at homes', but I often discovered a distinct apathy amongst many Welsh people to travel beyond the boundaries of their homeland. None of this bothered me in the slightest. I love to travel and I soon gained the reputation of being willing to journey to all four corners of the British Isles whenever required.

Surprisingly, especially to those who are unfamiliar with the funeral business, such situations were actually quite frequent. Many people desire to be buried or cremated in their hometown, even if they have long moved away to other parts of the country.

Likewise, death can often occur while people are on holiday or visiting family. It is therefore the task of the relevant funeral director to ensure that the body is transported from the place of death to the location of the funeral. And in Westport, this was where I came into my own.

These trips away were the best part of the job as far as I was concerned. They were certainly the sole aspect that could be considered anything approaching a perk. The only other benefit of working in the funeral industry is a free funeral upon one's demise, which can be, bearing in mind one's lack of consciousness by this stage, somewhat difficult to enjoy. I could never comprehend, therefore, the disinterest of my colleagues when the opportunity arose for a trip out of town. For starters, they meant the chance of a few hours away from the office. That in itself was a good enough reason for going. But there was also the equally tempting prospect of free food for the day as well. I enjoyed some outstanding meals on my travels, especially when I had time to leave the motorways and go in search of cosy little country pubs or tea rooms, where the food was so much nicer than the overpriced play food found at motorway services. And if that wasn't enough there was always the added interest of going somewhere different and seeing unfamiliar scenery. I've always found a thrill in seeking out and exploring new places so the opportunity this side of the job presented was right up my street.

I literally travelled the length and breadth of the country over the years I worked in Westport. From Newcastle and Carlisle in the north to Portsmouth and Dover in the south; from Lincoln and Ipswich in the east to virtually every major town across the midlands and south west, I clocked up thousands of miles over the years and enjoyed every single journey, particularly the frequent trips I made to London.

The more I drove across the British Isles the more I became convinced that Wales has been put in the wrong place. Either that, or back in the far distant mists of time a Welshman living in some isolated cave on a mountain clearly got his Celtic rituals mixed up and mistakenly performed a perpetual rain dance ceremony instead. Wales gets more than its fair share of rain. There are countries all over the globe who would give anything just for a small percentage of the vast quantities that seem to fall on South Wales. As far as I was concerned they could have had it for free. Grey, sodden skies seemed to be permanently camped out above Westport and it rapidly became a tiresome feature of living there. It was also uncanny how the weather would change as soon as I left Wales. I lost count of the number of occasions I would leave a soaking wet Westport in the morning, only to be welcomed by blue skies and sunshine once I'd crossed the Severn Bridge into England. I'm no climatologist but clearly the Welsh pay the price for having such beautiful mountain ranges running through their country.

As I said, the many trips away to places far and wide became my favourite part of the job. I would usually always make myself available whenever they came up, even if they were at short notice or required an early start and/or a late finish. I enjoyed the driving, I enjoyed the adventure, and I enjoyed the solitude. Technically there were supposed to be two drivers on such journeys, but with few exceptions I usually always travelled alone. There were two reasons for this. Firstly, I was willing, and secondly, there were very few colleagues who I wanted to sit in a confined space with for hours on end. I much preferred my own company and I've always enjoyed driving alone. For me, it is a rare chance to reflect, a time to ponder. Our lives are so hectic in this day and age that we are seldom able to sit quietly and deliberate life and its many directions. I found driving on these long runs afforded me the opportunity to do this, to slow down my mind and chill out away from the madness of the office.

And on this occasion I was relieved to be off to Ireland alone too. Travelling with someone you are not too keen on in a car is one thing, but spending a day and two nights with them would register pretty highly in the 'unbearable' category. As it was I had a fantastic time sailing to Ireland and back – a cosy cabin, exquisite food, and a whole day to explore a completely new location.

The opportunities of being able to go on a trip like this were rare. When circumstances necessitate it, coffins are usually always flown overseas. But in this instance the sons and daughters of the deceased wanted their Dad to go by boat because all of his life he had hated flying. It made sense and I certainly wasn't complaining. The only doubt was whether the shipping line would be willing to transport a coffin aboard the ferry. Paul had contacted them and was told that there would be no problem taking a coffin but it would need to be escorted by an employee of the funeral company concerned and the coffin had to remain on the estate car throughout the crossing. Neither was a problem to me. I was willing to be the escort and I didn't plan on taking the coffin up to dinner with me. Sorted.

And so that was how I ended up on a jolly to the Emerald Isle. It was an unusual situation but from that day onwards I harboured a strong hope that some eccentric European would die in Westport and have written in his will an insistence that he be transported by road back to Bavaria or Austria or Southern Italy, or some other gorgeous location on mainland Europe. Now that really would have kicked a free funeral out of contention in a 'perks of the job' competition.

The only other trip that could possibly compare with my jaunt to Ireland was a trip to Glasgow early on in my undertaking career. It was the only other journey I undertook that necessitated a stopover and one of the few where I had a co-driver to share the driving responsibilities. There was probably a touch of irony in the fact that it turned out to be an enjoyable excursion, despite my companion being the domineering Ceri Williams.

Ceri was a couple of years younger than me, rotund with short, sandy-coloured hair and dark-framed glasses. He possessed a propensity for cutting verbal responses to any situation and this gave him a demeanour that screamed 'don't mess with me'. As I have already mentioned during my description of the night of the horizontal rain, Ceri was an intimidating man and certainly at his worst when he had an audience to play to. But with only me to impress during the best part of nine hundred miles he clearly wasn't going to bother and for the duration of the trip was actually enjoyable company.

After an early start we arrived at the funeral premises in Glasgow at four o'clock in the afternoon, where we were met by a thickset man named Gordon with a creased face and tight lips. He was an assistant funeral manager and he showed us around his premises, which took over half an hour. We were both in awe of the huge operation involved, where they carried out forty plus

273

funerals *a day*. And I thought we were busy doing less than that a week.

After the tour Gordon clapped his hands and rubbed them together. 'Okay lads,' he announced in gruff Glaswegian. 'I'll tek you to the hotel noo. Then if you come back aboot half past eight in the morning, we'll load you up and you can set off for home.'

We followed him a short way to a very nice looking hotel on the edge of the city. Ceri and I exchanged glances. It looked a little too nice.

'This is the hotel we booked for you this morning,' said Gordon, approaching us as we got of our car. 'Ah hope it's okay. There are no' many decent hotels that close to the depot.'

"Well, actually', began Ceri, 'our gaffer told us to find a cheap Bed & Breakfast somewhere to keep the expenses down.'

'Oh aye? That would nae be Stewart Lewis would it?

We both nodded.

Gordon snorted. 'Ach, we had him phoning up yesterday afternoon, asking us to make sure you did nae stay anywhere too dear. That's why we booked this one for you, just to annoy him. And if the tight-fisted sod says anything when you get back to Westport, you bloody well tell him to give me a ring!'

I liked Gordon.

By now it was approaching five o'clock and our host escorted us to the hotel bar. 'Ah've time for a wee drink with you both before I go.' He then turned to the barman and ordered three pints of beer.

'Er....just blackcurrant and lemonade for me, thanks,' I interrupted.

'Eh?'

'Blackcurrant and lemonade please. I don't drink.'

From what I had seen of Gordon so far I figured it would be pretty difficult to render him speechless. But this is exactly what I achieved right at that particular moment. He stared at me open-mouthed as though I was of alien origin – coming across someone who didn't drink, I probably was to him – and then muttering to himself under his breath he turned again and amended the order.

Gordon's 'wee drink' turned into four pints in no time at all and Ceri, who was rather fond of the old sherbet himself, kept up admirably. But the session would probably have ended a lot sooner had it not been for, of all things, a funeral party arriving just before six. Thinking that we were part of the wake because of our black suits and ties, we were greeted and hugged by tearful Scots men and women and plied with offers of pints and shorts.

Sadly I failed to benefit a great deal from this outward pouring of generosity. But Gordon and Ceri, who by now were like a pair of long lost brothers, had reached a state of utopia and were accepting everything offered with cheerful gratitude. By the time Gordon finally tore himself away at half past seven, bidding us farewell until the morning, he looked decidedly well oiled. I found out later that he had done the honourable thing by getting one of the drivers back at the depot to pick him up and drop him home.

After he had gone I began trying to coax Ceri away from a particularly rough looking middle-aged couple who he was in animated conversation with. Even though he was nodding and agreeing with everything the couple said, I could tell he didn't have a clue what they were on about. It wasn't just the alcoholic mist descending over his weary eyes either. Their accent was strong enough to leave me floundering too.

I dragged Ceri into the restaurant, partly to save him from death by lager but also because I was starving. We enjoyed an extremely substantial three course meal, courtesy of Stewart Lewis's now severely wounded budget, and despite Ceri's rapidly advancing state of inebriation, the occasion passed by relatively incident-free. This was apart from him devouring three bowls of croutons – two of them from neighbouring tables – and being persistently roguish to the waitress. But generally his behaviour was bearable, especially as I'd seen him far worse at other work get-togethers.

At the conclusion of our meal we went upstairs to our rooms in order to get changed and go and have a look at Glasgow's city centre. It was now a lovely summer's evening and I looked forward to walking around some of this sprawling Scottish city. I knocked on Ceri's door a few minutes later. There was no answer so I figured he had gone on downstairs and was waiting in the lobby. But there was no sign of him there either. I went back upstairs and hammered loudly on his door once more. Still no reply. For the next twenty minutes I searched the hotel and grounds but he had seemingly vanished from off the face of the planet.

There wasn't a lot else I could do. I didn't particularly fancy walking Glasgow's streets alone and there wasn't a great deal on offer at the hotel. I toyed with the idea of taking the car and going to the cinema but I didn't like to go without Ceri, even though he had obviously disappeared somewhere without me. In the end I watched television in the hotel lounge for an hour, phoned my girlfriend, and then decided on an early night.

The following morning I was awoken by a sharp knock at the door. Yawning, I stumbled out of bed and opened it to reveal Ceri standing there smiling synthetically.

'Good morning, Mr Eldwin!' he greeted breezily. 'And how are you today?'

'I'm fine,' I grunted, marvelling at the irony of the scene. Despite the fact he had swallowed a lake's worth of beer last night, he now looked pristine and presentable. I, on the other hand, had consumed only three blackcurrant and lemonade's (and one pineapple juice for variety), and looked like a dog's breakfast.

'Where on earth did you get to last night?' I asked him.

Ceri pursed his lips into a confessional grin. 'I fell asleep on the bed when I went to get changed. It was that Scottish beer – lethal stuff. Nearly blew my cowin' head off.'

'You slept right through till now?'

'Nah, I woke up at quarter to eleven, went down to the bar again and had another few pints. Couldn't find you anywhere. Where did you get to?

'I went to bed early because I couldn't find you.'

'Well that was a stupid thing to do. You should have given me a knock.'

'I did. Several times actually.'

'Ah well. I couldn't hear you see. I was fast asleep. Right, come on then. Breakfast and back to work. It's nearly eight o'clock. Mmm, can you smell that bacon downstairs?'

And with that he was gone. Conversations with Ceri were often like this – an infuriating waste of time. But, as I say, despite usually being a difficult person to work with, we actually got on rather well for the two days we were away together. The swaggering, bravado-driven Ceri I knew had been left behind in Westport. It was almost like being with a different person. It was the one and only time I ever saw the more congenial side of Ceri Williams and it was a pleasant experience while it lasted.

Having worked with Ceri throughout the vast majority of my career in the funeral profession, there were always a multitude of stories and events surrounding him. Being such a colourful and opinionated character meant that controversy was never very far away. But the incident I will always associate him with involved…yes, you've guessed it…a walk in front of the hearse.

Ceri was one of the more flamboyant walkers on a funeral. But it wasn't so much his walking prowess that engaged attention: it was the spectacular gestures he would offer along the way. There were very few people he would not raise his top hat to with extravagant ceremony while executing a funeral walk. Whether it was those passing the cortege on foot, the car that had stopped to allow us through, the passengers on the bus across the street, or the workmen digging up the road, they all received the special treatment Ceri reserved for these occasions. I'm convinced that I once saw him doff his hat to a Yorkshire terrier one day as the fellow cocked his leg beside a lamppost. If it moved, Ceri acknowledged it.

Something else he liked to do was stop the cortege in front of a landmark that was unique to the family. We would pause for about thirty seconds before Ceri gave us the signal to move on again. Usually it would be the house where the deceased lived or the pub or club they may have frequented. Families would occasionally ask us to oblige them in such gestures but Ceri would do it as a matter of course.

In the case of the Burbeck funeral, the choice of pausing location was to be Cherrybrook Hospital. It was more or less on the way to the crematorium – only a slight deviation from our usual route – and as we approached the small convalescent hospital halfway up Cherrybrook Hill, Ceri prepared to swing into action. I slowed the hearse to a halt right outside the front entrance of the old, red-bricked building and Ceri got out of the hearse and stood silently upright for half a minute. Finally, he removed his top hat, bowed reverently towards the hospital itself, and returned to the passenger seat.

'Beautiful. Off we go, Tom.'

After a short service at the crematorium the funeral was over and the mourners milled around outside, talking, chatting, and catching up. Then after a few minutes, Mr Burbeck, son of the deceased, ambled towards Ceri and me as we stood beside the hearse. He was a burly, gruff looking man with bushy eyebrows and a mop of straw-like hair on his head. An amiable grin broke out across his podgy face as he extended a big meaty hand towards my colleague.

'Thank you, Mr Williams,' he grunted. 'You've done a grand job. Mam would have been happy.'

'It's been a privilege, Mr Burbeck,' Ceri replied warmly, pumping the man's hand.

'There is just one thing though,' he added, almost as an afterthought.

'What's that, Mr Burbeck?'

'Well we were all wondering why you paused outside Cherrybrook Hospital on the way?'

Ceri puffed himself up with pride and launched into his theatrical explanation. 'My reason, Mr Burbeck, was to acknowledge with respect the place where Mam took her leave of this world.'

Mr Burbeck nodded his craggy head slowly. 'I thought it would be something like that.' He stared thoughtfully at the ground and after a slight pause he looked up at Ceri with the hint of a frown on his well-creased face. 'But Mam didn't take her leave of this world at Cherrybrook. She collapsed and died outside Woolworth's.'

It was one of the very few occasions I saw Ceri speechless.

Bryn Llewellyn worked at Westport Crematorium and, as I stated earlier, was living confirmation that so many Welsh people do not seem to like venturing out of Wales. A hard-working crematorium technician – the posh title for those who work round the back and operate the cremators – Bryn had just turned thirty and was not a travelled man. He got anxious if he had to journey beyond the boundaries of Westport and went into hot and cold sweats if fate ever took him across the Severn Bridge. When the subject was broached, as it increasingly was, he just grinned self-consciously, revealing two rows of crooked teeth. 'What do I need to travel for? I've got everything I needs by yer.'

Possibly because of potential honeymoon destination issues, Bryn was still single. His mates had being trying to get him to go abroad for years and on a couple of occasions he did get close. One time he even went to the travel agent with them. But he walked out halfway through the arrangements, much to the combination of annoyance and amusement of his friends. Then one year, realising that he had to do something about his irrational reluctance, he agreed to see it through and go to the Costa Brava with two of his mates. I couldn't believe it when he told me it was all booked and he was flying out to Spain in eight weeks' time. I was even more surprised that he didn't cancel during those two anxious, sweat-inducing months. The build up amongst his colleagues was so big it was like anticipating the start of a British Lions rugby tour. It seemed that each time I saw him when I went round to the back of the crematorium to pick up cremated remains, his usually pallid complexion had turned a further shade paler as the big moment approached.

The merciless part of me would love to have seen what he was like on the day they left. But I was even keener to find out how Bryn had enjoyed himself in a foreign country with a different culture to experience, exciting places to explore, and new foods to try. It was with great curiosity therefore, that I headed round the back of the crematorium a couple of days after his return to hear about Bryn's coming of age. He greeted me with a huge, toothy grin but he didn't look tanned at all – he was still the pasty-faced Bryn I had got to know over the previous few years.

'Hey, Bryn!' I greeted. 'How did it go?'

I was taken aback by his enthusiasm. 'Tom, man, it was cowin' brilliant.

'You enjoyed yourself then?'

'Enjoyed it? I had the best time ever.'

I was impressed. 'So you enjoyed seeing somewhere new then, the views and the sun and stuff like that?'

Bryn's face clouded over slightly, like I'd just suggested something complicated. 'No, I didn't see nothing like that,' he said.

279

'Eh? So...what happened then?'

'Well we gets there and I thinks, this looks tidy. So I had a kip in our room and then we goes out in the evening for a walk, like. And guess what we finds just down the road from our hotel?'

'I've no idea, Bryn.'

'We finds the most amazing British pub. I spent the whole week by there, drinking, playing pool, and chatting to the other Brits. It was fantastic! And they did the best egg and chips ever.'

41

Although I returned to the role of driver after finally conceding defeat to my depression, the duties were no longer the same as when I had joined the company all those years ago. The whole structure had changed and instead of only two distinct roles – funeral director and driver – a third position had been created, that of ambulance man.

In earlier days all removals from hospitals, nursing homes, and residences were carried out by whoever was available at the time. But because of the amount of companies we were now responsible for, together with the increasingly vast area we were covering, it made sense to create a dedicated team whose job it would be to carry out all removals. Such a measure would leave the drivers to drive and the funeral directors to arrange and conduct. At least that was the theory. It worked most of the time but certainly not always. Because of the continual pressure brought about by staffing levels, colleagues were always being borrowed from other duties.

By now the Stapleton Road premises had been revamped and a large, purpose-built mortuary and cold storage area had been incorporated into the existing structure. Every removal our company attended within a thirty-mile radius could now be brought back to this central location. It made life a whole lot easier as far as embalming and preparation of the deceased was concerned, but it often created pressures of a different kind. We found we were continually working to unreasonable deadlines (again, no pun intended) in returning bodies to their respective chapels of rest so that viewings could be arranged.

Many of us, myself included, often felt a little uneasy with this whole new procedure. If Mr Jones passed away in the small town of Llanclwyd and his family phoned the local undertaker a quarter of a mile down the road, was it reasonable to then take the body twelve miles away to an unknown branch trading under a completely different name without their knowledge? Central hubs make commercial sense to the running of a business, but the public had no idea their loved one was being taken somewhere completely different to where they expected.

When I made the decision to become a driver once more I was actually given the choice as to where I wanted to work. I could resume the duties with which I started my career down at the garage in Tessum Street, or I could become an ambulance man. Although I wasn't overly enthused about spending my entire working day dealing solely with dead bodies, I chose to work on the ambulance for a number of reasons. The first involved the irritating Trevor Davies. Proving that management still possessed the uncanny ability to flout common sense and make jaw-dropping decisions, they had recently made Trevor the garage foreman at Tessum Street. I could not therefore vouch for the condition of my already frayed nerves if I had to work under him and his many fanciful fabrications. Stronger men than I had shown disturbing symptoms of insanity after having been in his presence for too long, so what chance would a man of my disposition have? On the other hand, the ambulance presented the opportunity of a new challenge. Also, the working environment in a new and dedicated facility was one of the best in the area. Such reasoning was sound on my part, but in the end it was the people I would be working with directly that sealed my decision.

Having been genuinely shocked and saddened by the attitude amongst many of my colleagues, it was not easy for me to return to their proximity in any position, whether it be as a funeral director, driver, or whatever. Apart from anything else I was feeling terribly humiliated by my very public failure. Working on the ambulance would give me reasonably limited contact with anyone save the three people working alongside me. And by chance, these three colleagues had probably been the most sympathetic – certainly the least insensitive – about my recent ordeals. They definitely weren't the lovey-dovey, group-hugging, new age man types. They were just genuine, trustworthy, down to earth guys with whom I felt far more comfortable and relaxed than any of the other so called 'in crowd'.

Because they were all single, Dai Proctor, Dafydd Phillips, and Joe Evans became known as the Bachelors. None of them were particularly lucky in love and had it not been for cupid finally taking pity on me, I would have been a fully paid up member myself. But whatever horror love stories I may have had to tell from the past, they could never compete with the tales of woe that plagued poor old Dai Proctor.

Dai was a tall, hulking man in his early forties who started with the company two years after me. He bore the obligatory funeral moustache (*could never be without it*) and the not so obligatory tattoos on his knuckles, which, in maturity, were something he wished very much he could do without. At first I was a little unsure of Dai but once I got to know him I grew to like him a great deal. This, again, was possibly the result of him not being very popular with Stewart Lewis. I always found myself drawn to those with a rebellious streak – kindred souls and all that – but Dai's ability to rub management up the wrong way came not so much from his personality but his position as our local trade union representative. As a result, Stewart considered him, with little justification, as some sort of treacherous threat.

Dai was uncomplicated in his desires for life – a self-rolled cigarette, a pint of beer, listening to music, and the love of a good woman. He had no trouble harnessing the first three but the fourth proved more elusive than a fox. He was a one-man disaster zone when it came to women, seemingly a magnet for romantic hassle of all kinds. Rather selfishly, it came as a relief to know that I had not possessed the copyright in such matters.

With his interest in music and a wry sense of humour, Dai and I got on well. This was important because we were a team on the ambulance, the only team of its kind in our set up. No one else worked in tandem the way the ambulance crew did and because of the structure now in place at Stapleton Road, we built up a smooth and enjoyable working relationship with both Dafydd Phillips and Joe Evans. I have already introduced you to the quirky, eccentric world of our champion embalmer, Dafydd. This just leaves Joe Evans, fastest coffin trimmer in Wales.

Joe was just about the most straightforward person I've ever met in my life. He took absolutely no nonsense from anyone whatsoever, no matter who they were. His dismissive contempt for management in particular was one of the most pleasurable spectacles of the working day.

Narrowing life's interests down to the bare minimum, Joe really only had three passions – beer, beer, and more beer. He lived on the stuff and many of us marvelled at the fact he remained alive, let alone fit enough to work. When five o'clock came we all went home. Joe just went straight to the pub. The sight of his balding head and dark red overalls disappearing into the Stapleton Arms opposite the Dean Street office was as routine to us as breathing. He had done it for years, mostly since the break-up of his marriage. It was at this difficult time that Joe moved into the small flat I had recently vacated. We remained neighbours for several years and I would often hear him staggering home a few minutes after closing time. He rarely disturbed me, although one night he did have me worried.

I had opened one eye in bed at the sound of the door closing downstairs as midnight approached. I then listened to the familiar rhythmic stomping as Joe eased his inebriated body up the uncarpeted stairs. Then suddenly there was a conspicuous gap in the staggering footsteps, followed by an almighty thud.

I leapt out of bed and raced to the front door. There, about halfway down the staircase lay Joe, upside down with his heavy boots pointing towards me. Fearing serious injury I rushed to his side.

'Joe! Are you okay?'

He muttered something incomprehensible and raised heavy eyelids, revealing a pair of glazed, watery blue eyes. After leering at me for a couple of seconds he closed them again.

'Come on, Joe. Can you stand up?' As I started to lift him up I nearly fell down the stairs myself, for Joe was a solid man in his late forties. I finally managed to get him into a sitting position when a flailing arm pushed me away.

'Bugger off!' he grumbled in his squeaky voice. 'I'm staying by yer.'

I tried again but it was no use. He rebuffed me once more with similar contempt and feeling mortally wounded that my boxer short-wearing mission of mercy had been ungratefully dismissed, I returned sulkily to bed. Of course, Joe remembered nothing the following morning. He did confess to a certain amount of surprise at finding himself lying down on the stairs when he awoke, but then claimed it was the best night's sleep he'd had for ages.

One day we arrived at work to discover the Stapleton Road premises had been broken into. It was a harrowing day for a number of reasons and as staff we were all required to provide a witness statement to the police. When Joe finished giving his he gave the Stapleton Arms as his contact address. "You've got a far better chance of finding me in there than at home," he told them. That was typical Joe. But the thing I liked about him most was his attitude towards Christmas cards.

Despite my Christian beliefs and support of the spirit of goodwill at Christmas, I have never understood the farce of Christmas cards in the workplace. The sight of everyone standing in the office handing cards to each other just for the sake of it is surely the height of absurdity. These are people who see each other every day of the year – why do they feel the urge to send cards? I wouldn't have minded so much if the messages written inside were even remotely interesting, like some sort of effort had at least been made. *To Tom and family – from Sian and family.* It hardly sends shivers of festive excitement down the spine, does it? For goodness sake, if people insist on sending cards to work colleagues, say something funny, something profound, something worth reading. In Joe I had found a Christmas card soul mate. He too believed that cards should only be sent to those from away who one would not necessarily be seeing over Christmas. But he had a far more effective way of dealing with the problem than I did. If anyone was ever daft enough to send Joe a Christmas card it would immediately be returned to the sender with the 'To's and From's' crossed out and swapped around. *To Joe, From Gareth* became *From Joe To Gareth*. His method was a masterstroke and it certainly stopped the rot.

And so Dai, Dafydd, and Joe became my closest working colleagues as I took up my new position on the ambulance. They weren't flash and they weren't pretentious. They certainly did not qualify as members of the trendy funeral jet set that seemed so important to some of the others. Yet their company to me was both enjoyable and trustworthy. For these reasons alone I knew I had made the right decision.

In all, I spent just over four years working on the funeral ambulance. I still kept my hand in with funeral directing and would always arrange and conduct funerals for friends or acquaintances when asked. And I was happy to oblige too, even though it caused the occasional pangs of regret as to what I'd had to give up. But my brief involvement also confirmed to me that I now had serious limitations following my two breakdowns. I knew there was no way I could go back to funeral directing full-time – not unless management were prepared to improve conditions and relieve stress levels. The job was already hard enough without the problems the company themselves were creating. The personnel department also needed to offer far more support instead of just raising the subject every so often in order to appear concerned. But none of this was going to happen in the real world. Things remained the same and I later found out that many more funeral directors and even drivers ended up suffering from stress-related illnesses in ensuing years.

Despite my disappointments and broken dreams, I genuinely enjoyed working on the ambulance with Dai. It was also a unique experience. Apart from continually touring the network of local hospitals, nursing homes, and house deaths, our responsibility was also to place the deceased in their coffins, dress them, and then take them to their respective chapels of rest. This full on task was now my new challenge. At times it could be extremely hard work. Heavy bodies, coroner's removals, and strict time frames all made for an often difficult working day. But there was always the consolation of being able to hit the road in our ambulance, turn on the radio, and drive away from the hassle and the gossip that remained rife throughout the company locally.

Having a purpose-built ambulance made a world of difference to the job too. The back had been converted into upper and lower decks with a variety of fixtures and fittings to allow the safe transportation of both stretchers and coffins. Amazingly, there were colleagues of ours who hated having an ambulance at all. They preferred using the estate cars to convey the deceased, the method that had always been used in Westport. Frankly, I found their attitude baffling. If someone gave me the choice of having a loved one transported in the back of a clean, dedicated, fully kitted out ambulance, or visibly bouncing around in the back of an estate car with the seats folded down, the response would overwhelmingly be in favour of the former.

Another advantage of the ambulance was its ability to accommodate every piece of equipment that might be required to effect a removal. Very often we had no idea what situation we would be faced with whenever we turned up at the scene of a death. It was time-consuming, unprofessional, and even embarrassing to have to leave again because the correct equipment wasn't on board. Using an ambulance eliminated this and I could never understand the apathy towards something that made the task easier and more professional. Like so many issues in the funeral profession, the 'change' word causes hearts to miss beats and bodies to perspire in head-shaking horror (I'm talking about live funeral staff here, not dead bodies. Just making sure). Granted, not all change is for good. But commonsense should convince the minds of even the most outdated of undertakers that an ambulance was a sensible, dignified, and hygienic idea.

Being a relatively new phenomenon back in the nineties, one of the teething problems of the ambulance was what to have written on the side. Personally I wasn't convinced there needed to be anything at all. The powers that be, however, insisted on having something and so more out of panic than anything else we opted for the words 'Funeral Ambulance.' But this never really sounded right. It came over as grandiose and invited a certain amount of unwanted attention. Eventually the decision was made to change the word 'Funeral' to 'Private.' I found it perversely amusing that men who were paid telephone number salaries actually needed to sit around and discuss such matters, especially as their initial decisions about anything always seemed to be wrong. 'Private Ambulance' was a definite improvement but the term still caused confusion amongst members of the public. Like the woman outside the dry cleaners in Brynmawr one day.

Dai had just picked up his spare suit and as he jumped back into the passenger seat, a woman approached us waving a hand at Dai to open his window. I had noticed her staring at the ambulance as she stood in front of the Post Office and I figured she was about to complain because we had stopped in a busy shopping street with a funeral vehicle. This had happened on many an occasion in the past. I have been shouted at, sworn at, and complained about, simply for parking a hearse outside someone's house for a few minutes. Talk about overreacting. It wasn't like I'd come to collect them, although after they'd finished their ranting I often wished I had.

Dai wound down his window and the elderly lady with fluffy white hair and a stoop smiled politely. She spoke in a whistling kind of voice.

'I've always wanted to know what a 'Private Ambulance' is?'

To which Dai replied spontaneously: 'It means it's mine.'

As I drove away trying not to burst out laughing, I looked in my mirror to see the little old lady standing there nodding her head thoughtfully as though one of life's great mysteries had finally been solved.

Dai was always getting me to stop somewhere in the ambulance – the dry cleaners, the bank, a supermarket to do his shopping, and then his house to take said shopping home. I didn't mind of course. Having been a bachelor living on my own for several years I knew that such small favours helped out and saved time. And Dai was a classic bachelor as far as eating habits were concerned. His palette seemed rather limited at the best of times, especially as he went through phases, discovering some wonderful meal or product that he would then buy in bulk and eat so often he eventually became completely sick of it.

Spam was the first such item that came to our attention. And yes, he was clearly influenced by the famous Monty Python sketch here because he would eat it with everything and anything. He then moved onto Kingsmill bread, rissoles, and mushroom omelettes from the local Chinese take-away. For months I was impressed that Dai regularly frequented his local Chinese until Joe informed me one day that the only thing he ever bought there was a mushroom omelette. Variety being the culinary spice of life probably wasn't Dai's strongest point. The craze that lasted the longest, however, was burgers in gravy. He began buying this tinned convenience food from a particular supermarket and I would often drop him off there during our various jaunts around the area. Five minutes later he would return to the ambulance with a carrier bag full of tins and a big grin on his tanned face.

With the mood and morale of the Westport unit seemingly diminishing on a weekly basis, Dai and I at least managed to maintain a sense of humour and we certainly enjoyed a few laughs along the way. It wasn't easy. Decisions and policies from above were becoming even more difficult to comprehend and the result was mass disillusionment amongst the staff. Trying to introduce a little humour into the working day became a vital ingredient of survival rather than just a recreational pastime.

Like the time we drove down to the chapel of rest in Llandulais to re-dress a body. As can often happen with the deceased, some changes had taken place and we needed to replace the sullied gown with a fresh one. Dafydd came with us to do his 'technical bit' and after he had attended to the problem we began to dress the body in the new coffin gown. When we had finished I felt the urge for a little rhythm before we left. The chapel organ was just a few feet away so I switched it on and pressed one of the rhythm buttons. It was a good job no one could see us as we swayed and hula-hula'd tastefully around the chapel in time to the slinky rumba beat. This was the defining moment when I knew that Dafydd's talents could have graced the television screens of the nation.

I should actually have been wary of switching the old organ on in the first place. It was possibly as old as the chapel itself and rarely used. Only a few months previously we had heard through the vibrant undertaker's grapevine that our old friend, Denzil Jenkins – who was now trying his luck as an independent funeral director – had bought himself a very old Welsh chapel to use as a chapel of rest. Apparently he had almost blown the place up, himself included, when the old organ he installed short-circuited the ancient wiring system.

But despite all the laughs and humour we enjoyed in our years working together, I will always remember my time on the ambulance with Dai Proctor for one memorable incident on a dark, winter's night, also, by chance, in Llandulais. I think I can safely say I will not remember the incident alone.

We were helping one of the funeral directors take a coffin home to a pleasant looking bungalow down near the estuary, the wide expanse of water poking its way between the small town of Llandulais and the village of Ruskin, where Gilbert Rees (Robbie the Robot) had nearly walked himself into trouble several years earlier. To make access a little easier the family had opened the patio doors for us and, relieved that this was going to be a simple, straightforward task, Dai and I began to carry the coffin into the home. As we entered through the patio doors, the widow, seated on an upright chair beside the fireplace, began to wail hysterically. Such scenes were always distressing but it was critical to remain professional and concentrate on the job in hand. Being distracted even for a split second while carrying a heavy coffin could lead to disaster.

We walked through to the back room and placed the coffin on the set of trestles that the funeral director had taken in ahead of us. The widow's sobbing was still audible and as we entered the front room again on our way back outside, other members of the gathered family had also started to weep. The emotional tension was almost visible.

Dai was making straight for the patio doors at a brisk pace. He hated scenes like this and just preferred to get out of the way as quickly as possible. I was following him more sedately when suddenly there was an almighty bang and Dai bounced backwards towards me. Realising immediately that someone must have closed the patio doors after we had entered with the coffin, I desperately tried to stifle an unruly giggle that bubbled rapidly to the surface. Making it worse was the sight of Dai, clearly dazed, trying to pretend nothing unusual had happened. It was no use. I was going to explode. I saw the hallway to the right that led to the front door. I might just make it before...

I heard a noise by my side and looked down at the widow still seated on the chair. Clutching a handkerchief to her mouth she was shaking and tears were rolling down her pale, wrinkled cheeks. But the cause was no longer grief.

It was an amazing sight. In just a few short seconds this lady had gone from overwhelming anguish to precious, healing laughter. As I glanced around the room I couldn't believe my eyes. There were the two daughters and the son, the grandchildren and other relatives all giggling helplessly. The atmosphere we had encountered upon arrival had been completely turned on its head. It was the most convincing argument for the power of laughter I had ever witnessed.

I still felt it was more ethical to take my own laughter outside so I stumbled through the front doorway and doubled up behind a small tree in the dark garden. Dai had made straight for the ambulance, which he hid behind in sheer embarrassment.

As we drove away a few minutes later, it suddenly occurred to me that not only had Dai been the cause of releasing the tension in that grief-stricken home, he had probably also written himself into the family's folklore. For generations to come they would be telling the story of the day the undertaker walked into the patio door while bringing the coffin home.

42

Throughout the many years I spent working in the funeral profession I met a whole legion of characters and individuals who added interest, humour, and occasionally downright irritation to the working day. I have already introduced several of them to you in the preceding chapters and pages. But there were many more. Some of these acquaintances were regular fixtures; others were fleeting. All left an impact or a clutch of memories along the way...

I have never met anyone like Ronald Bevan before. If he were spotted lurking in the background of a horror film, people would be very scared of him. At times one could be forgiven for exhibiting nervousness when he was around for real.

Ron was a skeletal-looking man in his late forties with mad, rolling eyeballs and a proclivity for verbal explosions that had to be seen to be believed. In fact, it would have been no surprise to see smoke emerging from his ears when he became annoyed. There is no question Ron had a problem with anger. The slightest thing would send him spiralling out of control and as long as you were not the victim, the spectacle could be highly entertaining. He possessed a very high-pitched West Wales accent to start with, but once he set off on one of his sermons of rage it was not unlike starting a car and gradually increasing the revs until the engine screams. His voice would steadily rise even higher until a piercing fever pitch was attained. Spontaneous combustion was not out of the question at its peak.

It is little wonder, then, that Ronald Bevan earned himself the nickname of 'The Furious One'. In some circles he was also favourably known as 'Fif-teen.' His use of the number fifteen during moments of frenzy was almost bizarre. Rarely was it technically correct in the way it was used: it was just a number that he favoured for some strange reason. An experienced psychiatrist may well have been able to shed some light on the phenomenon, but as far as we were concerned the number became inextricably linked with the name of Ronald Bevan. And he rarely let us down.

'I have been trying to get hold of that id-iot for fif-teen minutes!'

'That body weighed at least fif-teen stone!'

'I don't care if there is another fun-er-al to arrange. Fif-teen minutes I have had to eat my food!'

'The fam-ily only ordered two limousines. How am I supposed to get fif-teen people into two cars, I'm telling you!'

Because for some reason I was never the recipient of the wrath of Ron, I could often enjoy his outbursts from a position of relative safety. Like the time he was attending to a viewing in one of our outlying branches. By now the drivers were covering a very large area on call, including the two branches down west at Bronllan and Llangethin. On the weekend in question, Ron was the funeral director on call for this particular area and on the Saturday afternoon I was summoned to Llangethin by a peeved voice on the phone.

'Tom, we've got a re-move-al down by yer. Blood-y nuisance. Meet me at the chap-el of rest because that id-iot, Simon (the resident funeral director in Llangethin) has booked me a viewing there at half past three. It should only take about fif-teen minutes. Then we'll go and do the re-move-al straight afterwards.'

I took my time driving the thirty or so miles down to Llangethin. There was no point rushing there just to listen to Ron ranting on about Simon – the two of them disliked each other immensely. My plan didn't quite work, however. After a pleasant journey down in the pale, watery sun of late autumn, I pulled into the car park of the chapel of rest to see Ron pacing up and down the courtyard.

As I got out of the car I could hear cheering and shouting coming from the other side of the high wall to the rear of the chapel of rest. The funeral home backed onto Llangethin Athletic's football ground and by the sound of it a match was already in full swing, a game that probably involved Simon: he had played for Llangethin for a number of years.

Ron strode purposefully towards me, his face an unhealthy shade of crimson. He launched into a tirade of profanities and hysterics about Simon and his foot-ball with such zeal that I felt sure he would self-destruct at any second.

'Well I'm sure Simon didn't actually kick the ball over the wall himself,' I offered in defence of the accused. But it was no use. Ron had clearly made up his mind. Simon was standing right behind the wall and was deliberately kicking the ball over towards the chapel of rest every five minutes just to annoy him. After all, it had "happened fif-teen times already." When the violent finger pointing started I knew he was coming to the boil. His final, abuse-laden sentence was almost lost to the decibel count as The Furious One's voice reached soprano pitch.

And right at that moment the family chose to emerge tearfully from the chapel of rest. Fearing for their safety from the steaming Ronald I considered stepping forward to escort them from the premises. But even as the thought entered my head, Ron had started walking towards them a completely changed man. I watched with wry disbelief as he dealt kindly and sympathetically with the small group of people in the gentle, understanding manner that is the prerequisite of all funeral directors. The transformation was almost unnerving to witness.

Especially as he never once mentioned the word 'fif-teen' during his conversation with them.

In complete contrast to the personality of Ronald Bevan was Lucy Barnes, curate of St. Michael's and chaplain to the shops of Westport town centre.

I first encountered Lucy at the chapel of rest in Brynmawr one evening. The funeral director on call had arranged a viewing there that he was now unable to attend due to another call out, so he asked me to cover for him. Lucy Barnes was a friend of the family in question and they had invited her along for moral support.

The relatives of the deceased arrived shortly after I had checked that everything was ready and I showed them quietly to the coffin before retreating to the office. There was no sign of Lucy yet but the family assured me she would come. Five minutes later a miniature whirlwind breezed into the building.

'Well hello! How lovely to meet you! I'm the Reverend Lucy Barnes. I'm so sorry I'm late. Have the family arrived yet?'

I shook the tiny hand held out to me and marvelled at how small the rest of Lucy Barnes was too – she stood barely four and a half feet tall. The bun on the back of her head, neatly encased in a black hair net, somehow made her look even more minute and an eager pair of dark, twinkling eyes gave her a childlike quality that defied her half century of years. She wore a cassock of ankle length, which occasionally revealed the tiniest pair of feet I think I've ever seen on a grown woman. But what Lucy Barnes lacked in size she more than made up for with her huge personality. She positively oozed cheerful optimism and I learned within just a few minutes of meeting her that it was nigh on impossible to feel down or despondent in her presence.

'Yes, I showed them through a few minutes ago,' I replied. 'They said for you to go straight in when you got here.'

'I'm on my way!' she smiled. 'They are a lovely family. I'm so touched they've asked me to share this moment with them. Now then, what is your name?'

'I'm Tom, Reverend Barnes.'

'Oh, how delightful! Now, Tom, please call me Lucy. I hate formalities and all that nonsense. Shall we?'

I showed her to the viewing area and Lucy approached the family with quiet dignity. They greeted her warmly and she hugged each one of them with genuine feeling and concern. I was just about to return to the office and allow them the usual private time to themselves when the sound of Lucy's exuberant voice made me freeze in my tracks.

'Oh, isn't death wonderful!'

I spun round, not far short of horrified by what she had just said. She was staring adoringly into the coffin with the most beautifully radiant smile on her petite face. But I was even more surprised at the reaction of the family members gathered around her. They too were smiling, completely uplifted by the sheer heartening enthusiasm of this amazing little woman.

From that day on I always enjoyed my acquaintances with Lucy Barnes. There was never any question of her spirits being dampened by a sad funeral or a grey day: she was perpetually buoyant and friendly. She had that rare ability to uplift and inspire – the type of person who could listen to your problems and then make you feel as though everything would be okay. My father possessed this precious quality too. I could tell Dad anything that was bothering me and in his calm and natural way he would speak the words that sent the despondency a million miles away. Such people are a true gift to those fortunate enough to cross their lives.

And in dealing with the bereaved and the distressed, the Reverend Lucy Barnes had found the perfect way to use her wonderful personality to its full potential.

Mo Paynter was our cleaner – if this isn't too much of a contradiction in terms. Despite her lengthy stints in both the Dean Street and Stapleton Road offices, she never really seemed to clean very much. She would wipe the telephones with meticulous care; the picture frames too. And she often made a couple of encouraging movements along the desks and the backs of chairs. But everything else would barely receive a tickle from her yellow duster. We usually ended up doing it ourselves when she wasn't around, which somehow defeated the object of having a cleaner at all.

All this would have been far more irritating had Mo been a miserable, unfriendly woman. But she wasn't. She was an extremely nice person – pleasant, caring, and always concerned with the welfare of others. She was particularly kind to Connie Rees and did so much to help her as she advanced in years. Because of these qualities it was very difficult not to like Mo, despite her lack of enthusiasm towards the job for which she was paid. With a squat figure and somewhat ambling gait, Mo could never be classed as glamorous. Her penchant for the bouffant hairstyles of the sixties did her no favours either. But, as I say, her generous personality heavily outweighed everything else and she rarely caused me any problems. Except when she had a vacuum cleaner in her hand.

Most office cleaners start work when everyone has left the premises. Not Mo. She would turn up an hour early at four o'clock and whip round the place so she could finish the same time as us. I think this was possibly the main reason why very little ever got cleaned properly: we were all still there and very much in her way. It could be a nightmare for us, especially when the vacuuming began.

Mo had a system when she vacuumed. She would stop whenever the phone rang so we could speak uninhibited. While this might sound okay in theory, reality turned it into farce. Both offices were always very busy and the phones rang often so it got to the stage where we felt guilty for picking up the phone to make a call because we were interrupting the flow of Mo. But the scary part of Mo's vacuuming lay not in the implementation but rather the technique. She was a dab hand at the ankle tap and very few survived her 'vacuum cleaner cable across the room' ploy. I lost count of the number of times I would become entangled simply going from one room to the next. Vacuuming was the only aspect of Mo's cleaning routine that really got to me. And it was on one particular day in the Dean Street office – when I was in no mood for Hoover harassment – that I planned revenge with Johnny Morgan.

Mo was on a roll and nothing, it seemed, would stop her. The phone hadn't rung for ages and she was driving everyone nuts as she bustled around the still busy offices, poking the vacuum cleaner into corners and under chairs, banging legs, and tripping people up with the cable. I'd had enough. I couldn't concentrate on what I was doing with a howling Hoover gusting through my brain, so I took time out to indulge in a little skulduggery. I had disappeared into the middle office and shut the door to try and find some solitude but it was no use. The droning was still audible. Then Johnny Morgan walked in, a frown of anguish on his face.

'Can't we shut her up somehow?' he groaned. 'I can't hear myself think.'

'Yeah, I know.' Then an idea suddenly came to me. 'Johnny, go into the back office and answer the next phone call. I have a cunning plan.'

He disappeared with a puzzled look on his face. Then using the second line on the telephone in front of me I dialled the number for the line above. A few seconds later I heard the phone ring in the other office. As if by magic the vacuum cleaner stopped immediately and through the gap in the door I could see Mo poised, waiting to spring back into action.

'Hello, funeral service. Can I help you?'

'Johnny, it's me! But don't say my name!'

'Uh? What's going on?'

'This is my cunning plan! What can't you hear right now?'

I could almost hear the light bulb clicking on inside his head. 'Yes. Very good. Very good indeed.'

'Right,' I continued, 'now put the phone down and I'll dial again.'

'Certainly,' replied Johnny with glee in his voice. 'I'll be most happy to assist you, sir. Goodbye for now.'

Mo was like a vulture swooping on a dead carcass. Within a split second of hearing the phone go down the vacuum cleaner was back on. But seconds later the phone rang again and Johnny picked it up immediately. Off went the vacuum cleaner once more.

'Ah, good afternoon, Mr Morgan,' I greeted. 'This is Vacuum Busters Ltd, at your service.'

Johnny stifled a laugh and we talked nonsense for a few seconds before hanging up. And as Mo flicked the switch once more, I was already dialling the number for the third time.

'Brrring, brrring.'

This time I heard a distinctive tut of exasperation from Mo as the vacuum cleaner whirred to blissful silence yet again.

Our fake phone calls went on for several minutes until Mo finally gave up and decided to do a spot of quiet dusting. Unfortunately she chose to start in my office, but the inconvenience was nothing compared to the noise of that infernal vacuum cleaner.

'Phones are busy today, Mo,' I muttered. 'I just don't seem to be able to get on with my work.'

Mo grunted and flicked moodily at the offending telephone on my desk.

Johnny Morgan, like Dafydd Phillips, could be side-splittingly funny without really trying. He was a rotund young man a handful of years younger than me, but balding prematurely. His small brown eyes and slightly down-turned mouth gave him a hard-done-by expression and it was this downtrodden characteristic of the world on his shoulders that regularly doubled me up with laughter.

Johnny hailed from our northern most branch in the Westport valley town of Cwmfelin. Because the business there ran pretty much independently – the locals would have been more horrified at the knowledge of a takeover than most – I didn't see as much of him as I would have liked. He was a tonic for the soul with an intelligent wit that I loved.

Mostly because of where he lived and had been raised, Johnny Morgan was something of a man of the land. He would spend hours walking the bleak, exposed hillsides that stood guard over the string of small settlements running away north from Westport and his knowledge of the local wildlife was extremely impressive. Once, when Dai and I were with him at Sandacre Hospital's mortuary on removals one day, Johnny was telling us the names of a whole host of creatures portrayed on the large wildlife wall calendar behind James's desk. Dai was suitably impressed.

'You certainly know your animals,' he commented admirably.

'Well, I should do really,' came the nonchalant reply with that gloriously exaggerated grimace. 'I've shot most of them.'

Johnny soon became a hero amongst the meat-eating fraternity of the Westport funeral homes. His ability to provide a seemingly endless supply of fresh meat at reasonable prices made him a very popular figure and his droll claim of being a purveyor of fine sheep and hog products was no exaggeration.

Such enterprise also brought out the best lines from his humour stocks. One of the receptionists, who had pre-ordered half a lamb from Johnny, approached him after a few days with a slight hint of impatience in her voice.

'Any sign of my half a lamb?' she asked.

'As a matter of fact, yes,' said Johnny with his pained look. 'It was jumping around the field last night attached to somebody else's half.'

The human species had no monopoly on the characters found within the world of funerals. Some of the many vehicles I drove had their own distinct personalities too. Top of the list was undoubtedly The Beast of Bronllan.

The Beast was an unassuming looking Ford Granada saloon, a sort of 'free gift' as a result of our acquisition of a small funeral firm in nearby Bronllan. It was metallic silver and had apparently been used as the funeral director's 'run around' in

299

which to arrange funerals. Because of its colour and inability to do anything remotely useful like a removal it was assigned to a similar duty with us. But not for long.

The first time I drove this brute of a car I awoke the following morning feeling like I'd spent a week on a medieval rack. The steering column was so stiff it was like trying to negotiate a tank. Parking was almost completely out of the question – it took too long to locate a space that one could just drive straight into. Even then it was touch and go. Driving The Beast between two other vehicles was like trying to thread a needle while wearing welding gloves. But the most hazardous manoeuvre of all involved corners and mini-roundabouts. I know, because I saw the horror on the faces of other motorists as I appeared destined to hit them full on before somehow managing to wrench the steering wheel away from a huge insurance claim.

One by one we all drove The Beast and one by one we all refused to do so again. Eventually it was moved on to some unsuspecting funeral director hundreds of miles away. Whoever took delivery of the thing, I wished them the best of luck.

A couple of years later, Walter Turner's black Granada estate took over the mantle vacated by The Beast. Walter Turner was a local independent funeral director who we had also bought out. He had no premises or funeral vehicles in the way of hearses and limousines. But he did not come entirely alone. Walter owned a Ford estate car, which had a clutch so temperamental you could have put a pair of shorts on it and called it an Argentinean footballer. I tried every method I knew to handle the touchy thing – the strong approach, the gentle approach, the quick and the slow, and the downright violent. But each time the car would lurch uncontrollably forward and woe betide anything or anyone who happened to be in its path.

It reached crisis point when Walter insisted on doing a funeral in the estate one day and asked me to be his driver. It was not uncommon for some of the independents like Walter to use their estate car for a funeral instead of going to the expense of hiring a hearse. I slept very little the night before and when I did finally drift off I woke up in a cold sweat, having mowed down half the mourners in a very grisly nightmare. I actually escaped quite lightly at the real funeral. I only took out a small piece of hedge at the cemetery. But when one of the part-timers used it as a flower car on a big funeral and partly demolished a headstone and kerb set on a nearby grave, its days were numbered. The complaints were finally heeded and the ferocious lump of black metal suddenly disappeared overnight to terrorise some other funeral home with its bad-tempered clutch.

Aynsley Jenkins joined the company as a driver while I was a funeral director. He bore a head of thick, curly brown hair and had a habit of closing his eyes for the first few words of every sentence he uttered. Aynsley was actually a really nice chap but we soon discovered that he wasn't the sharpest scalpel in the mortuary. He would do really daft things – like when he soaked Paul Williams with a cup of tea. Paul was getting ready to go out and conduct a funeral and after changing he had sat down on a chair to give his shoes a quick polish. A few minutes earlier, Aynsley – who was Paul's hearse driver – had offered to make him a cup of tea before they left. He sauntered down the corridor from the kitchen and then inexplicably held the cup above Paul's head while announcing: "Here's your tea, mate." Paul sat up and knocked the cup out of Aynsley's hand with the top of his head, resulting in a deluge of tea all over his tailcoat. Paul went ballistic. Removing the colourful profanities, the gist of his reaction was to ask Aynsley what kind of idiot holds a cup of hot tea over someone's head when they're bending down.

Aynsley was a bit of a computer geek and we all fell for his claims of expertise in this embryonic field at the time. But after a while we came to the conclusion that the liberal use of words such as ROM and RAM in his technologically-themed conversations meant absolutely nothing at all. Our fears were confirmed one day when I found the address book he said he used to list all his favourite websites in. Upon flicking through the book I actually thought it was empty until I got to 'W'. All of his favourite websites were listed there all right, each one beginning with www...

And so these are just a few more of the characters that made up the colourful tapestry of my funeral life in Westport. There were others too. Like the superintendent of Murton Crematorium, a man so officious he had surely been diverted away from his more suited profession of traffic warden. Then there was Victor, the part-time driver we employed for a while who turned out to be so childish in his attitude that Chris Littlehales nicknamed him Victor Immature. And Rev Potts, the nervous vicar who got into a muddle when delivering a service at the graveside. Instead of saying: "Let light perpetual shine upon her", he uttered the immortal line: "Let light perpetual shine up her."

These, and the many others I have previously mentioned, raised a smile, caused a reaction, and provided endless topics of conversation for years to come. But soon not even this cast of many could dispel the gloom that had begun hovering incessantly above me like a huge, storm-laden cloud.

The job was changing beyond recognition. And certainly not for the better.

43

It was time to move on.

Ever since I embarked on my new and unusual career in Westport way back at the end of 1985, I had been aware of an undercurrent bubbling beneath the façade of the company I had chosen to work for. At times it was close to unbearable. On other occasions the problems melted away and morale rose, often the result of many of the incidents I have recorded over the pages and chapters of this book. But it was becoming increasingly harder to remain positive when everything around us appeared to be crumbling. Towards the end it was only my sense of humour that was getting me through each working day.

Mercifully, a small handful of my colleagues also felt that a little light relief was the best way to survive. But as time wore on they became fewer in number. Most of the people with whom I could identify had already deserted the sinking ship and despite continuous recruitment to replace them, the job was beginning to feel very empty. Chris Littlehales had been the latest to walk, totally fed up and disheartened with the direction the company was moving in. I missed Chris. There was something comforting in his no-nonsense approach and sharp, realistic wit.

I didn't realise it immediately but Chris's departure signalled the beginning of the end for me too. I began to question my role and my ambitions, but more crucially, my desire. The mental meltdowns I had experienced contributed greatly to all of these and there is no doubt that they had rocked my foundations. One of the cankerous effects of depression is that it undermines confidence and breeds self-doubt. I've never been particularly good at either anyway, but now I was tired too and the thought of calling it a day and trying something different began to appeal more and more. The additional benefit of this was that I would be able to escape the increasingly challenging environment in which I worked, because that in itself was making everything worse.

It had been an amazing journey and I knew deep down that I would miss this crazy job, this rollercoaster vocation of inspiration, anguish, and compassion. In spite of the difficulties I encountered over the years I do not regret for one minute the time I spent in this most rewarding of careers. I learned so much about people, about human nature, and probably most of all, about myself.

I saw firsthand the way people cope with the tragedy of death. I watched as they responded to something that is unprecedented amongst life's many trials. I observed with head-shaking admiration as they picked themselves up and continued to battle on with their lives in the face of almost overwhelming heartache. There were times when I could literally feel the despair, but their bravery was inspiring to witness and I was continually touched and uplifted by so many of these wonderful families and individuals who I had been privileged to help.

I also became very much aware of the wonderful army of people across the country, and indeed throughout the world, who take up the calling of the testing, taxing profession that is undertaking. I hope this book pays homage to the dedication of these amazing men and women and their willingness to help those at their lowest ebb. But my most important discovery of all was to realise how priceless a commodity is the ability to laugh, no matter what the situation or the circumstances. We all need to laugh and we need to laugh often. If I have been able to raise a chuckle or two at the stories contained within this book, I will have achieved what I ultimately set out to do.

As the world began a new century and a new millennium, the question was what to do next? Although I had absorbed and learned so much from my experiences as an undertaker, I felt strangely unarmed to take on the world again. Much of what the undertaker does feels of little use back in the real world.

'What skills do you think you can bring to our company, Mr Eldwin?'

'Well if anyone dies in reception I should know what to do.'

What are your strengths and weaknesses?'

'Umm, I don't particularly like it when the phone rings in the middle of the night. But I can dress a body in a coffin gown in four minutes flat.'

'We need team players here, Mr Eldwin. Are you a team player?'

'Certainly am. I played regularly for the Undertakers All Stars and we once went unbeaten for ten games.'

'We want 'go-getters' in this company. My colleague Angus, here, started at the bottom and is already nearing the top of the tree in just a handful of years. How do you feel about that?'

'Uh oh...Angus... You didn't use to be a (gulp) paperboy by any chance...did you?'

'We like dedication here in our little empire, Eldwin. Are you willing to go the extra mile?'

'Ooh well, that depends really. If you have an American client called Chuck Woods, then probably not.'

'I beg your pardon?'

'Nothing. It doesn't matter. I'll...er...close the door on my way out, shall I?'

There are many talents that those working in the funeral profession can carry over into other careers. For me, it was a case of deciding which path to take. There were certainly plenty of options open to me – perhaps trying my luck in New Zealand, the country of my birth; or maybe returning to live in England. I had missed England greatly during my time in Wales. The British Isles is such a diverse place – accents and cultures can change so dramatically, often literally within a handful of miles as one ventures across its winding roads and through its time-tinged towns and villages. That is certainly the case when crossing the Severn Bridge into Wales, this beautifully dramatic and rugged nation of such wonderfully entertaining characters. My life is all the more richer for meeting them, working with them, and living amongst them. At least the ones who weren't so anti-English anyway! But for the time being, my life beyond funerals is a tale for another day.

In an ideal world I would love to have carried on being an undertaker. But that had become impossible. Every day was a battle. Every week was more about office politics than the people we were supposed to be helping. The company had now started employing people in key positions with no knowledge or empathy whatsoever for the funeral business – people who possessed the man-management skills of a charging rhinoceros. They had little or no respect for what had gone before. The efforts of their hard-working predecessors – the Islwyn Thomas's, the Rhys Parry's, and the Arnold James's of the funeral world – were being ignored and treated with contempt. These pioneers had built up the business with respect, trust, and a deep and carefully nurtured knowledge of the funeral business. Now arrogant, know-it-all half-wits and their moronic corporate-speak had elbowed their way in and were smashing it all down.

For me, the final straw came within the space of a few months when ex-British Rail managers were employed to fill three local management positions.

The lunatics had finally taken over the asylum.

It was definitely time to go.

SONGS FOR FUNERALS

Another One Bites The Dust (QUEEN)

Going Underground (THE JAM)

Light My Fire (THE DOORS)

Smoke Gets In Your Eyes (BRYAN FERRY)

Who Wants To Live Forever (QUEEN)

(Don't Fear) The Reaper (BLUE OYSTER CULT)

Firestarter (THE PRODIGY)

Ashes To Ashes (DAVID BOWIE)

Body Talk (IMAGINATION)

Living In A Box (LIVING IN A BOX)

And there are, of course, many, many more. Feel free to add them below...

"The Burning Ring of fire"

ACKNOWLEDGEMENTS

It goes without saying that I would like to thank all those who have played a part in my undertaking existence – from my first day in the profession working as a casual bearer right through to my last. So, to be more precise: family and friends, for their support, understanding, and patience, especially those who have known about this labour of love for a while and had probably given up on me actually doing anything about it; former colleagues and acquaintances (well, most of them anyway); and the wonderful, inspiring clients it was my privilege to work for. Finally, my grateful thanks to the incredibly talented Dai Cable (www.daicable.com). His amazing cover artwork replicated exactly the ambience and tone I had hoped for. Cheers Dai. Hope you managed to mend the shed.

20803822R00175

Printed in Great Britain
by Amazon